"A major undertaking in Christian apologetics, this volume makes a most timely and welcome contribution. By labeling the apologetic task 'covenantal,' Scott Oliphint highlights throughout that the presuppositions of 'presuppositional apologetics' are the clear and indubitable teachings of Scripture and have nothing to do with the postmodern understanding of presuppositions as little more than the personal commitments, inevitably relativizing, of the individual apologist. Comprehensive in its scope, this balanced mix of principles and practice provides valuable instruction to a broad range of readers. I commend it most highly."

Richard B. Gaffin Jr., Emeritus Professor of Biblical and Systematic Theology, Westminster Theological Seminary

"In a day marked by shallow thinking, weak reasoning, and arguments lacking in both theological and biblical depth, Oliphint offers an arsenal of apologetic insight. His affirmation and exposition of a covenantal apologetic brings a vital biblical and theological dimension to the apologetic task. Believers seeking to give an answer for their hope will enthusiastically receive this book."

R. Albert Mohler Jr., President, The Southern Baptist Theological Seminary

"K. Scott Oliphint has done us a service in wonderfully translating the venerable Van Tillian apologetic approach into more accessible categories for the practice of apologetics in the contemporary world. Grounded in Scripture and Reformed theology, upholding the lordship of Christ in all of life, eschewing neutrality in our thinking, and tackling the hard cases of the problem of evil, naturalistic evolution, and Islam, Oliphint teaches us how to defend Christianity in a biblically faithful and persuasive manner. I highly recommend this work."

Stephen J. Wellum, Professor of Christian Theology, The Southern Baptist Theological Seminary

"Whatever your view and practice of defending your faith, *Covenantal Apologetics* will both motivate and equip you for the task in a way that is persuasive, winsome, clearly structured, thoroughly biblical, and most importantly, Christ-exalting. Dr. Oliphint roots us in the unequivocal authority of God's existence and his self-revelation, and brings principles down to earth by providing potential conversations with a humanist, an atheist, an evolutionist, and a Muslim. If you want to grow in your confidence in Scripture, your evangelistic fruitfulness, and your love for the Savior, read this book."

Bob Kauflin, Director of Sovereign Grace Music; author, *Worship Matters* and *True Worshipers*

"Engaging unbelief is the work of every believer in a post-Christian culture. In everyday conversations pluralism demands that we give equal value to all religious beliefs. To stabilize us in this culture, we turn to God's revelation in Scripture. Drawing from his own experience and offering concrete dialogues, apologist Scott Oliphint models a Christian response to unbelief and has delivered the type of book we desperately need—biblically grounded, God-centered, jargon-pruned, and clearly written. *Covenantal Apologetics* is an essential tool to meet unbelief with the hope of the gospel."

Tony Reinke, journalist; author, *12 Ways Your Phone Is Changing You*

"With seismic changes in our society's perception of life—and especially of human rights—the need for Christians to give reasons for their faith is even greater today. Scott Oliphint comes to our aid by bringing what is often food that only giraffes can eat (the field technically called apologetics) right down to the grasp of Christ's lambs. Here is a book that will enable you to argue intelligently from Scripture, in the midst of a plethora of false philosophies and religions, as to why the world needs Jesus Christ as Savior and Lord."

Conrad Mbewe, Pastor, Kabwata Baptist Church, Lusaka, Zambia

"*Covenantal Apologetics* places the defense of the Christian faith where it belongs—in a rich texture of appropriate contexts: the self-revelation of the triune God in the Bible and his created universe, the covenantal relationship of all people (rebellious and redeemed) with their personal Creator, the evangelistic mission of the church, the persuasive power of character and humility, and the give-and-take of interpersonal relationships and conversations. Instead of offering formulaic arguments to win debating points, Oliphint urges Christians to bring a full-orbed theology as we winsomely and forthrightly engage proponents of unbelief and other beliefs. Especially helpful are the sample dialogues with spokespersons for humanism, atheism, and Islam."

Dennis E. Johnson, Emeritus Professor of Practical Theology, Westminster Seminary California

"Few people have thought as deeply and carefully as Scott Oliphint about the relationship between confessional Reformed theology and Christian apologetics. There has been much talk in recent years about 'covenantal apologetics,' but it has consisted mainly of informal discussions scattered across the blogosphere. What has been sorely needed is a definitive book-length exposition by a well-regarded scholarly advocate. No one is better qualified than Dr. Oliphint to take on that task, and he has not disappointed. This book clearly explains the theological foundations of covenantal apologetics and illustrates its application in real-world conversations."

James Anderson, Carl W. McMurray Professor of Theology and Philosophy, Reformed Theological Seminary, Charlotte

"Oliphint's refreshingly Christ-centered approach to persuasively engaging unbelievers with the truth of God equips readers not merely for an intellectual contest of demolishing arguments, but also for a spiritual battle against the suppression of truth in the human heart."

Nancy Guthrie, Bible teacher; author, *Even Better than Eden*

"I am grateful to see Oliphint taking Reformed apologetics in a more accessible, less technical, and richly biblical-theological direction. His approach is uniquely centered on God's revelation in Christ and emphasizes persuasion aimed at the heart over argumentation targeting the head alone. The book goes beyond merely discussing principles to presenting thorough case studies demonstrating how covenantal apologetics can be put into practice. As a professor and pastor, I will recommend this to many people and assign it in my apologetics courses."

Justin Holcomb, Episcopal minister; author; Adjunct Professor of Theology, Reformed Theological Seminary

"Scripturally based, historically informed, theologically astute, and contemporarily relevant, *Covenantal Apologetics* equips one intellectually and spiritually."

Adriaan Neele, Professor of Historical Theology, Puritan Reformed Theological Seminary

"Dr. Oliphint elegantly displays the theological consistency of covenantal apologetics while demonstrating the practical usefulness of this method in addressing a variety of contemporary challenges to Christian faith. Perhaps most importantly, this book provides sturdy motivation for engaging nonbelievers, directing us to place our confidence not in our own apologetic prowess, but in the gospel's power, Scripture's authority, and the Holy Spirit's activity."

Jeff Purswell, Dean, Pastors College, Sovereign Grace Churches

"I appreciate the way Oliphint deals with the necessity of the lordship of Christ. He is Lord of all, which means that while truth is not relative, as God's truth it has relational implications and applications. Oliphint's emphasis regarding covenantal apologetics standing on the truth of Christ's lordship is critical to the task, especially in our postmodern culture."

Charles Dunahoo, Former Coordinator, Presbyterian Church in America Christian Education and Publications

"As a teacher I have been crying out for an apologetics primer that would help to demystify a presuppositional method, demonstrate the exegetical and biblical-theological basis for this method, and give some idea as to what this might look like in the real world with real people. Oliphint's *Covenantal Apologetics* fills this need. It is not only principled and practical, but also pastoral."

Daniel Strange, College Director and Lecturer in Culture, Religion, and Public Theology, Oak Hill College, London

"Every pastor and preacher is a persuader, and this book provides not only the theological rationale but also practical help in that task of persuasion. Those who are committed to a gospel-centered ministry will be both inspired and instructed by Scott Oliphint's insights. Ministries will be strengthened and made more effective by adopting this biblically based and God-honoring paradigm of covenantal apologetics."

Stafford Carson, Principal and Professor of Ministry, Union Theological College, Belfast, Northern Ireland

"Too often books on Christian apologetics get lost in a labyrinth of complications. Such is not the case with Scott Oliphint's book. It establishes the biblical basis for apologetics by showing how Scripture and the lordship of Christ are vital for the communication of Christian truth. With its accent on apologetics as covenantal, it is clear, practical, coherent, and persuasive—which is, after all, what one wants when looking for reasons for believing something. Oliphint's approach does not remain in a theoretical comfort zone, but tackles problems of unbelief that confront us every time we access the media. If you have never read a book on apologetics, this is it!"

Paul Wells, Emeritus Professor, Faculté Jean Calvin, Aix-en-Provence, France

"This book will become known as helpful among students and campus ministries. Oliphint effectively persuades the reader to defend the faith by his clear explanation of the loving covenantal relationship between God and his people, the redemptive work of Jesus, and the encouragement of the Holy Spirit."

Rod Mays, National Coordinator Emeritus, Reformed University Fellowship

"In attempting to put to rest the term 'presuppositional,' Oliphint integrates the best insights from his philosophical expertise in the Westminster Seminary tradition with the best insights from the Westminster Assembly theological tradition. The result: a book for both mind and heart. As a pastor, I welcome books that offer a consistently Reformed approach to a defense of Christianity. This may be the best one yet."

Mark Jones, Pastor, Faith Reformed Presbyterian Church, Vancouver, British Columbia

"What sets this book apart is Oliphint's insistence that the person and work of Jesus Christ take center stage in every apologetic discussion. Following Van Til, he relentlessly rallies us around the banner of the self-attesting Christ of Scripture. Although Oliphint's apologetic approach is theologically and philosophically sophisticated, he makes it understandable and practical for ordinary Christians."

Nathan Sasser, Assistant Professor of Philosophy, Greenville Technical College

"Dr. Oliphint has given us a very important presentation of Christian apologetics for our day. His discussions draw heavily from Scripture in ways that are accessible to a wide range of Christian readers. He stands in the stream of presuppositional apologetics, and he makes great strides toward dealing with contemporary challenges to the faith. Followers of Christ who want to reach the lost will find this book invaluable."

Richard L. Pratt Jr., President, Third Millennium Ministries

"*Covenantal Apologetics* succeeds in proving the biblical-covenantal terms for the framework of an unashamed Reformed apologetic. I heartily recommend it, especially to those seeking a thorough introduction to this vital discipline. Those in or aspiring to pastoral ministry will find help to prepare God's people for works of service and to provide reasons to a dying generation for our hope in our Savior. Those tasked with teaching in seminaries will find both academic stimulus and exegetical broadening. All of us already persuaded by Van Til will do well to recast our 'presuppositionalism' into this readily defensible and covenant-biblical frame."

Jim Wright, Principal, John Wycliffe Theological College, Johannesburg, South Africa

"Even those who do not embrace Reformed theology or presuppositional apologetics will realize that *Covenantal Apologetics* offers a consistent apologetic approach. It is internally coherent, but also in line with the scriptural message and with Van Til's heritage. The latter has often been discussed in highly academic terms. This text presents covenantal apologetics in an accessible way to church members, pastors, and others who may not have formal theological training. The book offers precious examples of apologetic practice and is therefore useful to equip every Christian to tackle concrete situations where a defense of the faith is needed. The more academically inclined, however, will enjoy the fact that the principles behind the concrete examples remain clearly visible and solid."

Renato Coletto, Professor, Philosophy of Science, North-West University, Potchefstroom, South Africa

"Here is an important contribution to the literature on Van Til's application of Reformed theology to the discipline of apologetics. Judicious, well written, and refreshingly accessible, Oliphint's analysis is a compelling 'translation' of an approach to defending the faith that insists, among other things, that because human beings are covenant creatures who live and move and have their being in the world created and providentially sustained by the covenant-keeping God, 'The only way properly to see yourself, the world, or anything else, is through the spectacles of Scripture.' Highly recommended."

Paul Kjoss Helseth, Professor of Christian Thought, Northwestern College, St. Paul, Minnesota

"In a pluralistic world, *Covenantal Apologetics* expertly equips pastors, teachers, parents, and students with a superior biblical and theological framework for defending the faith in the public square. For Christians who seek to have a credible voice at the 'Areopagus' of our day, this book will help them to dismantle unbelieving worldviews with razor-sharp precision while honoring God's redemptive mission. Oliphint reminds readers that any form of Christian apologetics divorced from the Triune God's covenant realities will send the church on a fool's errand. *Covenantal Apologetics* is faithful to the Bible, the gospel, and redemptive history. This book should be read widely."

Anthony B. Bradley, Professor of Religious Studies, The King's College, New York

COVENANTAL APOLOGETICS

*Principles and Practice in
Defense of Our Faith*

K. SCOTT OLIPHINT

Foreword by William Edgar

WHEATON, ILLINOIS

Covenantal Apologetics: Principles and Practice in Defense of Our Faith

Copyright © 2013 by K. Scott Oliphint

Published by Crossway
>   1300 Crescent Street
>   Wheaton, Illinois 60187

Cover design: Dual Identity, inc.

First printing 2013

Printed in the United States of America

Unless otherwise indicated, Scripture quotations are from the ESV® Bible (The Holy Bible, English Standard Version®), copyright © 2001 by Crossway. 2011 Text Edition. Used by permission. All rights reserved.

Scripture quotations marked NASB are from *The New American Standard Bible*®. Copyright © The Lockman Foundation 1960, 1962, 1963, 1968, 1971, 1972, 1973, 1975, 1977, 1995. Used by permission.

Scripture references marked RSV are from *The Revised Standard Version*. Copyright © 1946, 1952, 1971, 1973 by the Division of Christian Education of the National Council of the Churches of Christ in the U.S.A.

All emphases in Scripture quotations have been added by the author.

Trade paperback ISBN: 978-1-4335-7636-2
Mobipocket ISBN: 978-1-4335-7638-6
PDF ISBN: 978-1-4335-7637-9
ePub ISBN: 978-1-4335-7639-3

Library of Congress Cataloging-in-Publication Data

Oliphint, K. Scott, 1955–
Covenantal apologetics: principles and practice in defense of our faith / K. Scott Oliphint; foreword by William Edgar.
>   pages   cm
>   Includes bibliographical references and index.
>   ISBN 978-1-4335-2817-0
>   1. Apologetics. 2. Reformed Church—Doctrines. I. Title.
BT1103.O453   013
239—dc22
2013006320

Crossway is a publishing ministry of Good News Publishers.

CH		31	30	29	28	27	26	25	24	23	22
13	12	11	10	9	8	7	6	5	4	3	2	1

To John and Elise Maynard

Contents

Foreword

WILLIAM EDGAR

Slumber and Awakening

Apologetics, the defense and commendation of a Christian worldview, went into something of a hibernation, if not an eclipse, in the twentieth century. A number of factors contributed to this slumber. Following an age of relative confidence in the capacity of humankind to bring about the kingdom of God, the new century found so many reasons to put such confidence into question. It was a time of unforeseen upheavals and became the bloodiest of all centuries in human history. The tribulations of the First and Second World Wars, economic turmoil, revolutions, dictators, and global threats of hostilities meant doubts about the future even in the realm of theology. Artists such as Picasso or Mondrian depicted a world without any kind of trustworthy transcendent meaning. The strange, troubled Polish émigré to Britain Joseph Conrad (1857–1924) wrote powerfully about his discoveries, in various colonies, of the manifestation of human evil. With some exceptions, the twentieth century was a time of disillusionment and doubt.

Accordingly, theologians such as Karl Barth (1886–1968) simply dismissed apologetics as a weak-kneed concession to natural theology. Rightly critical of the nineteenth-century pretensions claiming to usher in God's kingdom in human ways, Barth went on, though, to argue that apologetics substitutes "human religion" for revelation, robbing the gospel of its inherent power. As he put it in the early parts of his *Church Dogmatics*, if Christianity takes up the weapons of apologetics, "it has renounced its birthright. It has renounced the unique power which it has as the religion of revelation. This power dwells only in weakness."[1] Apologetics, for Barth, only robs Jesus Christ of his freedom to make himself known directly. So great was Barth's influence that many seminaries or graduate schools simply eliminated their departments of apologetics.

Suspicions of apologetics could also be found outside the neoorthodox camp. No less an evangelical figure than Charles Haddon Spurgeon (1834–1892), and a number of his successors, thought the discipline a waste of time. "I question whether the defenses of the gospel are not sheer impertinences," he once said. He declared that if Jesus were not capable of fighting his own battles, then Christianity would be in a bad state indeed. Using the familiar illustration of the lion in a cage, he declared that the best strategy is not to defend the beast, but to let him out. The "prince of preachers" worried that apologetics would simply compromise the authority of the gospel preached.

Similarly, certain exegetes argued that the apostle Paul decided when he came to Corinth "to know nothing among [them] except Jesus Christ and him crucified" (1 Cor. 2:2) because he had tried apologetics on Mars Hill and failed to achieve any results (Acts 17:16–34). F. F. Bruce comments that some see Paul's statement to the Corinthians as a "confessed decision . . . as though he realized that his tactics at Athens were unwise." But Bruce comments that this was likely not the case, since Paul was no novice at Gentile evangelization. Rather, he was simply assessing two different contexts and responding appropriately.[2] William Ramsey goes so far as to say that Paul was "disappointed and perhaps disillusioned by his experience in Athens. He felt that he had gone at least as far as was right in the way of presenting his doctrine in a form suited to the current philosophy; and the result had been little more than naught."[3]

Are these not various cases of throwing out the proverbial baby with the bathwater? Barth's dialectical theology found little room for celebrating any kind of natural revelation; he feared it could lead to natural theology, wherein nature would be seen as *predisposed* to grace. In his estimation the opposite is the case: nature only resists grace.

---

[1] Karl Barth, *Church Dogmatics*, 1.2, *The Doctrine of the Word of God*, ed. G. W. Bromiley and T. F. Torrance, trans. G. W. Bromiley and R. J. Ehrlich (1956; repr., Edinburgh: T&T Clark, 2004), 333.

[2] F. F. Bruce, *Paul, Apostle of the Heart Set Free* (Grand Rapids: Eerdmans, 1977), 246.

[3] William Ramsay, *St. Paul the Traveller and the Roman Citizen* (London: Hodder & Stoughton, 1892), 252.

Barth's extreme view finds no warrant in Scripture, which is very insistent on the authority, necessity, sufficiency, and clarity of God's revelation in the creation and in human consciousness, as well as in special revelation. Romans 1:18–23 makes it clear that unbelieving people not only know *about* God and his standards, but also know God himself. Even Barth's fellow neoorthodox colleague Emil Brunner accepted the reality of a consciousness of God in the natural man, although in my view he did not deal fully with the implications of Romans 1:18ff.[4] Barth's polemical booklet *Nein* replied to Brunner's timid suggestions.[5]

Spurgeon's case is different. Perhaps like Barth he had read only the rationalist apologists of the nineteenth century, to which he rightly reacted. Unlike Barth, however, Spurgeon's theology was not dialectical. Rather, his zeal was to protect the gospel from the overgrowth of philosophical reasoning and preach it in all its "naked simplicity." The problem with that, however, is that it appears to eliminate all media— from the humanity of its carriers, to the requirement for adapting the message to particular audiences and cultures. After all, 1 Peter 3:15 enjoins the believer to respond to interlocutors with *apologia*. Making ourselves "all things to all people" does not necessarily compromise the gospel (1 Cor. 9:22). There really is no naked, simple gospel. It must be spoken in human language and argued carefully. Ironically, there is plenty of argument and apologetics in Spurgeon's sermons. The same might be said of Barth's work as well.

As to the view that Paul was disappointed in Athens and decided apologetics could not accomplish the task, we can find no evidence for any of that in the New Testament. While his time on Mars Hill was only brief, the result was the same as it was when he could stay in a place longer: some mocked, some wanted to hear more, and some joined him and believed (Acts 17:32–34). Besides, telling the Corinthians he would know only Christ and him crucified is a typically Pauline way of making his point. He is hardly telling them that he won't reason anymore and that he'll settle instead for repeating Christ and the cross like a mantra. His arguments for moral purity, for sound

---

[4] Emil Brunner, *Natural Theology*, trans. Peter Fraenkel (Eugene, OR: Wipf & Stock, 2002), 32.
[5] For a thoughtful discussion of this very public debate, see Trevor Hart, "A Capacity for Ambiguity: The Barth-Brunner Debate Revisited," *Tyndale Bulletin* 44 (1993): 289–305.

marriage, for eating food from the public market, for order in worship, and for the resurrection of the dead are among the most involved discourses found in the New Testament.

Some apologetics was being done in the twentieth century despite these wet blankets. Roman Catholics remained active in responding to the surrounding culture with a defense of the faith. One thinks of Maurice Blondel (1861–1949) in France, or the remarkable G. K. Chesterton (1874–1936) in Great Britain. We can also think of the neo-Thomists, or the "restorationists," who produced such fertile thinkers as Jacques Maritain (1882–1973) and Étienne Gilson (1884–1978). And there were a number of lay apologists from Great Britain, the most influential being the Anglican C. S. Lewis (1898–1963), specialist in medieval and Renaissance literature, storywriter, and apologist for the gospel.[6]

Neo-Calvinism

Then there was another kind of voice from within Protestantism, one that is represented in the present volume. Stemming from the awakening in the Netherlands (*Het Réveil*) and the so-called neo-Calvinist movement in Holland and then in North America, a special kind of apologetics was born. Unlike some of the awakenings, *Het Réveil* touched a good number of theologians, philosophers, and historians. One of the founding fathers of this inventive approach was Guillaume Groen van Prinsterer (1801–1876). Something of a Renaissance man, Groen was a statesman, historian, and chronicler, and, for a time, secretary to King William I of Holland. He grew to become one of the most articulate opponents of political liberalism. The basis for contemporary liberalism was what he considered to be the spirit of revolution, represented by politicians such as Johan Thorbecke. Much of this spirit was bolstered by the French Revolution, about which he wrote a penetrating analysis.[7] Following several conservative historians, Groen argued that while the revolutionary spirit in France no doubt stemmed from understandable frustrations, its underlying motive was a revolt

---

[6] Many other names could be added, including Hans Urs von Balthassar. For a comprehensive overview of the most important schools, see Avery Cardinal Dulles, *A History of Apologetics* (San Francisco: Ignatius, 1999).
[7] Guillaume Groen van Prinsterer, *Lectures on Unbelief and Revolution*, ed. Harry van Dyke (Toronto: Wedge, 1989).

against God's authority. In this way trends and historical movements could be understood in terms of their profound religious roots.

Such an approach became an inspiration for Abraham Kuyper (1837–1920), Groen's collaborator in the work of the Anti-Revolutionary political party (the ARP). Kuyper had grown up in rather "modernist" theological circles and studied in a fairly liberal seminary, the Leiden Divinity School. But his life changed during and just after his doctoral studies. Through a number of circumstances and readings he began to think that God is much more directly involved in human affairs than he had previously thought. Kuyper longed for a deeper piety than he had known. As the Reformed pastor in the small village of Beesd, he encountered a simple peasant girl, Pietronella Baltus, who dared tell him he was not a believer! Instead of scorning her, he listened and eventually gave his life fully to God.

Kuyper became a thoroughly Calvinist theologian. In addition, he was a statesman, a journalist, and the founder of the Free University of Amsterdam. Among his many accomplishments, one of the most important for our purposes is the groundwork he laid for the type of apologetics set forth in the book you are reading. Indeed, in some ways, Kuyper is the father of Reformed apologetics. He believed that the Christian world-and-life view could be compared and contrasted with other, unbelieving worldviews, and that this could be done in all the different disciplines, from science to politics to the arts and beyond. To get a good grasp on his approach, one ought to read his *Lectures on Calvinism*, presented at Princeton University in 1898.[8] The Christian university he founded was based on the same conviction that one could engage in every kind of study as a Christian believer.

There is considerable irony in attributing to Kuyper such a crucial role in the development of Reformed apologetics, since he regularly condemned apologetics as an obscure endeavor, unable to answer the issues of the day! A number of questions are involved here, which space forbids exploring. At least one reason he saw little benefit in the discipline of apologetics is that his approach to worldview meant opposing massive system to massive system, whereas much apologetics was concerned, it seemed to him, only with narrow polemics and details. There

---

[8] Abraham Kuyper, *Lectures on Calvinism* (Grand Rapids: Eerdmans, 1943). This is the best introduction to Kuyper's thought.

were also theological reasons. His sense of the antithesis between belief and unbelief was so great that it left no real room for communication across the barriers. While he strongly believed in common grace, he saw its purpose as, first, to restrain sin and, then, to allow Christians to engage in social and cultural activity, such as labor reforms and furthering the good purposes of science, the arts, and so on.[9] Common grace was not for Kuyper a basis that allowed bridge building and apologetic persuasion to take place. Here, though unlike Barth, he differed with the majority Reformed tradition. For example, John Calvin believed that Romans 1:18–23 means all human beings possess a *sense of deity* to which the Christian apologist may appeal. Nonetheless, what Reformed apologists have been able to take away from Kuyper, more than his objections to the discipline, is his insight into worldview and the way in which we must oppose the deep principle of belief to the deep principle of unbelief, rather than simply arguing from the details.[10]

Presuppositionalism

Here enters Cornelius Van Til (1895–1987). He was born in the Netherlands, but moved with his family to Highland, Indiana, when Cornelius was ten years of age. They were farming people. The Van Tils attended the Munster Christian Reformed Church. Cornelius was educated at Calvin College, then spent a year at Calvin Seminary, followed by Princeton Theological Seminary and finally Princeton University, where he obtained the PhD in 1927, having written his dissertation on "God and the Absolute," which interacted with Idealist philosophy. After a year in the pastoral ministry he returned to teach at Princeton Seminary in 1928. The next year he left to teach at the newly formed Westminster Theological Seminary, where he labored for more than forty years as professor of apologetics.[11]

[9] For a thorough study of Kuyper on common grace, see S. U. Zuidema, "Common Grace and Christian Action in Kuyper," http://www.reformationalpublishingproject.com/rpp/docs/S_U_Zuidema_on _Kuyper.pdf.

[10] For more on Kuyper's relation to Reformed apologetics, see the introduction to Abraham Kuyper in *Christian Apologetics Past and Present: A Primary Resource Reader*, vol. 2, *From 1500*, ed. William Edgar and K. Scott Oliphint (Wheaton, IL: Crossway, 2011), 331–35. Kuyper's sphere of influence was considerable. He is behind the Amsterdam philosophy represented by Herman Dooyeweerd, H. G. Stoker, and D. H. Th. Vollenhoven.

[11] A first-rate biography of Van Til is John R. Muether, *Cornelius Van Til: Reformed Apologist and Churchman* (Phillipsburg, NJ: P&R, 2008). This study covers many aspects of Van Til's thought, but it also describes him as a churchman through and through.

Building on the great Reformed theologians past and present, in-cluding John Calvin, Abraham Kuyper, Herman Bavinck, Benjamin B. Warfield, Geerhardus Vos, and C. W. Hodge, Van Til began to construct a truly biblical apologetic for the twentieth century. "Apologetics," as he puts it in several places, "is the vindication of the Christian phi-losophy of life against the various forms of the non-Christian philoso-phy of life."[12] This statement is significant at several levels. Van Til's project was to take the Christian worldview ("philosophy of life") and defend it over against unbelief. Notice he describes the "non-Christian philosophy" as coming in various guises. At bottom, though, unbelief is based on the dialectic of rationalism and irrationality at the same time. The term "vindication" should not throw us. It means justifica-tion rather than merely exoneration. Such justification takes the form of arguments for the truth of the Christian position that are different from the typical approaches in more traditional apologetics. Van Til said at least two things about the right kind of argument. First, there is no neutrality. You cannot "prove" the gospel simply by appealing to evidence or to some sort of logical demonstration, however sophisti-cated. Unless you embed evidence and logic in a framework that has authority, you have, in effect, sold the farm. You have not really chal-lenged unbelief. The second thing, however, is that we may indeed build bridges to the unbeliever. Because unbelievers know God and have the sense of deity in them, we can appeal to that consciousness. We do that not by building on their philosophy, since despite having a knowledge of God they suppress the truth (they process it wrongly), as Paul explains in Romans 1:18; instead, we may and must appeal to their conscious knowledge of God and his requirements.

Accordingly, the apologetic procedure set forth by Van Til is to get over onto the ground of the unbeliever for argument's sake, and then to show how such a position simply cannot square with its own claims. Jean-Paul Sartre (1905–1980), for example, affirmed that to be truly au-thentic, one's views could not begin with any preset rules. The trouble is, then, how do we know Sartre is truly authentic, free of rules? The requirement to be without rules is a rule! Indeed, Sartre took moral

---

[12] Cornelius Van Til, *Christian Apologetics*, 2nd ed., ed. William Edgar (Phillipsburg, NJ: P&R, 2003), 17. A number of Van Til's books were originally class syllabi handed to the students for discussion.

and political positions, which were most often leftist. When the "iron mask is off," Van Til says, we can then invite an unbeliever to see how in the Christian worldview you may find meaning and grace to think and to live.

Though Van Til did not use the term much, his approach has become known as *presuppositionalism*. The reason is that unless one presupposes the ontological Trinity (as he often referred to God), then it is impossible to make intelligible predications. Pierre Courthial, the dean of the Reformed Seminary at Aix-en-Provence, in my hearing called Van Til "the most original apologist of our times." A principal reason for his originality is that he thought about philosophy and apologetics biblically and theologically. This earned him the criticism of some who believed the genres should not be mixed. Yet he insisted that unless one begins from God's authority, revealed in the world and in the Scriptures, then we will always have an inadequate foundation for our views and our lives.

Van Til directly or indirectly inspired several generations of pastors, theologians, and laypersons. Some of them, like Francis Schaeffer (1912–1984), while not fully absorbing all of his teacher's views, have had an extraordinary impact on those they instructed. Others adopted certain aspects of Van Til's thought—say, the antithesis—but without detecting the radically gospel-driven aspect of his teaching. *Covenantal Apologetics: Principles and Practice in Defense of Our Faith* is written by a man who has not only absorbed what Van Til stood for, but developed and applied it in ways Van Til was unable to do, simply because he was a pioneer more than a consolidator.

Covenantal Apologetics

With the present volume, as with his other writings, K. Scott Oliphint has made a remarkable contribution to apologetics in the Reformed tradition. To begin with, much more than Van Til, who was usually satisfied merely to assume it, Oliphint does a good deal of biblical and theological explication for the reader. There are substantial sections here on the Trinity and the incarnation, as well as on biblical passages such as Acts 17 and many others, with which he substantiates his points. Oliphint, himself a rather original apologist, courageously puts into question the usefulness of the expression *presuppositional apologetics* and suggests instead that because the project of Van Til and his school was to defend the faith within the larger structure of the relation of the Creator to the creature, a more apt name for this task would be *covenantal apologetics*. Taking his beginning point from the way God condescends to his creatures, Oliphint argues that apologetics should be conducted by reaffirming the way God remains God and yet truly (covenantally) relates to the real world that he has made. And then he shows how our response should be "lost in wonder, love, and praise."[13] Accordingly, Oliphint highlights a feature of the *locus classicus* for apologetics, 1 Peter 3:15, not always noticed: its call first to lift up Christ in our hearts.

Oliphint spends considerable time on issues often ignored by typical books on apologetics. For example, he writes extensively of the role of the Holy Spirit in our lives and in our apologetics. This may sound like a no-brainer, except that most books I know, if they mention the Holy Spirit, ask us to choose between pure argument and somehow letting the Spirit do all the work for us. Oliphint explains the numerous roles of the Holy Spirit in apologetics.

Oliphint conducts various specific arguments with considerable depth. Rather than the usual sound-bite responses to skeptics and relativists, he takes on individual philosophers in sometimes imaginative ways. For example, he interacts with skeptics like Richard Dawkins, who got himself into trouble by telling a young woman who had been propositioned in an elevator that her plight was far less serious than that of women living in countries where the law allows female mutilation. Dawkins sensed that there was a difference, but the outraged woman did not, nor could she get him to show why there was. In fact, Dawkins's skeptical philosophy cannot produce a reason.

Oliphint addresses a number of problem areas that any apologist must address, and he does it by using the foundational theological principles that ought always to be at work in our arguments. This does not mean he simply quotes scriptural prooftexts so as to gag the interlocutor. Oliphint's primary training outside of theology is in philosophy. Thus, he addresses the problem of evil as it is often discussed

---

[13] From the hymn by Charles Wesley, "Love Divine, All Loves Excelling," 1747.

by philosophers. He thoughtfully interacts with Alvin Plantinga's *God, Freedom, and Evil*. He looks into the relation of science to the Bible. He has important thoughts on Islam. Yet, instead of trying to cover every possible issue, he explains that a covenantal apologetic is not an encyclopedia of answers but a wise approach to the art of persuasion.

The word *practice* is part of the subtitle. In view of that, Oliphint has made every attempt to show how all of this works. That is, again, something less present in Van Til's corpus, but a badly needed extension. We are given here ten principles that should guide our practice in various conversations. He discusses the use of legitimate *ad hominem* arguments. Indeed, Oliphint gives us a number of sample dialogs between believers and unbelievers.

Not everything in this book is easy. Certain parts of it will require concentration. Yet, no one could miss the general flow. Altogether, this book is timely and full of encouragement. It accomplishes what it commends: persuasion. If my hunch is right, this book represents the next step and an assured future for the movement that began so long ago in Holland.

Acknowledgments

This book is the product of decades of thought and teaching on the apologetic approach of Cornelius Van Til. Over time and through many readings and rereadings of his works, I continue to gain an ever-increasing awe and appreciation of his deeply insightful and faithful application of the Reformed theology that he saw as the lifeblood for a defense of the Christian faith.

I must first acknowledge Van Til's patience with me. As a young buck from Texas, out of the blue I once wrote him a letter to ask him questions about what I had been reading in his *Defense of the Faith*. Not only did he respond immediately, answering my questions graciously and humbly, but he even ended his letters with the remarkable phrase "Please write again," which I did, often. There is no substitute for the kind of humble and encouraging interaction that I received from him in those nascent days of apologetic discovery.

I must also thank my wife, Peggy. Even though she had deep suspicions about me as I began to think about these things when we were first married, she not only encouraged me to press on, but has become my most ardent helpmeet and supporter. She was the first one to read and critique each chapter in this book, and her comments helped make the end product much better than it would have been otherwise.

There have been, of course, colleagues, friends, and students along the way who have urged me to write a book like this and encouraged me. In that vein, I must mention my Westminster partner in apologetics, Bill Edgar. It is an honor to have Bill pen the foreword to this book. Bill has been a faithful friend and colleague, and has done nothing but encourage me in all my endeavors. It is no overstatement to say that I would not be fulfilling my calling in apologetics, humanly speaking, were it not for Bill's efforts in my behalf. I want also to thank my mentor and friend Richard B. Gaffin Jr. Dick has always urged me on and been most helpful in my theological pursuits over the last few decades.

I am thankful also to the Board of Trustees of Westminster Theological Seminary for granting me a study leave in which I could focus on this project and bring it to completion.

This book is affectionately dedicated to my longtime good friends John and Elise Maynard. John has always wanted a book like this, and he has, as only he can, *continually* urged me to get to writing. His disappointment will likely be that I did not choose him as a coauthor. My only excuse is that it would have ended our long and fruitful friendship.

Thanks, finally, to Allan Fisher and Crossway. I began my publishing career with Allan when he was with Baker Book House. From then to the present, he has been a faithful encouragement to me. This book would not have come to fruition without his efforts.

Introduction

All Divine Religion (say the Atheists) is nothing else than a human invention, artificially excogitated to keep man in awe; and the Scriptures are but the device of man's brain, to give assistance to Magistrates in Civil Government. This objection strikes at the root and heart of all Religion & opposeth two main principles at once: (1) that there is a God; (2) that the Scripture is the word of God.[1]

A few years ago I was involved in a conference overseas. The theme was the relationship of faith and reason. Most of the presenters were academicians and professors who came from an Eastern background. They were intensely curious about the various ways that the Western tradition thought about the relationship of faith and reason.

The paper I presented included a critique of Immanuel Kant's view of faith and knowledge, but it also included an argument for a theory of knowledge that had God's revelation as its ultimate ground. In the course of that presentation and discussion, I also wanted to make it clear to the other presenters that what I was urging was not simply a change of mind, although that was necessary. What I was urging was a total transformation that could be had only by way of faith in Christ. So I moved from a critique of Immanuel Kant to the *true* Immanuel, the Lord Jesus Christ.[2]

During the discussion immediately after my presentation, one of the other presenters was particularly agitated. It seemed obvious to him that all I was saying with respect to the relationship of faith to reason was that such a relationship could not be truly understood unless

---

[1] Edward Leigh, *Treatise on Divinity* (1646), 2.1, quoted in Richard A. Muller, *Post-Reformation Reformed Dogmatics: The Rise and Development of Reformed Orthodoxy, ca. 1520 to ca. 1725*, vol. 3, *The Divine Essence and Attributes*, 2nd ed. (Grand Rapids: Baker Academic, 2003), 192.
[2] The full text of this presentation can be found in K. Scott Oliphint, "Using Reason by Faith," *Westminster Theological Journal* 73, no. 1 (2011): 97–112.

one accepted the Bible as true. He went on to ask me just why he or anyone else should accept the Bible as an authority. He was perplexed that I seemed to be arguing in a circle.

I admitted to him that I certainly was arguing in (some kind of) a circle. I was arguing that unless one accepts the Bible for what it says and what it is, there would be no real solution to the faith-and-reason problem. Then I made clear to the other presenters that they were all asking that their own views, based on their own reasoning and sources, be accepted as true. In every case, I said, every other presenter appealed to his own final authority. "So," I asked, "on what basis should I accept your circle over mine?"

At that point there was an awkwardly long silence, after which one of the presenters said, "Maybe we should look again at the way Buddhism views these issues." In other words, the only response to my query was to deflect it and to suggest perhaps that a more mystical approach would be a better way to think about these things.

That evening some of us at the conference took a riverboat tour after dinner. Two of the attendees at the conference were eager to discuss my presentation. They were adherents of Kant's view, and they wanted to hear more about why I thought his view was so deficient. That more-than-three-hour conversation provided a wonderful opportunity to further discuss the reality and necessity of the gospel of Jesus Christ, and all that it entails, if one is interested in thinking properly about philosophy, or about anything else. The entire day, and into the evening, was one long apologetic discussion. I was attempting to defend the truth and faith of Christianity.

A number of presenters at this conference argued for some kind of generic theism. Their arguments were less than controversial. All they were saying, in effect, was that there might be a proper way to think about the possibility that a god could exist. Responses to these arguments mirrored the manner in which they were given—cool, pensive, and abstract. There was nothing in those kinds of arguments that required anything more than a response of, "Hmmm, perhaps," in contrast to an all-day discussion.

The approach I took at that conference is the approach that will be developed in these pages. The beauty of this approach—and what sets it off from any other apologetic method—is that it is naturally and centrally focused on the reality of God's revelation in Christ, including, of course, the good news of the gospel.

What was so distinctive about the argument I gave at that conference was that it called for a radical commitment, a commitment that included a change of mind and heart, a commitment every bit as religious as the context in which these presenters had been reared.

That kind of argument could never settle for a response of, "Perhaps," but was more conducive either to passionate objections or utter surrender. No abstract response would do in this case. The only way to think properly about faith and reason, I was arguing, is to take every thought captive to the obedience of Christ (2 Cor. 10:5). No other way can provide what my fellow presenters were hoping for.

That conference was an academic one, so it needed an academic presentation. But the approach that I was employing at the conference fits just as comfortably in a more normal setting. What I hope to accomplish in this book is to set out (what has been called) a presuppositional approach to apologetics. As will become clear, however, I hope to do that in a way that is relatively free of technical vocabulary. You will rarely see the word *presupposition*. Not only so, but I will suggest another label for this approach; I will try to make the case for retiring the label *presuppositional* and adopting the label *covenantal*. The reasons for this will be laid out in chapter 1.

This book seeks to do a number of things. It is an attempt to move past a somewhat common *description* of apologetics and apply a new label. In applying a new label, it will argue why that label, and the content included in it, is more apt for the method advocated here.

We are also attempting to move discussions about a "presuppositional" approach to apologetics past simply laying out the *principles* that must be included in it. Those principles are important. As a matter of fact, they are central and crucial to the approach itself. But in my experience, many students of apologetics are growing weary of an almost interminable discussion of principles only. This is understandable. An apologetic that can do little more than continually talk about itself is not worth the effort exerted or ink spilled over it. An apologetic that leaves us in the dark as to exactly *how* it might be practiced will not encourage the saints and will be of little use to the cause of Christ in the face of opposition.

So this book is not meant to be, technically speaking, another "introduction." My publisher tells me that the word *Introduction* in a book title is so broad these days that it says very little about the contents of a book. Rather, this book is meant to be a basic translation. To translate means, literally, to "carry across." There are two aspects of translation that I hope to accomplish in this book. First, translations usually refer to a "carrying across" from one language to another, for example, from Greek to English, in the case of the New Testament. What this book will do is translate the language, concepts, and ideas set forth in Van Til's Reformed apologetic into language, terms, and concepts that are more accessible. Second, translations have to do with "carrying across" the meanings of words, phrases, and so forth. I hope to translate much of what is *meant* in Van Til's own writings from their often philosophical and technical contexts to a more basic biblical and theological context. Part of that translation of meaning will include dialogs designed to show what it means, for example, when a defense of Christianity focuses on an opponent's presuppositions.

As with any translation, there will, nevertheless, be some differences from the original. The differences will not be substantial. That is, they will not (as far as I know) change or negate any of Van Til's central concerns. The differences, rather, will be of language and of style. While, for the most part, avoiding technical terminology, I will explain methodology by using some of the basic categories given to us in Scripture and in the Reformed theology that flows from Scripture. In that way, I hope that the discussion and development in this book will take a Reformed apologetic and move it forward.

Because my approach has its roots in biblical and theological truth, I will begin, in chapter 1, with some of the basic biblical content that informs that approach. Chapter 2 will then explain how that content applies specifically to the activity and discipline of apologetics. Chapters 3 and 4 lay out the methodological impetus behind a covenantal approach. I will argue that, given its theological roots, covenantal apologetics is better seen as the art of persuasion than as the science of demonstration.

Chapter 5 will attempt to show how (what is sometimes called) the "Achilles' heel" of Christianity—the problem of evil—can be adequately and biblically addressed in a way that moves, naturally and inexorably, to the good news of the gospel. Chapters 6 and 7 are, in the main, expositions, with example dialogs, of what it means for us to do apologetics in a way that requires that we "walk in wisdom toward outsiders." The "outsiders" in chapter 6 will be those who hold to naturalistic evolution. In chapter 7, the "outsider" will be a convert to Islam.

The "movement" of the book will progress from the simple to the more complex. Each chapter is designed, in its own way, to build on the ones before it. So it just may be that the latter chapters will introduce ideas and concepts not yet familiar to some.

In the discipline of apologetics, however, there is a constant need for thoughtful, meditative practice. Such practice itself may be new to many. However, I am confident that the more complex material will become more and more obvious and familiar as readers give it more and more thought and meditation. In most everything that I say in the dialogs, all that is needed is a thoughtful commitment to the truths given to us in Scripture, and then the practice of probing the assumptions and foundations of any opposing position will come more readily.

In all of these chapters, there is a dual goal. I am attempting to explain the focus of our approach and then, through sample dialogs, show the approach "in action." My hope is that this combination of "principles and practice" will move readers significantly forward in their interest in and practice of a defense of Christianity.

This, then, is the bottom-line truth that must be central in everything we discuss: Christianity is true, so anything opposing it is false. This means that whatever opposition to Christianity we face, it is by definition an opposition that is false. Even if we have no idea what the central tenets or teachings are in such opposition, we know at the outset that it cannot sustain itself in God's world. The rest of this book is an attempt to explain the implications of that central truth.

One more note must be mentioned. As stated above, the approach that will be set out in this book is one that reached its halcyon days during the career of Cornelius Van Til. I have read virtually all of the significant criticisms of Van Til's approach and am well aware of the problems that some see. However, none of those criticisms is convincing enough to provoke a change in Van Til's basic approach. Whatever the critiques, Van Til's application of Reformed theology to the discipline of apologetics is obvious in everything he wrote; any advance on his discussion must reckon, first, with the theological roots of his approach.[3]

I am convinced that much more *biblical and theological* discussion is needed with respect to this approach. So much of the material related to this method is mired in deep and complex philosophical concepts and verbiage that it has remained, by and large, inaccessible to any who are not interested or schooled in such things. The change of terms and labels in this book is, therefore, not meant to be mere window dressing. It is meant to begin to alter discussions of how we understand and do apologetics. I remain convinced that if one embraces the theology that came out of the Reformation era, then this approach to apologetics is the only consistent option available. Discussions about that, then, ought to begin with the possibility of *theological* disagreements, and not with mere differences in *philosophy* or in philosophical jargon.

Though this book is a translation, it is not meant to eclipse its original source. Any who are interested in moving on—theologically and apologetically—after reading this book, should begin to collect the volumes listed at the end of chapter 1, for a start, and to work through those in light of the material presented here.

I am confident that no other method so naturally and clearly sets forth a defense of the *Christian* faith as this one does. The application of this approach is the best apologetic means to bring glory to God; it encourages others to know and understand that glory, as they see it in the face of Jesus Christ (2 Cor. 4:6).

Sure I must fight if I would reign;
Increase my courage, Lord.
I'll bear the toil, endure the pain,
Supported by Thy Word.[4]

---

[3] For an excellent picture of Van Til's career, including the central focus of his theology on his work in apologetics, see John R. Muether, *Cornelius Van Til: Reformed Apologist and Churchman* (Phillipsburg, NJ: P&R, 2008).
[4] Isaac Watts, "Am I a Soldier of the Cross," 1724.

1

Always Ready

Reformed theology, as worked out by Calvin and his recent exponents such as Hodge, Warfield, Kuyper, and Bavinck, holds that man's mind is derivative. As such it is naturally in contact with God's revelation. It is surrounded by nothing but revelation. It is itself inherently revelational. It cannot naturally be conscious of itself without being conscious of its creatureliness. For man self-consciousness presupposes God-consciousness. Calvin speaks of this as man's inescapable sense of deity.[1]

Christian apologetics is the application of biblical truth to unbelief. It's really no more complicated than that. But it *is* complicated by the fact that there are so many theological permutations of biblical truth and almost no end to the variations and contours of unbelief. Not only so, but there have been, are, and will continue to be attacks of every sort that seek to destroy the truth of the Christian faith. So as one thinks about and commences to defend the Christian faith, things can become complex.

What we hope to accomplish in this book is more modest than some might wish. We will not seek to knock down every argument, or even every main argument, that has been brought against Christianity. Nor will we seek to lay out every *way* such attacks and objections have been or can be addressed. Normally, there are various ways to respond to objections that come our way. Rather, what we will set out to do, first of all, is to lay out the primary biblical and theological principles that must be a part of any covenantal defense of Christianity and then

---

[1] Cornelius Van Til, *The Defense of the Faith*, 4th ed., ed. K. Scott Oliphint (Phillipsburg, NJ: P&R, 2008), 114.

to demonstrate how these principles might be applied against certain objections.

Therefore, the intent of this book is to be both principial (foundational) and practical. The principles can be seen as the fence outside of which one should not go, and the actual responses to objections can be seen as specific paths within the fence line. No doubt there are other paths as well, so there will usually be other ways one might approach objections that are proffered against Christianity.

The fact is, there is no one way or even five ways properly to address objections against Christianity. There are as many ways as there are people with objections. What you might say to one person could be very different from what you might say to another, even if their basic objections are identical. But in each and every case, what must be understood are the fundamental biblical and theological tenets or principles that guide, direct, and apply to whatever attacks, objections, and questions may come to the Christian. With those principles in place, a proper, covenantal defense of Christianity can be pursued. So we must stay within the fence line (i.e., the principles), but we have ample room to move inside its borders.

The biblical and theological principles that will be laid out below belong, historically, to the theology that gained its greatest clarity during the time of the Reformation. Thus, the principles will have a certain specificity to them that may not be the case, for example, in a more general evangelical context. Our entire discussion will assume that Reformed theology is the best and most consistent expression of the Christian faith.[2] First, however, to ensure that we are all on the same page, some basic truths about Christianity and apologetics will be broached here and will come up later as we proceed.

Christian Truth

The true God—Father, Son, and Holy Spirit—created the heavens and the earth, and he created them good. There were no flaws in God's creation. Because it was all the work of his perfect hands, it was all very good. But then creation changed, because we changed it.

---

[2] For a summary of Reformed theology, see, for example, the Westminster Confession of Faith.

The entrance of sin in the world was also the initiation of a cosmic war. Scripture gives us no details as to why the serpent decided to tempt our first parents. Perhaps there was a Job-like scene in the heavenlies, where Satan asked for permission to attack Adam and Eve. Or perhaps it was just a natural part of the devil's now-fallen nature.

Whatever the reason, the temptation of Adam and Eve was an attack on their right relationship with God. And the attack was successful. Eve was utterly deceived (2 Cor. 11:3), ate the forbidden fruit, and convinced Adam to do the same, and all of creation fell.

It would have been perfectly acceptable and expected if God had determined at that point to do away with creation altogether. Because the fall of creation was ruinous to its original status as "very good," and because the reality of sin in the world was despicable to a holy God, he could have simply determined to eliminate the universe, setting things back to where they were prior to his creative activity. God could have continued happily and eternally to exist without creation and all of its now-sinful aspects.

But this was not to be; it was not a part of God's eternal plan, a plan he freely decided to initiate. Instead, the Lord determined freely to condescend and extend his grace. He came down to the garden. But this time, he did not come down to have fellowship with Adam and Eve. Rather, he came down as their Judge and as their only hope. Not only so, but he came down to judge Satan as well for what he had done in Paradise.

> The Lord God said to the serpent, "Because you have done this, cursed are you above all livestock and above all beasts of the field; on your belly you shall go, and dust you shall eat all the days of your life. I will put enmity between you and the woman, and between your offspring and her offspring; he shall bruise your head, and you shall bruise his heel." (Gen. 3:14–15)

It may be that the full impact of these horrendous words escapes us. We should remember that prior to this event everything was just as it should be. God had created a place and people in that place, all of which were there to bring him glory and to work in relationship to and with him.

But after the fall he said, "I will put enmity between you and the woman, and between your offspring and her offspring." This is horrible news. This marks the beginning of a radical and all-encompassing war. From this time forward, no one is excluded from this war; no one is left out. Prior to Adam's sin, Adam and Eve worked toward the one goal of bringing glory to the God who had made all things. Now there are two goals, not one. There are two cosmic powers working in creation. The power of God and his plan are now battling against the power of Satan and his legion. These powers are not at all equal; one depends upon the other. Anything Satan does, he does only because the Lord sustains him. So the battle is not among equals. Even so, the battle rages on until the close of history.

In this light, and basic to everything else that we will say, we should recognize that every person on the face of the earth is defined, in part, by his relationship to a covenant head. That is, there are two, and only two, positions that are possible for humanity, and only one of which can be actual for each person at a given time. A person is either, by nature (after the fall into sin), *in Adam*, in which case he is opposed to and in rebellion against God, or he is *in Christ*, in which case by grace a person is not guilty before God but is an heir of eternal life. This is the covenantal status of humanity, and it assumes, in each case, a relationship to God. It assumes as well the ongoing battle against evil in which God is making his enemies a footstool for Christ's feet.

But why didn't God, when sin entered the world, simply squash Satan and his legion and finish the battle? Why does he put up with, even actively join the fight against, such rebellion when he could stop it at any time? The only answer we have to such questions is that all things are still working to and for his own glory, even though sin has ruined his creation (Rom. 11:36). Everything that happens, happens according to his all-wise and perfect plan.

But we shouldn't minimize the fact that he is actively fighting. Though he has the power to finish it all, the Lord continues to wage war against the powers in the heavenlies. Not only so, but those who are in Christ have the privilege and responsibility to fight with him (Eph. 6:10–18). Included in that fight is the activity of defending the faith (a faith, we should remember, that we have been graciously given—cf. Eph. 2:8; 1 Pet. 3:15; Jude 3). This is the task of apologetics; it is the task of defending and commending the truth of Christianity.

Required to Respond

We should pause here for a moment to consider our place in God's cosmic battle. A non-Christian friend of mine recently returned from a trip overseas. When I asked him how his trip was, he looked me in the eye and, with finger pointing and shaking in my face, steadfastly declared, "There is no God." That was the first thing he wanted me to know. He knew I was a Christian, and he was anxious to give me one more reason why he was not. He reasoned that if there were a God, the places that he had seen on his trip would not be in the wretched and Augean conditions that he saw. For him, the suffering he witnessed was so overwhelming that it was a sure indication God could not exist. My response was very simple, and it stopped the conversation (at least for a while). I simply said to him, "What makes you think that God is responsible for such things?" That question was in itself a kind of defense; it was calculated to make my friend think of the destructive power of sin.

The first epistle of Peter is written to a group of suffering Christians. These are Christians who have been "grieved by various trials" (1:6), who are in exile (1:17), and who thus are living in places foreign to them. They are encouraged not to be surprised when fiery trials come upon them (4:12)—not *if* fiery trials come, but *when* they do. The Christian perspective on suffering is in diametrical opposition to my friend's. This is not surprising. There is an antithesis between Christian and non-Christian; as we said, one is either in Christ or in Adam. That antithesis is not merely theoretical. It applies to the way we think, the way we act, and the way we view the world. In the midst of his readers' suffering, Peter gives this command: "Sanctify Christ as Lord in your hearts, always being ready to make a defense to everyone who asks you to give an account for the hope that is in you, yet with gentleness and reverence" (1 Pet. 3:15, NASB).

The command is to "sanctify Christ as Lord." In the previous verse, Peter refers to Isaiah 8:12–13, which includes a command to regard

Yahweh as holy. Peter attributes the prerogatives of Yahweh to Jesus Christ here. The New Testament application of Isaiah 8:12–13 is that Christians, in the midst of their suffering, are to set apart, remember, and recognize in their hearts that Jesus Christ is Lord.

Instead of looking at the overwhelming suffering around them and declaring that there is no God, they are rather to declare, "Jesus is Lord." They are to "sanctify" or "set apart" the lordship of Christ in their hearts by showing his lordship when suffering comes. Peter then goes on to tell them (and us) that the command to set Christ apart as Lord is fulfilled as we ready ourselves for a defense of what we believe. Peter is telling us here that, when objections and attacks come our way, we are required to respond to them.

If we are honest with ourselves, our mindset may often be more in sync with my friend's than with Scripture. It may be that, when suffering comes, or when it threatens to overwhelm us in some way, we think that belief in God seems foolish. How could God allow such a thing to happen? Why wouldn't he prevent this?

Perhaps the most significant point of Peter's command is the reason he gives for it. It is as simple as it is profound: "For Christ also died for sins once for all" (3:18, NASB). The ironic twist, one that points us to the transposition of the gospel, is not that when we see suffering, we should conclude there is no God. Rather, it is that when we see suffering, we should remember that God himself, in the person of his Son, did exactly that so that suffering and sin would one day cease. Suffering is clear evidence that Christ is Lord; it is not a testimony against that truth. The suffering that is the cross of Christ—the very thing that, on the face of it, might lead us to believe there is no God—is, as a matter of fact, the deepest expression of his sovereign character as Lord.

It is the clear and steadfast conviction that Christ, and Christ alone, is Lord that has to motivate our Christian defense. Peter's point is clear. In commanding us to set Christ apart as Lord, Peter is not talking about whether one has received Christ as Savior, or as Savior and Lord—not at all. Peter's point is that, if one is to be adequately prepared to give an answer for one's Christian faith, the lordship of Christ must be a solid and unwavering commitment of one's heart.

But why? Again, the answer is as simple as it is profound: because that is what he is! The specific command that Peter gives can be stated more generally. We are to think about and live in the world according to what it really is, not according to how it might at times *appear* to us. As Peter writes to persecuted and scattered Christians, he recognizes that one of their paramount temptations is to interpret their circumstances in such a way that would not acknowledge Christ as Lord. In the midst of their persecution and suffering, it may begin to look like someone else is in charge. After all, if Christ were Lord, how could these things be happening?

As a matter of fact, the lordship of Christ explains why these things are happening. The lordship of Christ is the conclusion to, the end result of, his own suffering and humiliation. It is *because* he was obedient, even to death on a cross, that he has been given the name that is above every name. It is *because* he suffered that every knee will bow and every tongue confess that he is Lord. The road to his exaltation was paved with blood, sweat, and tears. If we are to be exalted with him on that last day, ours will be so paved as well.

With all of the attendant mysteries surrounding the suffering of Job, two words from God himself—"my servant" (Job 1:8; 2:3)—initiate our understanding of what Job was called to endure. As Job was called to be a suffering servant, Christ was the quintessential Suffering Servant (Isa. 53). Those who know that their Redeemer lives (Job 19:25), who are called to be united to him, will be suffering servants with him as well.

The lordship of Christ is basic to our defense of Christianity. Christ now reigns. He is Lord. All authority in heaven and on earth has been given to him. That authority is the prerequisite to the command to make disciples. Without that authority, baptism and disciple making in and for the church are meaningless. All things have been placed under his feet, and Christ has been given "as head over all things to the church" (Eph. 1:22). The process of history is the process of making Christ's enemies a footstool for his feet. That footstool is being built because he is Lord. Just like Jesus's earthly father, his heavenly Father is a carpenter. He is building a footstool for his Son (see, for example, Acts 2:35; Heb. 1:13; 10:13).

So wherever you go, to whomever you speak, Christ is Lord there, and he is Lord over that person. Since he is Lord, his truth is truth in every place and for every person. All persons are in a covenant relationship with Christ the Lord. They owe him obedience. The same Christ who rules over you, rules over those who oppose him. The fact that someone has not set Christ apart as Lord in his heart in no way detracts from or undermines the central point that he is Lord over all. At least two implications of this truth are important to remember.

The first is that truth is not relative. Most Christians agree with that point, even if they don't quite understand it. I remember years ago reading Allan Bloom's best seller *The Closing of the American Mind*. Bloom began that book by noting what was patently obvious then (and what is even more pronounced today). He said that there was one cardinal affirmation that every college student believed: "Truth is relative." He went on to say that it was such a part of the fabric of our culture and our way of thinking that it was thought to need no argument; and to demand an argument would be to misunderstand the status of that truth. The bedrock conviction that truth is relative, Bloom asserted, was as ingrained in the American psyche as baseball and apple pie; it was the air that we breathed. "Truth is relative"—ironically, that proposition alone seemed to be universally affirmed and thus *not* relative.

The sinful power of self-deception cannot be underestimated in this regard. The power of sin in us makes us adept anosognosiacs (people unaware of, or denying, our own disease). In our sins, we have an uncanny ability to fashion a world that has all the substance of an ethereal fog. If anything is patently obvious, it is that truth cannot be relative. The notion itself betrays a decided lack of self-awareness and a stubborn blindness to the big picture. At the micro and the macro levels, we live and move and have our being in the God who alone is truth. Anyone who wants to argue that truth is relative betrays, by that argument, that it cannot be. Anyone who wants to hold that truth is relative, but pretends apathy about the matter and thus eschews argument, is like David Hume,[3] who played backgammon even though he knew that such an act annihilated his own philosophy. So the relativ-

---

[3] David Hume (1711–1776) was the most famous and radical exponent of the empiricist school of philosophy. I'll say more on Hume later.

istic worldview that we think is real turns out to be a sleight of hand, a magician's illusion.

The point for the Christian, however, and the point to stand on in a covenantal apologetic, is that Christ's lordship—which includes not only that he now reigns, but also that he has spoken and that all owe him allegiance—is true for anyone and everyone. Christ is Lord even over his enemies, and ours. And part of what this means is that the authority of Scripture, which is the verbal expression of Christ's lordship, is authoritative even over those who reject it.

The Bible is authoritative not because we accept it as such, but because it is the word of the risen Lord. It has a claim on all people. Its truth is the truth for every person in every place. Why, then, would we be reluctant to communicate that truth in our apologetics? Perhaps because we have not reckoned with the actual lordship of Christ. Perhaps we haven't really set him apart as Lord in our hearts.

The second implication, which we have already raised, is that we must base our defense of Christianity on reality, and reality is what God says it is. What we dare not do in a covenantal apologetic is let the enemy choose the weapon. Any enemy worth his salt will choose a weapon that fires in only one direction. But we are called to use the weapons that the Lord himself has given us. "For the weapons of our warfare are not of the flesh but have divine power to destroy strongholds" (2 Cor. 10:4). The weapons of our warfare are divine weapons, and they have their focus in the sword of the Spirit (Eph. 6:17).

Why choose these weapons? Because they are *God's* weapons, given to us by God so that we can "destroy arguments and every lofty opinion raised against the knowledge of God, and take every thought captive to obey Christ" (2 Cor. 10:5). In other words, they are the real and true weapons that God has given to us to fight the good fight. They are the weapons through which God is building his Son's footstool. And they are the weapons that alone have the power to subdue the enemy.

There is more to be said on these points, and more will be said later. But the basic principle is this: a covenantal apologetic must proceed on the basis of reality and not on the basis of illusion. We must proceed according to what Christ, who is the Lord, has told us, not according to what our opponents have decided is "appropriate" for a defense of

Christianity. We view our apologetic and we proceed in it, as in the rest of life, through the corrective lenses of Holy Scripture. Anything less would be like choosing to walk in a fog in order to see more clearly.

What Is Covenantal Apologetics?

As we saw in 1 Peter 3:15, apologetics is a biblical and theological notion taken directly from Scripture. In that way, *apologetics* is a term much like other biblical words such as *justification* or *sanctification*. The difference with apologetics, however, is that it necessarily deals with a relationship between Christian faith and unbelief that is not the focal point of most other biblical notions. Many, if not most, of our Christian doctrines relate specifically to what we as Christians believe. Not so with the notion of apologetics.

So, for example, if one wanted to be an expert on the biblical teaching of justification, one would concentrate on texts that deal specifically with that teaching. The doctrine of justification is a doctrine for the church; it is Scripture's teaching on how we can be declared not guilty before God. It relates directly to the Christian and his relationship with God. In order to think carefully about apologetics, we begin with Scripture as well. But we pursue Scripture in such a way that we have at the forefront of our minds how biblical doctrines—especially the doctrines of God, Christ, sin, and salvation—relate to what Scripture says about unbelief. In other words, the concern of apologetics is biblically to answer challenges that come to Christianity from unbelief.

What I hope to show throughout this book is that apologetics must (1) be *Christian* and (2) have a *theological* foundation. If these two things are integral to Christian apologetics, then it might be best to give it a proper label. Though the approach I advocate is a version of what some have called presuppositionalism, that label as an approach to apologetics needs once and for all to be laid to rest. It has served its purpose well, but it is no longer descriptively useful, and it offers, now, more confusion than clarity when the subject of apologetics arises.

There are various reasons for this confusion. For one, there are a variety of ways to understand the notion of presupposition, as well as a variety of presuppositionalists whose approaches differ significantly. Francis Schaeffer, Gordon Clark, and E. J. Carnell, just to mention three, were all concerned with presuppositions in their apologetic argumentation. Their respective approaches, however, differ in ways that relate to their use and understanding of biblical truth.

Moreover, there is also the post-Kuhnian[4] predicament in which we find ourselves, such that paradigms and presuppositions have come to be equated, and have come into their own, in a way that would serve to destroy Christianity in general, and Christian apologetics in particular. "Presuppositionalism" has been thereby dispossessed of any clear meaning and has often died the death of a thousand qualifications. It is time, therefore, to change the terminology, at least for those who consider the approach of Cornelius Van Til to be consistent with Reformed theology and its creeds.

Because what Van Til was arguing had its roots in historic, Reformed theology, it would be natural to delineate his apologetic approach simply as Reformed. However, there is a breadth and depth to the adjective *Reformed* that may make it too ambiguous as a modifier for apologetics. I propose, in light of the above, that the word *covenantal*, properly understood, is a better, more accurate, more specific term to use for a biblical, Reformed apologetic. I hope in what follows to explain Van Til's presuppositional apologetics and in the process to make a case for a terminology switch, a switch to a *covenantal apologetic*.

To understand this approach to apologetics, as well as to justify the change in terminology, we need a clear understanding of the word *covenant*. For that, we begin with the Westminster Confession of Faith 7.1, "Of God's Covenant with Man":

> The distance between God and the creature is so great, that although reasonable creatures do owe obedience unto Him as their Creator, yet they could never have any fruition of Him as their blessedness and reward, but by some voluntary condescension on God's part, which He has been pleased to express by way of covenant.

We need to highlight the most important ideas in this section. First of all, we are reminded that, in the beginning, *and quite apart from the entrance of sin*, the distance between God and the creature is "so great."

---

[4] Thomas Kuhn's *Structure of Scientific Revolutions*, published in 1962, made the notions of paradigms and presuppositions much more commonplace than they were before.

But just what is this distance? Is it an actual spatial distance between God and humanity? That doesn't seem possible, given that God is everywhere; there is no place where he is absent. So the "distance" referred to here must be metaphorical. It should not be interpreted as primarily spatial.

Rather, it might be best to think of it as a distance based on the character of God himself in relation to the character of man. The "distance," in other words, might be analogous to the distance between man and a snail. There are similarities between a man and a snail—both are capable of physical motion, both depend on the necessities of life. But it is not possible for a snail to transcend its own character in a way that would allow it to converse, communicate, and relate to man on a human level. We could call this an *ontological* difference; a difference according to the *being* of the snail relative to the *being* of man. Or, perhaps better, there is a necessary and vast *distinction* between the two kinds of beings.

This is the case as well with respect to God and man, according to this section of the Confession. There is a vast, qualitative distinction between God's character and ours, between God's being and the being of man. God is One "who is infinite in being and perfection, a most pure spirit, invisible, without body, parts, or passions; immutable, immense, eternal, incomprehensible . . ." (WCF 2.1). He is not restricted or confined by space; he is not subject to the passing of moments; he is not composed of anything outside of his own infinite character; he does not change; he cannot be fully understood.

We, however, are none of those things. We have no analogies of what those attributes are, and we are unable completely to comprehend them. We are finite, bodily, mutable, and constrained by time and space. This disparity is impossible to state adequately, but it is a difference, a vast difference, and one that includes a kind of "distance" between us and God.

There is a great chasm fixed between God and his creatures, and the result of such a chasm is that we, all of humanity, could *never* have *any* fruition of God, unless he saw fit, voluntarily (graciously), to condescend to us by way of covenant.[5] That condescension includes God's

---

[5] For a fuller and more technical discussion of God's covenantal condescension, in light of his "distance" from us, see K. Scott Oliphint, *The Majesty of Mystery: Celebrating the Glory of an Incomprehensible God* (Bellingham, WA: Lexham Press, 2016).

revealing himself in and through his creation, including his word, to man. We begin, therefore, with respect to who we *are* and to what we can *know*, with a fundamental distinction between the Creator and the creature.

Contrary to some opinions, God is in fact Totally Other. But there is nothing intrinsic to this truth that would preclude God from revealing himself to his creatures. Since God is Totally Other from creation, our understanding of him and our communication and communion with him can take place only by his initiative. That initiative is his condescension, including his revelation. Such revelation, as the exclusive means of knowledge of and communion with God, *assumes* rather than *negates* God's utter "otherness."

So God decided to create. He did not have to create, but he determined that he would. The high point of that creation was the creation of man, Adam and Eve. These were the only aspects of all of God's creation that were called "image of God" and were meant to show off God's character.

In creating man, God voluntarily determined, at the same time, to establish a relationship with him. That relationship is properly designated a *covenant*; it is established unilaterally by God, and it places obligations on man with respect to that relationship. It comes to man by virtue of God's revelation, both in the world, defined here as every created thing, and in his spoken word.

This has sweeping implications for apologetics. Given that all men are in covenant relationship to God, they are bound by that relationship to "owe obedience unto Him as their Creator." That obligation of obedience comes by virtue of our being created—we were created as covenant beings. We are people who, by nature, have an obligation to worship and serve the Creator. That much has been true since the beginning.

But as we have said, something went terribly wrong. Man fell from his original state and consequently lost the ability and the will to worship and serve the Creator. The covenant relationship that, prior to the fall, existed in harmony with the Creator's will was, after the fall, a relationship of animosity and rebellion on our side, and was one of wrath on the side of the Creator.

But there was still a relationship. It is not that man ceased to be a covenant creature after the fall. He was still responsible to God to obey and worship him. He turned this responsibility, however, into occasions for rebellion. Instead of walking with God in the cool of the day, man began to try to hide from God, to fight with God, to run from him, to use the abilities and gifts he had been given to attempt to thwart the plan of God and to construe for himself a possible world in which he was not dependent on God at all.

So God provided a way in which the obedience owed him and the worship due his name could be accomplished. He sent his own Son, who alone obeyed the spirit and letter of the law, and who also went to the cross to take the penalty we deserve in order that those who would come to him in faith would be declared not guilty before the tribunal of the covenant Judge. And those who thus put their faith in him, as a part of their obedience to him, may be called on, and thus required, to answer the challenges and questions that come from those who will not bow the knee to Christ.

Enter apologetics. To whom is the faith "once for all delivered to the saints" to be defended? Given the above, it is to be defended at least to those who are *covenant breakers*—those whose relationship to God is defined by rebellion and denial. The apostle Paul gives us something of the psychology of these covenant breakers in Romans 1 and 2; we will highlight some of his main points in those chapters here. Given the importance of Paul's discussion, however, it will be necessary for us to elaborate on his themes in these passages throughout this book.

Paul begins, first of all (Rom. 1:18–23), by asserting that the attributes of God have been both clearly seen and understood since the creation of the world. That is, Paul is telling us here, part of what it means to be created in God's image is that man *inescapably* knows God. It is not simply that he knows *that a* god exists. But, says Paul, man—*every man*—knows God, the true God, the God who made all things. We can say unequivocally, therefore, that by virtue of man's being created in the image of God, by virtue of man's being a covenant creature, *every human being on the face of the earth since creation and into eternity* has an ineradicable knowledge of God—a knowledge that is given *through the things that were made*, which includes, of course, *everything* (except

God himself). In order for man to have this ineradicable knowledge, he must know the things created, for it is through those things that the knowledge of God comes. So in knowing a particular thing, man knows God who reveals himself in and through that thing (including man himself). Thus, man knows God if and when he knows anything else.

This was in part Calvin's point in beginning the *Institutes* as he did. "Nearly all the wisdom we possess, that is to say, true and sound wisdom, consists of two parts: the knowledge of God and of ourselves."[6] There can be no separation between the knowledge of God and the knowledge of ourselves. To the extent that we know ourselves truly, to that extent we know God truly; the two are inextricably moored. This is part of what it means to be *image* of God. To try to know ourselves without knowing God would be like trying to know our image in a mirror when we were not standing in front of it. There would be no image because the "original" would not be there. True self-knowledge depends on God-knowledge (and vice versa). So it is also that in the act of knowing, to the extent that we know something truly, we know it as created, that is, as having its origin and its sustaining existence in God.[7] To claim to know something while thinking it to be independent of God (or to deny that there is a God) is to fail to know it for what it *really* is. Whatever it is, it is created and sustained by God at every moment.

But Paul introduces a problem in this passage. Man does not willingly submit himself to the knowledge of God that comes in and through creation. On the contrary, God's wrath is revealed from heaven precisely because man, in knowing God, suppresses the truth of that knowledge in unrighteousness, worshiping and serving the creature rather than the Creator (Rom. 1:18, 23, 25). As a covenant creature, man takes his relationship to God, graciously initiated by God's condescension, and attempts to hold down its truth and the implications of that truth, fabricating for himself idols to take the place of the God whom he knows to exist and to whom he knows he owes worship (cf. WCF 21.1, 7).

---

[6] John Calvin, *Institutes of the Christian Religion*, ed. John T. McNeill, trans. Ford Lewis Battles, 2 vols., Library of Christian Classics (Philadelphia: Westminster Press, 1960), 1.1.1.

[7] Van Til speaks of "false knowledge," which is knowledge but which refuses to acknowledge the ground and source of knowledge, namely, God himself.

It is not the case, then, as Thomas Aquinas supposed, that knowledge of the existence of God is not self-evident to us[8]; rather, such knowledge is an integral aspect of our covenant relationship with God and can no more be eradicated from our souls than can our souls themselves be annihilated. The problem is not with the *evidence*, but with the *"receptacle,"* (i.e., the sinful person) to which the evidence constantly (through creation) comes.

It is this covenant dynamic of always knowing while suppressing (what I will call a *sensus/suppression* dynamic) that a Reformed, covenantal apologetic seeks to incorporate. It may be helpful here to elucidate the application of this "knowing while suppressing" principle by attempting to make some distinctions.

Man (male and female) did not cease to be human after the fall. There were certain aspects after the fall that were in continuity with the pre-fall situation. It should be obvious from our reading of Scripture that while every aspect of man was affected by sin, so that we are all *totally* depraved, we still remain *people* made in God's image. Whatever was essential to being a person prior to the fall was retained after the entrance of sin. And since one essential aspect of man was his being created in the image of God, that image, at least to some extent, remained after the fall. We are still, by virtue of our very constitution, covenant creatures even after the fall; we are still accountable to God and we still owe God unqualified allegiance. This is true for all people everywhere and at all times, so that the *universal situation* is such that we all live as creatures of God, knowing him, and responsible to him.

In terms of our *actions* (including our thoughts, attitudes, motives, and desires), however, there was *radical* change. Whereas Adam and Eve gladly served God in the garden, once sin entered the world "every intention of the thoughts of his heart was *only evil continually*" (Gen. 6:5). It is no longer the case that man is able not to sin (*posse non peccare*), as it was before the fall. Rather, his entire direction is changed; it is subverted and perverted, so that now for man it is not possible not to sin (*non posse non peccare*). This depravity, this sinfulness, which extends itself to the entire person, is rebellion in the face of the knowledge of

---

[8] Cf. *Summa theologica*, 1.2.1.

God. It is *covenant* sinfulness—before the face and in the context of the clear, distinct, and personal knowledge of God.

So we remain fundamentally who we are as image of God. We will always be image of God. We will be image of God even in our eternal existence, whether in hell or in the new heaven and new earth. The very reason we are made to live eternally has to do with our character as image. None other of God's animate creation will live eternally as covenant creatures. Only man was given that gift.

But since the fall, given the above, we became, in the truest sense of the word, *irrational*. That is, we sinfully and deceptively convince ourselves that what is actually true about the world is *not* true. We create a world of our own making, where we are all gods. What we now seek to do and how we seek to live and think are set in polar opposition to the world as it actually is. Our actions are in opposition to what they were originally intended to do.

So also, the image that we are becomes something horrific. Trying to make ourselves out to be gods, we distort both who we are and who God is. We are at war with our true identity. Always and everywhere in covenant relationship with God our Creator, we seek the utterly impossible and unobtainable; we seek autonomy.

If this is really the way things are since the fall, then the apologetic task is always, or at least *should* always be, set within and controlled by that covenant relationship which is a universal condition of every person. Man's denial of God is not something done in ignorance. It is evidence of the suppression of the knowledge of God within us. Our refusal to acknowledge God is not, as has been supposed, an *agnostic* refusal—that is, it is *not* a refusal based on ignorance—but it is culpable rebellion. Since the fall we are and remain, as Paul clearly states, without excuse.

This is, as we said, irrational. It militates against the way the world actually is. So it is incumbent on the apologist to ask the unbeliever to justify his own position. Suppose the unbeliever is convinced of his own autonomy. We could ask how, for example, it can be that he thinks himself worthy of complete trust so that he is the origin of truth itself.

Even as we begin to ask some probing questions, though, we cannot simply accept the unbeliever's self-diagnosis, as if in his sin he is able and willing to assess his own condition accurately. Embedded in the sinful heart is the paradox of self-deception—the steadfast commitment to knowing but suppressing; a commitment to deny the world as it is, even with regard to one's own fundamental identity, in order to attempt to assert our supposed autonomy. So we should not expect that the unbeliever will properly analyze his own sinful condition in the world. He will, as far as he is true to his own sinful principle, seek to suppress the actual situation and set forth the (literally) make-believe world that he is working so hard to build.

It will not do, then, for the apologist simply to start on the Yellow Brick Road with his unbelieving friend and assume that it will lead to Kansas. Once one begins on a make-believe road, it can only lead to more of the same; one cannot leave the land of Oz by taking a road that is, *in its entirety, within* Oz. The only way back to the real world of Kansas is to get off the road altogether and change the mindset that trusted in the Yellow Brick Road in the first place.

This is what a covenantal apologetic seeks to do. It seeks to take the truth of Scripture as the proper diagnosis of the unbelieving condition *and* challenge the unbeliever to make sense of the world he has made. Scripture tells us that a world built on the foundation of unbelief does not exist; it is a figment of an unbelieving imagination, and thus is basically irrational.

If we want to use a philosophical term for this approach (which is not necessary but could be useful at times), a covenantal apologetic is *transcendental*. A transcendental approach looks for the (so-called) *preconditions* for knowledge and life. It does not simply assume that knowledge is the same for believer and unbeliever alike. Instead, this approach asks questions about the basic foundations of an unbelieving position. In asking those questions, it also recognizes that what Scripture says is true. It recognizes, for example, that the only reason there can *be* an unbelieving position is that God is who he says he is, people are what God says they are, and they all, even unbelievers, "live and move and have [their] being" in the triune God (Acts 17:28).

So the unbelieving position *both* has its own presumed foundations *and* needs Christian foundations in order even to oppose the latter. There are two worlds colliding in every unbelieving position, therefore. There is the world the unbeliever is attempting to build, a world that is illusory. And there is the *real* world, the world where the triune God reigns, controlling whatsoever comes to pass—even the unbelieving position itself. This apologetic approach, then, tries to make obvious both the presuppositions of the unbelieving position itself and the covenantal presuppositions that are at work in order to challenge the unbelieving position at its root. In that sense, it is a *radical* (from *radix*, "root") approach. It attempts as much as possible to get to the root of the problematic position.

In the chapters below, we will be looking at examples of how these truths might be applied to unbelief.

The Ten Tenets

Having looked at the most basic Christian truths and the biblical mandate for a covenantal approach to apologetics, I would like to set out ten crucial theological tenets for a covenantal, Christian apologetic that will be necessary to keep in mind throughout the rest of the book. The list itself is not exhaustive, and as in much theology, there could be useful debates on the relative priority of each of them. But what should be noncontroversial are the tenets themselves, each of which is a substantial part of a covenantal approach to apologetics. These tenets will make their appearance in different ways and contexts as we proceed, some more applicable or obvious than others.

It will be important to keep these tenets at the forefront as we work through the rest of this book. For that reason, I will also list them at the end of this chapter and it might be useful to copy that list and have it within one's purview while reading. In that way, it will soon become more obvious which tenets are being applied in later chapters, and how.

The ten tenets certainly deserve more space than I am giving them here, but there are excellent resources already available for most of them. A book could easily be written on each one. Readers unfamiliar with (some of) them may fruitfully consult other literature to gain a fuller understanding of them. When resources come to mind, I will mention them below. However, I will be mentioning resources with which I am most familiar (e.g., my own), and a more thorough search will produce other, perhaps better resources than I have highlighted. I will provide a short list of recommended titles at the end of this chapter for anyone interested in pursuing the theological and apologetic backdrop to these tenets.

The primary reason I prefer at this point simply to summarize these tenets is twofold. First, the tendency with a covenantal approach to apologetics is to talk or write *about* it and its principles, rather than to demonstrate how it might look in action. I hope in this book to explain the biblical rationale for a covenantal approach as we move along in each chapter, but I also want to *show* at least one way to respond to some attacks and objections that have been lodged against Christianity. In that way, I am not primarily concerned just with the tenets, but am concerned with their actual use.

Second, and following on the first, I am assuming that readers will be (more or less) familiar with the basic thrust of these tenets. Readers completely unfamiliar with them can begin by working through the recommended resources at the end of this chapter. My concern, again, is primarily with these tenets as foundational for *application* in defending the Christian faith. The aim here is to *apply*, as much as to present, these crucial and central tenets of a covenantal apologetic.

In light of this, the ten tenets are as follows:

1. The faith that we are defending must begin with, and necessarily include, the triune God—Father, Son, and Holy Spirit—who, as God, condescends to create and to redeem.

Generic theism is no part of the Christian faith. Why this is the case will become clearer later on. At this point we need only recognize that any defense that does not include the triune God is a defense of a false theism. And theism of this sort is not a step *toward* Christianity, but an idolatrous reaction to (suppression of) the truth. Thus, a belief in theism that is not Christian theism is a sinful suppression of the truth. It masks, rather than moves toward, true knowledge of the triune God.

In saying that we "must begin with" the triune God, we are not saying that a covenantal apologetic must always *begin its apologetic discussion* with the triune God. Rather, we are saying that we must never assume that we are defending anything but what God himself, as Father, Son, and Holy Spirit, has accomplished in creation and redemption. To "begin with" and "necessarily include" the triune God means that we stand squarely on Christian truth, including a Christian understanding of God, when we engage in our defense. Again, this *does not* mean that all of our conversations or discussions have to articulate this at the start. How this looks will become clearer as we move along.

2. God's covenantal revelation is authoritative by virtue of what it *is*, and any covenantal, Christian apologetic will necessarily stand on and utilize that authority in order to defend Christianity.

As we have seen, God's revelation is covenantal because (1) it initiates a relationship between God and humanity and (2) it entails obligations. This means that we cannot begin our discussion with the assumption that the intellectual, moral, or conversational ground on which we and the unbeliever are standing is the same. The very *reason* there is a debate between us is that our respective authorities are in conflict. Just as an unbeliever will stand on his own chosen ground in order to debate and discuss, so also will we.

This is an important point, in that its most consistent expression is found in Reformed theology. Thus, it is intrinsic to a covenantal apologetic. The point itself is put concisely and most helpfully in the Westminster Confession of Faith 1.4 (and, verbatim, in the Savoy Declaration and the London Baptist Confession): "The authority of the Holy Scripture, for which it ought to be believed, and obeyed, depends not upon the testimony of any man, or Church; but wholly upon God (who is truth itself) the author thereof: and therefore it is to be received, because it is the Word of God." This is one of those truths that forms the foundation of our apologetic approach. However, it is another one of those truths that we do not necessarily or in every case present as an integral part of our actual discussion or argument. But as Christians, we need to have this teaching firmly in place.

Note that the Confession is focusing here on Scripture's *authority*. That authority is not something that comes to it from the outside; it is not something *given to* or *imposed on* Scripture by another, external authority—not by "any man or church." Rather, Scripture's authority is tied inextricably to its author, God himself. As Christians, therefore, we accept the authority of Scripture, and we believe and receive it "because it is the word of God."[9]

So while there can be arguments given for Scripture's authority (the next section in the Confession gives a partial list of those), those arguments seek to *explain* and not to *establish* the authority itself. This has deep implications for apologetics, as we will see.

3. It is the truth of God's revelation, together with the work of the Holy Spirit, that brings about a covenantal change from one who is in Adam to one who is in Christ.

The import of this tenet is that it encourages, even requires, us to communicate the truth of God, since it is just that truth that the Holy Spirit uses to change hearts. We must remember here that we are attempting to defend the *Christian* faith, not a generic theism. So, as in evangelism, there needs to be a communication of that faith if there is going to be any hope of a change of mind *and heart*.

4. Man (male and female) as image of God is in covenant with the triune God for eternity.

We noted this above, but the importance of this can hardly be overstated. What it means is that all people, just because they are image of God, are responsible to God for everything they are, do, and think. They are, therefore, in *covenant* with him for eternity. Every person lives *coram Deo*, that is, before the face of God, and thus is responsible to God for his every thought and action. This responsibility is presumed in the final judgment. God will judge *all men* on that day. Those who have rejected him will be eternally punished for that rejection, and those who have trusted him will be eternally rewarded. This judgment assumes that the entirety of humanity is responsible to the same God; all are *obligated* to obey him because he is their Creator and Sustainer. God, then, has a sovereign right over all humanity.

5. All people know the true God, and that knowledge entails covenantal obligations.

As we noted above, this tenet is concise but is crucial to grasp. It does not mean that all people *can* know God. Nor does it mean that all peo-

---

[9] See K. Scott Oliphint, "Because It Is the Word of God," in *Did God Really Say? Affirming the Truthfulness and Trustworthiness of Scripture*, ed. David B. Garner (Phillipsburg, NJ: P&R, 2012).

ple know that something, somewhere is bigger than they are. Scripture is clear that all people *know God* (Rom. 1:18–20). All people know the true God because God makes himself known. The knowledge that we all have is sufficient so that if we refuse to respond to it properly, we will stand without excuse before God on the day of judgment.

This knowledge is not knowledge that we, through some process of inference, may acquire for ourselves. The point that Paul makes in Romans 1:19 is that all of us have this knowledge *because God gives it to us*. In other words, the revelation of God and his character that is given in all of creation is also given to each and every person by virtue of God's own revelatory activity.

6. Those who are and remain in Adam suppress the truth that they know. Those who are in Christ see that truth for what it is.

God gives sufficient knowledge of himself to all of his human creatures. That knowledge is true knowledge; it is not a vague or imprecise feeling or a sporadic experience of something greater. It is true *knowledge* of God. But because of the effects of sin in our hearts, we seek, if we are in Adam, to hold that knowledge down. In our sins, we will not acknowledge it. Instead, we deceive ourselves into thinking that there is no God, or that we cannot know him, or that we can get by on our own, or a million other falsehoods that serve only to mask the clear truth that God continually gives to us through the things he has made (Rom. 1:20).

7. There is an absolute, covenantal antithesis between Christian theism and any other, opposing position. Thus, Christianity is true and anything opposing it is false.

This should be obvious to any Christian, but it is oftentimes not as prominent in our thinking as it ought to be. When we claim to be Christians, we are doing more than just listing a biographical detail. We are claiming that the truth set forth in God's revelation describes the way things *really and truly* are in the world. That is, we are saying that what God says about the world is the way the world *really* is.

Any view or position that opposes what God has said is therefore, by definition, false and does not "fit" with the way the real world is. This means that the views of any who remain in unbelief are, in reality, illusions. They do not and cannot make sense of the world as it really is. Not only so, but, we should notice, there are at bottom only two options available to us. Either we bow the knee to Christ and affirm the truth of what God says, or we oppose him and thus attempt to "create" a world of our own making. No matter what kind of opposition there is to Christianity, before we even know the details of that opposition, we know that it cannot make sense of the real world. We know that it is self-destructive.

This is a great comfort and should help us to be more confident of our defense. We need not fear or be threatened by any view that we encounter. Even before we know the details of that view, we know from the outset that it cannot stand of its own weight; it cannot match the way the world is. When we begin to learn the details of an opposing view, then, we do so with the initial conviction that there will be no way for that view to actually make sense of the real world. Any view that opposes Christianity cannot be consistently thought or consistently lived.

8. Suppression of the truth, like the depravity of sin, is total but not absolute. Thus, every unbelieving position will necessarily have within it ideas, concepts, notions, and the like that it has taken and wrenched from their true, Christian context.

In properly understanding the biblical doctrine of sin as total depravity, we affirm that *all* of man is affected by sin (total depravity), but we also affirm that man is not as bad as he could be (absolute depravity). In the same way, when someone suppresses the truth in unrighteousness, that suppression is total. There is nothing that he knows, thinks, and does that is not affected by it. *But it is not absolute.* He cannot completely eradicate or submerge the knowledge of God that is always his and always being given by God.

Thus, there will be aspects of the truth of the knowledge of God that surface in those who are in Adam. So, for example, even though an unbeliever will recognize that two plus two equals four, the very fact that he would hold that truth to be independent of God's creating and sustaining activity means that he does not know that truth *as it really is.* This may not affect the equation itself, but neither will God say to him on judgment day, "Good for you; you got that part right." Those who die in Adam will be held responsible for every fact (even two plus two equals four) that they took from God's world, even as they refused to acknowledge the facts to be God's facts in the first place. So just as the man who remains in Adam can continue to think, work, and so on, that thinking and working will only serve, in the end, to further condemn him.[10]

9. The true, covenantal knowledge of God in man, together with God's universal mercy, allows for persuasion in apologetics.

Some might want to argue that if tenet 7 above is correct, then there is no use discussing, debating, or arguing about the truth of Christianity, since man is either in one "world" or in the other. If there is such a divide, it might be asked, how can we even reach those who live in a world of their own making?[11]

The answer is twofold. First, because people always and everywhere know the true God, whenever we speak God's truth to them, it "gets through" and "connects" to that knowledge that God is continually giving to them. Second, because God's universal mercy restrains their sin in various ways, the depravity that might otherwise hinder our conversation is also restrained.

If we think of persuasion as an opportunity to take what the other person himself might hold or believe and to reframe that belief in a way that is consistent with Christianity, then we can begin to think about the best approach to someone who wants to reject Christianity altogether. I will provide examples of this as we go along, but initially we can point to Paul's use of the Greek poets in his address at the Areopagus (Acts 17:16ff.; more on this in chapter 4). Paul co-opted those quotations and gave them Christian content, thereby drawing his audience in (by quoting and using what was familiar to them and was an aspect of their own worldview) while also pointing them to the truth of Christianity.

10. Every fact and experience is what it is by virtue of the covenantal, all-controlling plan and purpose of God.

This means that in every case, those who are outside of Christ, who remain in Adam, are nevertheless thoroughly embedded in the world

---

[10] See K. Scott Oliphint, "The Irrationality of Unbelief," in *Revelation and Reason: New Essays in Reformed Apologetics*, ed. K. Scott Oliphint and Lane G. Tipton (Phillipsburg, NJ: P&R, 2007).
[11] See K. Scott Oliphint, "A Primal and Simple Knowledge," in *A Theological Guide to Calvin's Institutes: Essays and Analysis*, ed. David Hall and Peter A. Lillback (Philipsburg, NJ: P&R, 2008).

that Christ created and controls. The breath they breathe, the lives they live, the people they know—all of it belongs to God and is therefore meant to be used to and for his glory. The facts of the world display God's glory (Ps. 19:1ff.; Rom. 1:20). To take those facts for selfish use is to twist them and pervert them. This is culpable rebellion against God, and it takes place as those in Adam "live and move and have our being" in the triune God.

So in order for someone to understand one fact properly, that fact needs to be seen in the context of God's plan and purposes. The explanation of the fact itself is not sufficient unless and until the context and purpose of that fact is known and acknowledged. For example, it is not enough simply to say that lions instinctively seek their prey because they are such good hunters; the real story includes the fact that

> the young lions roar for their prey,
>   seeking their food from God. (Ps. 104:21)

It is God who provides for the animals, not instinct.

> Crowns and thrones may perish, kingdoms rise and wane,
>   But the church of Jesus constant will remain.
>   Gates of hell can never 'gainst that church prevail;
>   We have Christ's own promise, and that cannot fail.[12]

Tenets and Texts

The ten tenets above will surface in various discussions and examples as we continue. It is crucial to keep them in mind.

I promised, above, to provide a list of the ten tenets, as well as an initial collection of recommended sources for further reading. Those lists follow.

---

[12] Sabine Baring-Gould, "Onward Christian Soldiers," 1865.

The Ten Tenets

1. The faith that we are defending must begin with, and necessarily include, the triune God—Father, Son, and Holy Spirit—who, as God, condescends to create and to redeem.

2. God's covenantal revelation is authoritative by virtue of what it *is*, and any covenantal, Christian apologetic will necessarily stand on and utilize that authority in order to defend Christianity.

3. It is the truth of God's revelation, together with the work of the Holy Spirit, that brings about a covenantal change from one who is in Adam to one who is in Christ.

4. Man (male and female) as image of God is in covenant with the triune God for eternity.

5. All people know the true God, and that knowledge entails covenantal obligations.

6. Those who are and remain in Adam suppress the truth that they know. Those who are in Christ see that truth for what it is.

7. There is an absolute, covenantal antithesis between Christian theism and any other, opposing position. Thus, Christianity is true and anything opposing it is false.

8. Suppression of the truth, like the depravity of sin, is total but not absolute. Thus, every unbelieving position will necessarily have within it ideas, concepts, notions, and the like that it has taken and wrenched from their true, Christian context.

9. The true, covenantal knowledge of God in man, together with God's universal mercy, allows for persuasion in apologetics.

10. Every fact and experience is what it is by virtue of the covenantal, all-controlling plan and purpose of God.

For Further Reading

The resources below have varying levels of complexity. I list them (roughly) from easy to more complex.

Oliphint, K. Scott. *The Battle Belongs to the Lord: The Power of Scripture for Defending Our Faith*. Phillipsburg, NJ: P&R, 2003.

Edgar, William. *Reasons of the Heart: Recovering Christian Persuasion.* Grand Rapids: Baker, 1996.

Pratt, Richard L., Jr. *Every Thought Captive: A Study Manual for the Defense of Christian Truth.* Phillipsburg, NJ: Presbyterian and Reformed, 1979.

Frame, John M. *Apologetics to the Glory of God: An Introduction.* Phillipsburg, NJ: P&R, 1994.

Notaro, Thom. *Van Til and the Use of Evidence.* Phillipsburg, NJ: Presbyterian and Reformed, 1980.

Oliphint, K. Scott. "The Irrationality of Unbelief." In *Revelation and Reason: New Essays in Reformed Apologetics,* edited by K. Scott Oliphint and Lane G. Tipton, 59–73. Phillipsburg, NJ: P&R, 2007.

Oliphint, K. Scott, and Lane G. Tipton, eds. *Revelation and Reason: New Essays in Reformed Apologetics.* Phillipsburg, NJ: P&R, 2007.

Frame, John M. "Van Til and the Ligonier Apologetic." *Westminster Theological Journal* 47, no. 2 (1985): 279–99.

Bahnsen, Greg L. *Van Til's Apologetic: Readings and Analysis.* Phillipsburg, NJ: P&R, 1998.

Edgar, William. "Two Christian Warriors: Cornelius Van Til and Francis A. Schaeffer Compared." *Westminster Theological Journal* 57, no. 1 (1995): 33–56.

Van Til, Cornelius. *The Defense of the Faith.* 4th ed. Edited by K. Scott Oliphint. Phillipsburg, NJ: P&R, 2008.

Van Til, Cornelius. *An Introduction to Systematic Theology: Prolegomena and the Doctrines of Revelation, Scripture, and God.* 2nd ed. Edited by William Edgar. Phillipsburg, NJ: P&R, 2007.

Oliphint, K. Scott. *The Majesty of Mystery: Celebrating the Glory of an Incomprehensible God.* Bellingham, WA: Lexham Press, 2016.

2

Set Christ Apart
as Lord

> There is not an atom of the universe in which his everlasting power and deity are not clearly seen. Both from within and from without, God's witness speaks to us. God does not leave himself without a witness, either in nature or history, in heart or conscience, in life or lot. This witness of God is so powerful, accordingly, that almost no one denies its reality. All humans and peoples have heard something of the voice of the Lord.[1]

We have seen that the lordship of Christ provides the foundation for our defense of Christianity. If we have not set Christ apart as Lord (1 Pet. 3:15), then we cannot be adequately prepared to give an answer for the hope that is ours in him to anyone who asks. It is nearly impossible to overstate the importance of this truth. Given its central importance, therefore, it might be useful to elaborate on it so that we are all on the same biblical-apologetical page.

The first thing to recognize is that the lordship of Christ is conferred on him by the Father and is the reward and outcome of his obedience as the Son (Phil. 2:1–11). Just why this is important is a multifaceted and fascinating study, but it would take us too far afield to pursue this in great detail. It is important, however, to highlight some of the main contours of this truth, especially as they relate to our defense of Christianity.

---

[1] Herman Bavinck, *Reformed Dogmatics*, vol. 2, *God and Creation*, ed. John Bolt, trans. John Vriend (Grand Rapids: Baker Academic, 2004), 90.

I Am

Since it is Christianity that we aim to defend, some central aspects of it need to be kept in mind as we proceed. Fundamental to all that we will say in the pages ahead is the way in which we think about God.[2] Since God's existence (rightly) lies at the heart of so much apologetic literature, it is necessary for us to be clear about exactly how, biblically, we understand that existence.

Historically, Christian theology has derived the character and attributes of God initially and primarily from his names. We learn who God is, first of all, by virtue of the names he gives himself. Supremely, we learn who he is by way of the name Jehovah, or Yahweh.[3] This name tells us something of who God is essentially. Though it is God's covenant name, in that he reveals it in the process of establishing the Mosaic covenant (Ex. 3:14), it nevertheless tells who God is quite apart from his relationship with his people.

> This explains his name Jehovah, and signifies, that he is self-existent; he has his being of himself, and has no dependence upon any other: the greatest and best man in the world must say, By the grace of God I am what I am; but God says absolutely—and it is more than any creature, man or angel, can say—I am that I am.[4]

This name of God, Yahweh (Jehovah), is used over five thousand times in Holy Scripture.[5] So though there are relatively few passages that speak of the Lord specifically as "I am," the fact that his own name is taken from that ascription and that it is used with such frequency indicates that we are, on every page of Scripture, to think of the Lord

---

[2] Discussions of all that we will discuss in this initial section can be found in K. Scott Oliphint, *The Majesty of Mystery: Celebrating the Glory of an Incomprehensible God* (Bellingham, WA: Lexham Press, 2016); see also K. Scott Oliphint, *The Battle Belongs to the Lord* (Phillipsburg, NJ: P&R, 2003). Worth noting in this regard, which I will elaborate on later, is that Paul begins his apologetic address at the Areopagus with the biblical teaching of God's aseity and sovereignty.

[3] Jehovah is a name formed by adding the vowels of the Hebrew word for Lord—*Adonai*—with the consonants of the name of God given in Exodus 3—*YHWH*. One common theory is that in the sixteenth century, Petrus Galatinus argued for the combination of the consonants with the vowels, thus forming *YeHoWaH*, which comes into English as Jehovah. This was not the common Hebrew pronunciation, which today is thought to be something akin to Yahweh. The two, however, are interchangeable, in that they both refer to this revealed name of God in Exodus 3.

[4] Matthew Henry, *Matthew Henry's Commentary on the Whole Bible: Complete and Unabridged in One Volume* (Peabody, MA: Hendrickson, 1996), Ex. 3:14.

[5] Most English translations render the Hebrew word Yahweh with large and small capital letters, as Lord. Whenever the word Lord or (less often) God appears that way, the divine name Yahweh lies behind it.

as essentially *a se*. It is this *aseity* (absolute independence) of God that must be affirmed in the first place.

This is the case because before there was anything else, there was only the triune God—Father, Son, and Holy Spirit. Because God exists in and of himself, he exists as one who is in need of nothing (cf. Acts 17:25). God did not create because he was in need of fellowship; he has perfect fellowship with himself, as triune. Not only so, but the fact that God created does not in any way alter his aseity; he remains who he is. God does not begin to be in need of anything because he creates. Creation does not change God's character as *a se*.

But creation does bring about a new relationship with God. It brings about a relationship to which God *commits* himself for eternity. This commitment is binding on God.[6] As the author to the Hebrews reminds us:

> So when God desired to show more convincingly to the heirs of the promise the unchangeable character of his purpose, he guaranteed it with an oath, so that by two unchangeable things, in which it is impossible for God to lie, we who have fled for refuge might have strong encouragement to hold fast to the hope set before us. (Heb. 6:17–18)

The covenant that God has established is a covenant that, by God's own free decision, binds him. That "binding of God" is guaranteed "by two unchangeable things." It is guaranteed because the God who cannot lie has taken an oath.

How, then, ought we to think about a God who, at one and the same time, is absolutely independent (*a se*) and also has freely chosen to commit himself to his creation? The God who is in need of nothing is also the God who is "with us" to move and act in the world, including to *reveal himself*, in order to carry out his perfect plan. How can this be?

We get a hint of this twofold idea in that quintessential passage in Exodus 3 where Moses sees a bush that is on fire, yet not consumed. As Moses approaches the bush, it is clear that he is in the presence of God himself (Ex. 3:5). As the Lord then begins to explain to Moses

---

[6] This point is important in its own right, but will also be an important point in our dialog with a Muslim in chap. 7.

his covenant purposes for his people, Moses asks the covenant Lord to reveal his name, so that Israel might know that Moses is the Lord's chosen mediator. And the Lord reveals his name as "I am."

Surely this name refers Moses, and Israel, to God's utter independence. Only God can say that he is "I am" in and of himself. Anything else is what it is by virtue of something or someone else. Every experience that we have in all of creation is an experience of utter *dependence*. But the Lord is not one who depends on anything; he, and he alone, is who he is. And yet the Lord has also announced himself to Moses, initially, as the God of the covenant (Ex. 3:6). How can this Lord, who alone is who he is, also commit himself to his covenant?

The revelation that Moses has of what is really the *unburning* bush is, in part, designed to reveal to Moses both of these truths. The fire, which represents the Lord himself, is in no way dependent on the bush in order to burn. The fire is, in that sense, *a se*. It does not need the bush for fuel; it is able to burn in and of itself. But it is also *with* the bush. It could easily appear on its own, because it is in need of nothing to burn. Or it could appear beside the bush. Instead, it is linked inextricably *with* the bush, even as the Lord himself—who is who he is—has bound himself inextricably to his people.

So what we have in this central and determinative event in the Old Testament—the event of God's announcement to save his people from their slavery—is a revelation, both in word and in deed, of God's twofold character. We have God revealing and explaining to Moses his very name—the "Lord"—and we also have God announcing to Moses his identity as the God of Moses's fathers, the covenant God.

It is also worth noting in this passage that the One who appears to Moses is designated as "the angel [messenger] of the Lord," and then, without any hint of discontinuity, as he speaks to Moses he is simply "the Lord" (Ex. 3:2–4). So now we have One who is both the Lord's messenger and, at the same time, "the Lord" himself. There is identity, but there is also distinction. The One who appears to Moses is "the Lord" and is "the angel of the Lord."

Alert readers will likely begin to see where this is going. If the One who appeared to Moses is both the Lord and the angel, or messenger, of the Lord, then surely we have One who is both God and sent from/by God. "So the Jews said to him, 'You are not yet fifty years old, and have you seen Abraham?' Jesus said to them, 'Truly, truly, I say to you, before Abraham was, I am.' So they picked up stones to throw at him, but Jesus hid himself and went out of the temple" (John 8:57–59).

In this passage the Jews are arguing over Jesus's true identity. True to form, they could not be further from the truth. The audacity and ignorance of their question may escape us. They ask, "Are we not right in saying that you are a Samaritan and have a demon?" (John 8:48). Not only are they convinced that Jesus could not be a descendant of Abraham, but they also accuse him of having a demon. No stronger description of Jewish opposition to Jesus could be imagined. Physically, he is not "one of them," and spiritually they think he is the embodiment of evil itself!

So Jesus answers their question in a way that could not have been imagined by any of them. He answers them not by denying that he is in opposition to them (they have that part right), but rather by telling them that the opposition is a result of *their* spiritual problem, not his. He tells them that the One who identified himself to Moses on Mount Moriah as the "I am" is the very One standing before them at that moment! And they understand, without question, exactly what Jesus is claiming, so we're told, "they picked up stones to throw at him." He is immediately charged with blasphemy, and his execution is imminent.

The point we need to set squarely in our minds is that the One who appeared to Moses and who is revealing himself throughout covenant history, is himself the second person of the Trinity, the Son of God. Jesus makes that clear in John 8, and it is a point that will help us begin to understand our apologetic task as we move along. In order to know who this God is that we are discussing and defending, we cannot lose sight of the fact that it is the triune God revealed throughout history in the Son.

In the previous chapter, we highlighted the notion of covenant as given in the Westminster Confession 7.1. It is a notion that includes God's free decision to condescend. This condescension of God is a metaphorical way of speaking. It cannot mean that God literally began to occupy a space that he did not previously occupy. He is not coming down to a location wherein he was otherwise absent. What, then, does *condescension* mean when used this way?

It means, at least, that the *way* in which God occupies a particular place is different from his omnipresence. God, as Spirit, is present everywhere. There is no place where God is not present. His free decision to condescend, however, includes a presence that is *covenantal*. It is a presence that is designed to accomplish the purposes to which he has eternally bound himself in his covenant. In Genesis 3:8, for example, the Lord God condescends to walk in the garden in the cool of the day. In that instance, the fellowship that he had with Adam and Eve has been broken by them, so his condescension is in order to judge. But in Exodus 3, the Lord says that he has "come down to deliver" Israel from her slavery in Egypt (v. 8). In this case, he condescends as Israel's deliverer.

The Bible, from beginning to end, is replete with instances of God's covenantal condescension. The Bible itself is a product of that condescension. Covenantal condescension is a necessary aspect of his binding himself to his creation. Once he (freely) chose to create, he would need also to "stoop down" in order to relate himself to his creation. This "stoop" in no way modified or diminished his aseity. Rather, it gave us, his human creatures, a revelational way to understand his majestic character. It revealed that character to us, and it required us to see his condescension for what it really was—his merciful determination that we have fellowship with him. Apart from that condescension, as the Confession says, "we could have no fruition of him as our blessedness and reward."

In the opening verses of John's Gospel, we begin to see more clearly the condescension of God in the Son. That condescension, John makes clear, is both *cosmic* and (since Gen. 3) *redemptive*. John highlights both of these aspects in the prologue to his Gospel.[7]

The first thing we notice in the prologue is that John is alluding to Genesis 1:1. His "in the beginning" is meant to highlight the same reference that we see at the beginning of the Bible. So, "In the beginning, God . . ." is meant to be seen as identical to "In the beginning

---

[7] Readers interested in the connections between God's condescension and the person of the Son may want to consult Oliphint, *The Majesty of Mystery*. For a detailed exposition of the prologue, see the entirety of the Vos article cited below.

was the Word." This, of course, means that the second person of the Trinity, the One whom John calls "the Word" (*logos*) is himself God. Lest there be any confusion, John tells us explicitly that in the beginning, "the Word was God."

But we also read that this One who was God in the beginning, was also "with God." As in Exodus 3, where the angel of the Lord is himself the Lord, so also here in John's prologue, we are introduced to One who is *both* God *and* distinguished from God. Given what we understand explicitly in the New Testament, we can see that John is explaining to us part of what it means that God is triune. We have three persons in the Godhead, who are God and yet are distinguished from each other. There is unity and there is diversity in God's essential character.

The fascinating and rich way that John goes on to explain the activity of this Word is developed in a few short verses of the prologue. Without moving through the details of John's discussion, we can perhaps best focus his discussion by noticing what he says about this Word in 1:9: "The true light, which gives light to everyone, was coming into the world."

John's reference to "the true light" here is a reference not to the *redemptive* activity of the Word. John will certainly be concerned with that activity throughout his Gospel. Initially, however, his concern is for the Word's *cosmic* activity as the "light." And as such, the Word "gives light to everyone."

Obviously, this cannot mean that the Word gives *saving* light to everyone. Neither does John's language allow for a notion that the Word *might* or *could* give light to everyone, if they would respond properly to him. John's language is quite clear here, and it refers us back to what he said about the light of the Word in verse 5: the Word, as light, shines in the darkness. The "darkness" here is a reference to the sin-darkened world. Having affirmed the Word's creative power (v. 3), John wants also to affirm that the cosmic "light" of the world continued to "enlighten" even in the midst of the darkness that sin brought into the world. Not only so, but this cosmic enlightening of the Word in the world is universal; *it enlightens everyone.*

In his unparalleled exposition of John's prologue, Geerhardus Vos says this with respect to verse 9:

> Here the Logos-revelation is actually mediated through the subjective life which man in dependence on the Logos possesses. The life here naturally produces the light. The meaning here is . . . that the life which man receives carries in itself and of itself kindles in him, *the light of the knowledge of God*.[8]

In other words, part of the activity of the life-giving and enlightening Word, who himself is God and is with God, is to reveal the light of the knowledge of God to all people. We can see here an extension, centering in the second person of the Trinity, to what Paul affirms in Romans 1:20.

The point thus far is this. God who is *a se* is and always has been the Lord. His lordship has its focus in the life-giving and revealing activity of the Son, who, from the beginning, has condescended to and in his creation. His *cosmic* activity has always been, in part, to reveal God. So God's revelation has, from the beginning, had its focus in the Son (though in the Son, it is *God* who is revealed).

There is also, since Genesis 3, a *redemptive* activity of God that has had its focus in the Son. We saw this explicitly in Exodus 3. When the Lord (who is the angel of the Lord) says that he has "come down to deliver" (v. 8), we are meant to see that deliverance as a type of the full and complete deliverance that will come to all of God's people. The cosmic activity of the Word is presupposed in his redemptive activity. All of the "deliverances" of God in the Old Testament look forward to that one, final deliverance from sin that can be accomplished only in Christ. From Genesis 3, history looks forward to God's final revelation in the person of Christ. From that revelation forward, history looks back on his accomplished task. History can be properly defined only in light of what the second person of the Trinity has condescended to do—both in creation generally and for his people more specifically.

At this point, we can begin to see what Scripture means when it teaches us that the One who, from the beginning, is the Lord has also been *made* Lord. In Acts 2:36, Peter concludes his Pentecost sermon with this admonition: "Let all the house of Israel therefore know for

---

[8] Geerhardus Vos, "The Range of the Logos Title in the Prologue to the Fourth Gospel," in *Redemptive History and Biblical Interpretation: The Shorter Writings of Geerhardus Vos*, ed. Richard B. Gaffin Jr. (Phillipsburg, NJ: Presbyterian and Reformed, 1980), 76, my emphasis.

certain that God has made him both Lord and Christ, this Jesus whom you crucified." Peter declares this just after quoting from Psalm 110 (the most quoted psalm in the entire New Testament). How can it be, we could ask, that the One who was from the beginning, who identifies himself with the "I am" of Exodus 3, who is himself "the Lord" throughout the Old Testament, could be *made* Lord by God?

The all-too-brief answer to this question is that the lordship that is now Christ's is a lordship that assumes the completion of his redemptive work. It is a lordship that could only take effect once the Son of God took to himself a human nature, walked in perfect obedience to his Father, gave himself up to save his people from their sins, and was seated at the Father's right hand. It is, we could say, the full and complete *redemptive* lordship of the Son of God become man.

This can be understood most clearly in the so-called *status duplex*, the two states of Christ. Those states consist of his humiliation and his exaltation, and the latter follows from the former. The apostle Paul lays these states out most concisely in Philippians 2:6–11. Speaking of Christ, the apostle says that

> though he was in the form of God, [he] did not count equality with God a thing to be grasped, but emptied himself, by taking the form of a servant, being born in the likeness of men. And being found in human form, he humbled himself by becoming obedient to the point of death, even death on a cross. Therefore God has highly exalted him and bestowed on him the name that is above every name, so that at the name of Jesus every knee should bow, in heaven and on earth and under the earth, and every tongue confess that Jesus Christ is Lord, to the glory of God the Father.

The Son of God, the second person of the Trinity, did not unduly hold on to what was rightfully his, but instead he "emptied himself." By that Paul means that the Son became what he was not; he, as Paul says elsewhere, "became poor" (2 Cor. 8:9) that we might become rich. He did not, we should emphasize, become something other than God. God cannot deny himself (2 Tim. 2:13). But he emptied himself of his prerogatives *as God* in order to take on the burdens, and ultimately the penalty, that sin brought into the world.

It was the accomplishment of this task—a task that was decreed before the foundation of the world—that brought about his redemptive lordship. It was because he was humiliated that God exalted him to his right hand. It was because he accomplished all his Father's will that he was able to sit down at the place of both cosmic and redemptive authority (cf. Heb. 1:1–4; Rev. 5).[9]

So this lordship of Christ, which Peter commands us to set apart in our hearts, includes both his cosmic lordship—by which he sovereignly ruled and rules his creation from the beginning—and his redemptive lordship—which is his because his work of deliverance is completed, and thus God has highly exalted him.

This must be firmly embedded in our minds and hearts if we are to think rightly about the apologetic task.

Condescension and Apologetics

What is the import of all of this? Why spend time on the theological and covenant-historical truth of the cosmic and redemptive lordship of the Son of God?

The primary reason is that it is central to the gospel and to the very truth of God, and for that reason alone it should be a central aspect of our own thinking and living in the world, to the glory of God. The more we can grasp the extent of God's condescending love to us, the more we will be motivated to honor him in all things, to eat and drink to his glory. This truth of the lordship of God in Christ should wash over the totality of who we are until all that we do is, in our own minds, inescapable from the wonder of that truth. And that is exactly what Peter has in view in 1 Peter 3:15. When he commands us to set Christ apart as Lord in our hearts, he is giving to us a crucial and all-encompassing mindset that itself is necessary if we are to engage the battle that rages in the heavenly places.

We can perhaps illustrate the importance of this covenant condescension of God by looking briefly at the philosophy of Immanuel

---

[9] It is worth noting, with respect to the "two states," that Bavinck admits that this doctrine "may very well be expanded to include Scripture's entire doctrine of Christ. In the Old Testament, we already encounter traces of it in the figure of the Servant of the Lord." Herman Bavinck, *Reformed Dogmatics*, vol. 3, *Sin and Salvation in Christ*, ed. John Bolt, trans. John Vriend (Grand Rapids: Baker Academic, 2006), 424–25.

Kant.[10] In fact, it is just this very covenant condescension that ought to form the basis of our response to any objection that has its roots in Kant's critical philosophy. Discussions here can be overly complex, but a few predominant points will illustrate the way forward in defending Christianity.

Immanuel Kant is arguably the most influential philosopher since the Enlightenment.[11] Many, if not most, of the post-Enlightenment arguments against traditional Christianity have as their backdrop Kant's monumental work *The Critique of Pure Reason*. In that work, Kant hoped to assign to reason its proper place. He was aware that rationalism (Descartes, Leibniz, Spinoza) had failed; he was awakened, by his own account, from his own dogmatic slumber by the empiricist David Hume. But he was also aware that Hume's empiricism necessarily resulted in utter skepticism. So he set out to remedy both schools (the rationalist school and the empiricist school) by developing his own "critical" philosophy.

In his *Critique*, Kant hoped to show the relationship of knowledge and faith. In the preface, he says, "I have therefore found it necessary to deny knowledge in order to make room for faith."[12] What Kant means by this will occupy the entirety of the *Critique*.

Kant begins his *Critique of Pure Reason* this way:

> There can be no doubt that all our knowledge begins with experience. For how should our faculty of knowledge be awakened into action did not objects affecting our senses partly of themselves produce representations, partly arouse the activity of our understanding to compare these representations, and, by combining or separating them, work up the raw material of the sensible impressions into that knowledge of objects which is entitled experience? In the order of time, therefore, we have no knowledge antecedent to experience, and with experience all our knowledge begins. But though all our knowledge begins with experience, it does not follow that it all arises out of experience.[13]

---

[10] Immanuel Kant (1724–1804) attempted to synthesize rationalism and empiricism. He is the most influential philosopher of the modern and contemporary eras.

[11] The Enlightenment is understood, roughly, as the "Age of Reason," which began in the eighteenth century. For an in-depth understanding of the Enlightenment and its influence, see, for example, Jonathan Irvine Israel, *Radical Enlightenment: Philosophy and the Making of Modernity, 1650–1750* (New York: Oxford University Press, 2001).

[12] Immanuel Kant, *Critique of Pure Reason*, trans. Norman Kemp Smith (New York: St. Martin's, 1958), 29.

[13] Kant, *Critique of Pure Reason*, 41

Kant's point here is that the source of much of what we know, and its status, transcends experience. That is to say, in order to know *anything*, two aspects of knowledge have to be in place. There must be experience, and that experience must be synthesized with our own internal "categories." So knowledge and understanding necessarily include the application of our mental categories to the experiences of the world.

In this way, Kant thought he was proposing a "Copernican Revolution." The "Copernican Revolution" in Kant's philosophy was this: all previous philosophy had assumed that knowledge comes to us when our external experiences impose themselves on our minds; Kant was now arguing that, on the contrary, *we* impose our mental categories on those experiences in order to know or understand them. Knowledge is not from the outside in; it is from the inside (mental categories) out (experiences).[14] These matters need not detain us here; they are important, but not directly relevant to the discussion at hand.

In the third section of his *Critique* (the "Transcendental Dialectic"), Kant wants to focus on the faculty of *reason*. (The previous two sections focused on the faculties of understanding and intuition). In this section, Kant argues that there are other things, things outside our experience, to which we cannot apply the mental categories that are necessary for knowledge. Those things outside our experience are (1) God, (2) the soul, and (3) the things in themselves. These three categories transcend experience altogether, so our mental categories are not able to be applied when it comes to these three things.

For Kant, then, it is the faculty of reason that produces the higher, purer concepts such as God and the soul. As Kant analyzes reason, therefore, he is forced to conclude that there can be *no real knowledge* of those things that reason alone assumes. This is why Kantian philosophy bifurcates into a "phenomenal" realm—which is the realm where we *can* impose our mental categories, since we *experience* the phenomena around us—and the "noumenal"—which is the realm where we do posit some things such as God and the

---

[14] It is easy to see how Kant's philosophy has had so much influence on relativistic thinking, with its primary emphasis on the *subject* of knowledge.

soul, but which, by definition, cannot be *known*; there is no *experience* of such things.

Now we can begin to see the explanation, and the titanic impact, of Kant's dictum: "I have therefore found it necessary to deny knowledge in order to make room for faith." Since it is not possible to *know* God (because he is a part of the noumenal realm), our positing of the existence of God can only be a matter of *faith*, and faith can have nothing to do with real knowledge and understanding.

This conclusion with respect to reason is the foundation from which Kant begins to critique the historic proofs for the existence of God. He critiques both Anselm's "ontological" proof and Thomas Aquinas's proofs. He begins with a critique of the ontological proof because, he surmises, if that one is deficient, then any of the others will be as well, since the ontological proof deals with *existence* itself (and all other proofs have to assume *existence* in order for one to argue).

Without spelling out the details of Kant's critique of the ontological argument, we may note two points in his conclusion that give us all we need at this juncture. First, Kant argues that the concepts of reason are nothing more than concepts:

> Such transcendent ideas have a purely intelligible object; and this object may indeed be admitted as a transcendental object, but only if we likewise admit that, for the rest, we have no knowledge in regard to it, and that it cannot be thought as a determinate thing in terms of distinctive inner predicates. As it is independent of all empirical concepts, we are cut off from any reasons that could establish the possibility of such an object, and have not the least justification for assuming it. *It is a mere thought-entity.*[15]

Any idea that has no experience undergirding it is "a mere thought-entity." Thus, and secondly, when we speak of God, we should be aware that we will never be able to move from an idea in the mind to an external reality. So, says Kant,

> If, now, we take the subject (God) with all its predicates (among which is omnipotence), and say "God is," or "There is a God," we attach no

---

[15] Kant, *Critique of Pure Reason*, 484, my emphasis.

new predicate to the concept of God, but only posit the subject in itself with all its predicates, and indeed posit it as being an object that stands in relation to my concept.[16]

That is, since there is no experience of God, all that we are able to produce by the category of reason is a *concept*. If we want more than a concept, that can only come by "making room for faith." But that faith can have no access to real knowledge; it cannot be known, only (blindly) *believed*.

The implications of Kant's philosophy are vast, deep, and wide, and we could spend the rest of our time mapping those out in various strands of postmodernism, postconservatism, liberalism, Barthianism, and so forth. The point that needs to be stressed, however—and this is a point that can be applied to countless objections to the Christian faith—is that, for Kant, there is *absolutely no category* for the Christian reality of God's covenantal condescension.

But why should there be such a category? Isn't Kant simply attempting to show that reason is not able to move from the finite to the infinite? Isn't his argument against an experience of the noumenal designed to highlight the vast difference between what we experience in this finite world and a world beyond our experience? Perhaps, and taken at face value, this is a considerable argument for reason's deficiencies (if reason is thought to be autonomous). But the serious and central problem with Kant's discussion is that if it is the *Christian* God that he has in view (and there is every indication that it is), then there is no basis (1) for assuming that we humans have no experience of God and (2) for thinking that faith has been given its proper room by divorcing it from knowledge.

Or, to put it more positively, the only way that Kant can make sense of a God of whom we have no experience is if it is a god who has not come down to reveal himself to us. And that kind of god is no real God at all; it is an idol manufactured by an unbelieving heart. Not only so, but the only way that Kant can pronounce a divorce of faith from knowledge, so that each has its own separate room, is by ignoring the Christian tradition altogether.

---

[16] Kant, *Critique of Pure Reason*, 504

If Kant had given due credit to Christ as Lord, he would have seen and known that, as a matter of fact, all men everywhere, at all times and in all places, have deep and abiding, continual, and persistent experiences of God such that every person, by virtue of being made in God's image and living in God's world, *knows* God. And that knowledge of God comes because God has condescended, covenantally, to reveal himself "in the things that have been made" (Rom. 1:20), in his Son (Heb. 1:1–3), and in his Word. The second we know about anything at all, God is known as well, and that knowledge comes by way of our living and moving and having our existence, in this world, in *him* (Acts 17:28).

So Kant's philosophy, with all of its substantial influence, is singularly unconvincing as an analysis of God's existence. He is right that we cannot move from the finite to the infinite, but he has not considered that the infinite has moved to the finite. In that light, Kant hasn't even broached the most basic truths of the Christian God.

Only a god who has not condescended to be the Lord could be reduced to a pure concept. The true, triune God, who is the Lord, has come from the infinite to the finite. He has condescended, covenantally, so that we might have "fruition" of him. Apart from that condescension, there is no hope of knowing him; he would only be, at best, "a mere thought-entity." But since he has condescended, and since the One who condescended is the cosmic and redemptive Lord, we are guaranteed, for eternity, to have true and certain knowledge of him. Whether we suppress that knowledge (in Adam) or rejoice in it (in Christ), in either case we know him. And that knowledge is, in either case, indicative of our covenant status before him.

It is high time, now, in light of what we have set forth thus far, to put some actual flesh on the bones of the principles we have been discussing. We need to begin to see what an application of what we have laid out to this point might look like. In the remainder of this chapter, we will give two examples of how a covenant apologetic might relate to those who oppose the Christian God. In the first, we will illustrate one way in which a refusal to acknowledge Christ as Lord will end in the self-destruction of the views that are held. In that way, we can see how a rejection of the Christian God is self-defeating. In the second, we will notice what happens when a supposed critique of the Christian

God winds up being nothing of the sort. In both cases, because the lordship of Christ, including his covenant condescension, is not taken into account, the arguments and positions that stand against him are shown to be altogether without merit.

He Who Is Not with Me

Family Feud

Christ—who himself is both fully divine and fully human—is Lord. That truth will shape all that we say in response to objections that come against Christianity. Moreover, what Christians affirm as central to their faith will play a central and significant role in our responses to unbelief. Two examples may help us to see how we might formulate answers to objections that come our way. The first example is not, in the main, an objection to Christianity, but it is very helpful in pointing out (some of) the essential problems that plague those who commit themselves to their own lordship rather than to Christ's.

Recently a feud developed between a group of admitted and committed skeptics and the atheist Richard Dawkins. In an online article about that feud, Brandon K. Thorp began with this:

> Biologist, philosopher, and atheist prophet Richard Dawkins really put his foot in it. *The New Statesman* says Dawkin's [*sic*] career as a public intellectual is kaput. *The Atlantic Wire* has him losing a flame-war against his very own fan base. In the blogosphere, the most devoted Dawkinsians—people who've spent their adult lives in adoration of his every utterance—are boycotting his books and calling him a buffoon.[17]

So Richard Dawkins, who is arguably the (nonexistent) god of all things atheist, recently found himself on the wrong end of a verbal baseball bat. To summarize: at a conference of skeptics, one of the lead "dubitantes" found herself being propositioned on an elevator at 4 a.m. As is our (post)modern custom, the first thing one does when such traumas occur is blog about it.

---

[17] "Richard Dawkins Torn Limb from Limb—by Atheists," accessed July 7, 2011, https://gawker.com/. Readers should be warned that the tenor and language of this article are themselves offensive.

The woman's blog, however, failed to garner the emotional empathy of Dawkins. In a comment on the incident, Dawkins used the woman's blog complaint to attempt his own complaint. Given the mutilation of Muslim women, commented Dawkins, a mere proposition on an elevator at 4 a.m. seems a relatively meaningless and petty problem.

But Dawkins bit off more skepticism with his comments than his atheist stomach could digest. Even after an apology to her, followed by an apology to the skeptics, Dawkins was ill-prepared for the wrath that the rationalist regime rained down on him. The vitriol was relentless, and Dawkins found his own god-like status in serious question. He simply could not understand how his prioritizing of evil deeds could have caused so much caustic consternation. Of particular interest to me was Thorp's concluding comment on the "Skeptics vs. Dawkins" discussion: "That's skeptics," said Thorp. "Rational about everything except themselves, self-preservation, and manners."

By their own admission, these skeptics pride themselves on their commitment to rationality and evidence-based reasoning. However, what *ought* to be perfectly clear in this kerfuffle is that "being rational" is insufficient to deal with things like personal offenses, human preservation, and any statement or belief with an "ought" implied in it. More specifically, "being rational" or "evidential" provides no help or information to someone who is inappropriately propositioned in an elevator. The woman who was propositioned, and who, on her blog, names herself the "Skepchick," assumed that the mere mention of her plight on her blog would rally the rationalist troops with appropriate, rationalist responses. But Dawkins dared to compare the Skepchick's scare with Muslim mutilation and then to apply arbitrary standards of moral equivalence. What Dawkins discovered is that such equations don't compute for the Skepchick and her supporters. How can it be, we could ask, that so many committed to nothing more than being rational and evidential find themselves in such turmoil?

This might be a good place to introduce a sometimes useful apologetic tactic. So-called *ad hominem* (literally, "to the man") arguments are generally considered to be fallacious. There is no question that such arguments *can* be fallacious, but there is also no question that logical fallacies are not fallacious in every case. An *ad hominem* argument, when used in a fallacious way, is an attack on a person's personal character *rather than* a response to that person's arguments. It is, in sum, character assassination. In a charged political atmosphere, for example, such arguments are typically in abundance.

An *ad hominem* argument that is not fallacious is one in which a person's position is challenged *based on what that person claims*. It is an *ad hominem* argument because it goes to the challenger's own beliefs; it seeks to question the consistency of what someone believes, argues, or maintains in light of other beliefs or arguments that he claims to hold. This point is an important one and bears restating. An *ad hominem* argument *does not* compare, for example, an unbelieving position with Christianity in order to show the unbelieving position to be wanting. In an *ad hominem* argument, the comparison is between a person's basic claims or commitments, on the one hand, and that same person's behavior, complaints, assertions, on the other. The problems detected are that the person's basic commitments cannot be consistent with his other claims or complaints. This serves, in part, to provide significant pressure on the truthfulness or applicability of one's basic commitments.

So, we could ask, what is it about Dawkins's response that violated the rational or the evidential foundation of the skeptics? Dawkins tried to make the point that the Muslim mutilation of women is a level of evil with which a 4 a.m. request to have coffee on an elevator can hardly compare. In using the skeptic's basic principles, then, we could ask, is Dawkins's argument an *irrational* argument? If it is, then the Skepchick might have provided the specific law(s) of reasoning that Dawkins violated in his complaint. Or, we could ask, does Dawkins's complaint violate a commitment to evidence-based reasoning? If so, then it would have been useful for the Skepchick to spell out just how evidential principles were transgressed in what Dawkins was saying.

The fact of the matter is that the fact of the matter transcends the rational and the evidential. To what rational law or evidential fact could the Skepchick point that would show Dawkins to be out of bounds in his comparison? There are no such laws or facts, based on the skeptic's worldview. There is something at work in Dawkins's argument, and in the Skepchick's response, that goes beyond their basic commitments, something that their own basic commitments cannot account for. The *ad hominem* question to ask here is just what it is about Dawkins's complaint that violates rationality or evidential reasoning.

No legitimate response will be forthcoming from such a question because none could be. One will search the plethora of logic textbooks in vain hoping to discover a rational law or evidential fact that would vindicate the Skepchick and her supporters. The basic problem is that she had to move beyond her own foundational worldview commitments in order to lodge her lament against Dawkins. To make her complaints, she was, consciously or not, depending on principles that did not comport with her own basic commitments.

There are, then, deep and inviolable forces at work in this debate, forces that go way beyond laws of rationality and evidence. For Dawkins, there is the obvious *scale of evil*: what is done to Muslim women is *more evil* that what was done to the Skepchick. But how would Dawkins account for *any* evil, much less evil on a scale? For the Skepchick, there is a *code of morality* that must be taken by all with utter seriousness *when she is the one violated*. But what rational law or evidential fact provides this code to all people? As the article says, there really does seem to be no common rational or evidential commitment between Dawkins and the Skepchick when it comes to their own personal lives, the way they ought to act, and what constitutes acceptable behavior between people.

This is inevitable. Anyone who determines to base his life on something other than the lordship of Christ and all that his lordship entails will discover that whatever foundation he thinks is holding him up is actually, even if sometimes slowly or imperceptibly, crumbling to dust underneath him. Thus, the *ad hominem* argument is an attempt to show the crumbling foundation in its true light. The supposed basic foundation chosen cannot bear the weight of real life in God's world as God's creatures. It is utterly impotent and so cannot begin to accomplish the task it has been assigned.

The article by Thorp is useful in that it points out, in a real-life, tangible way, just what it means when we say that atheists (skeptics included) cannot, on the basis of their own worldview, make a credible judgment on moral issues. With respect to the skeptics, Thorp himself sees the problem clearly. The fact that their own foundational commitments cannot account for their own personal lives, or for how people *ought* to behave, is no small matter. It destroys the entire approach. Any commitment that cannot account for the way that I and all others should live is doomed at the outset.

Dawkins's argument makes some moral sense; it certainly seems to be true that the mutilation of women is more serious than a man asking a woman to have coffee, even if the request came at 4 a.m. in an elevator. But in order to make *that* evaluation, there must also be a cogent understanding of what and who people are (i.e., image of God), and why and how such things constitute *real*, and not just subjective, evil (i.e., because God, as the only and ultimate good, determines what things are evil and what are not). But neither Dawkins nor the skeptics have a universal standard; the best that they can do is argue for their own relative moral code. Dawkins may want to point to the "common sense" notion that mutilating women is worse than propositioning them. But that notion is anything but common among Muslims. And it apparently gains little traction with offended skeptics.

On the positive side, we can see that Dawkins could set out a gradation of evils only because he knows, deep down, that people are more than rational laws and material composites. They have characteristics that transcend their thinking and their constitution; they are image of God. Dawkins wouldn't put it that way, of course. He could not do so without a healthy commitment to repent of all that he has stood for. But it is just that repentance, and that alone, that can resolve the tension between Dawkins and the Skepchick. It is, to put it rather bluntly, *only* repentance that will give to both Dawkins and the Skepchick what they so desperately want—a cogent and consistent way to understand "themselves, self-preservation, and manners."

So what have we observed in this example? There are two primary aspects of any argument (which we will develop later) that need to be a part of one's analyses and responses to that argument. First of all (though the order here is not important), it is crucial to attempt to articulate just why and how the position one is opposing cannot do what it purports to do. Let's call this the Quicksand Quotient. In applying the Quicksand Quotient, we attempt to show that the position that we are opposing is sinking sand and cannot stand on its own.

There are basically two ways that one could go about this kind of analysis. One way would be to state that the position cannot stand because it does not agree with the Christian position. That way is true enough, but it typically carries no persuasive value; it serves only to show that there are (at least) two competing positions. It is, we could say, too obvious to be argumentatively useful on its own. That there is a discussion in the first place assumes such disagreements. The other, more persuasive and effective way to apply the Quicksand Quotient is to show that the position, *based on its own principles*, cannot stand. The "ground" chosen by the position is insufficient to support its own principles. In that context, the solution of Christianity can take its proper, persuasive place.

In the example above, Thorp has provided the Quicksand Quotient for us. Certainly more could and should be said, but minimally he has argued that the position of skepticism is unable to deal with some of the most basic problems and conundrums that people face. Skepticism may be a comfortable position to hold as long as principles and positions remain in the abstract. But once they are supposed to support matters relating to "themselves, self-preservation, and manners," a commitment to the rational and evidential begins quickly to sink.

Further, if we translate Thorp's categories of "themselves, self-preservation, and manners" into the more general categories of "human beings, life, and behavior," the conclusion is nothing less than devastating. A commitment to the rational and evidential is unable to pronounce on the basic meaning and motivation of life in this world. Once the Quicksand Quotient is in place, then it is useful to demonstrate how Christianity itself is alone able to do justice to the concerns of the skeptic; in Christianity alone do we find a universally applicable way to navigate *how* the rational and evidential relate to "human beings, life, and behavior." We can move, then, from the Quicksand Quotient to the covenantal (Christian) context.

Incompatible or Incomprehensible?

But sometimes people want to turn the Quicksand Quotient in the Christian direction. Sometimes the claim is that Christianity has no foundation, that it sinks of its own irrational weight. Let's take one example of this and see how we might go about addressing it.

In "Omniscience, Eternity, and Time,"[18] Anthony Kenny sets out, in part, to show why the traditional contention that God is immutable cannot be compatible with the traditional notion of God's omniscience. In other words, he is arguing that there are basic Christian tenets that cannot rationally be held, and if a Christian insists on holding both, his Christianity sinks of its own weight; it cashes out as an absurdity. In this argument, the Quicksand Quotient is leveled at traditional Christianity.

We cannot do justice to Kenny's entire article here; the full import of his point can only be had by reading his entire chapter. But we can lay out at least one of the basic tenets—a tenet that, if true, would require the conclusion that (the traditional) God of Christianity does not exist—in order to demonstrate how a Christian could respond.

First, a summary of the argument.[19] Kenny sets out seven propositions:

(1) A perfect being is not subject to change.
(2) A perfect being knows everything.
(3) A being that knows everything always knows what time it is.
(4) A being that always knows what time it is is subject to change.
(5) A perfect being is therefore subject to change.
(6) A perfect being is therefore not a perfect being.
(7) Ergo there is no perfect being.[20]

Given these propositions, and after some discussion, Kenny concludes:

> If a changeless being cannot know the time, then it cannot know either what is expressed by tensed propositions. Knowing that "Christ will be born" is true (roughly) throughout the years BC and that "Christ has been born" is true throughout the years AD will not . . . enable one to know which of these two propositions is true now,

---

[18] Anthony Kenny, "Omniscience, Eternity, and Time," in *The Impossibility of God*, ed. Michael Martin and Ricki Monnier (Amherst, NY: Prometheus, 2003).

[19] The reader should keep in mind that there are twists and turns to Kenny's argument that will not be pursued here. Kenny is actually evaluating an argument set out by Norman Kretzmann. We will avoid those complexities for the sake of simplicity. But we should note that the chapter is more complex and multifaceted than our summary. However, the summary itself is true to what Kenny's argument is intended to conclude.

[20] Kenny, "Omniscience, Eternity, and Time," 212.

unless one also knows the date. . . . A believer in divine omniscience must, it seems, give up belief in divine immutability.[21]

Because this essay comes in a book entitled *The Impossibility of God*, it is clear that its editors see this argument as a refutation of the traditional notion of God. To agree to Kenny's conclusion would require a radical redefinition of the God of Christianity. Thus, *that* God's existence would be impossible.[22]

How might we go about responding to this argument? Kenny has applied the Quicksand Quotient to us and supposes that our belief in Christianity is sunk. There is more than one way to respond to this, of course. We could begin by questioning the notion of a "perfect being." We might want to argue that Christianity cannot abide a generic notion of a perfect being without further necessary qualifiers (e.g., that God is a perfect *triune* being). That, I think, is absolutely right. But there is also a way to respond to Kenny that might serve to highlight some of the central truths of Christianity without involving us in initial semantic debates.

First, Kenny is quite clear that he is arguing against the God of Western theism. His primary interlocutor is Thomas Aquinas. So this puts Kenny squarely in a Christian context, which is vitally important to recognize. Second, because Kenny is interacting with Aquinas, we should recognize that his view of God comports with Thomas's view. We will discuss that view more in another chapter, but it may help just to mention the primary problems with it here.

Thomas Aquinas was convinced that one can know God's existence and his "oneness," or simplicity (as well as some other attributes) by reason alone, without the need for revelation. So Thomas's initial discussion of God is a view that, initially, since it is acquired by reason alone, any Muslim or Jew could affirm, and one that is content with a list of (abstract) attributes that supposedly follow from God's simplicity (as that simplicity is understood by reason alone).[23] This, we should

---

[21]Kenny, "Omniscience, Eternity, and Time," 218.

[22]It seems clear as well that Kenny (along with Kretzmann) is not satisfied with Thomas's response to this predicament in *Summa theologica*, 1.14.15.

[23]It is sometimes supposed that since Thomas does quote biblical passages in his arguments, his natural theology has its foundation in biblical revelation. This question would occupy too much time for us to do it justice here. However, since Thomas is clear that he wants to "demonstrate" God's existence

see, is a problem. It is a problem that we will return to later, but that has served unduly to handicap apologetics in significant ways.

But our response need not suppose the god of Thomas's natural theology. As a matter of fact, our response *should not* suppose that god, since the Christian view of God has a ready response to objections such as Kenny raises.

Since Kenny supposes the God of Western theism, it is no stretch to ask him how exactly we come to know that this God is eternal, immutable, omniscient, omnipotent, and so on. Given Kenny's knowledge of Aquinas, he might reply that such things can be known "by reason alone." Even if we grant that point (for argument's sake), we can then ask Kenny if the attributes delineated by Thomas in his natural theology were contradicted by supernatural revelation. According to Thomas, they were not. That which was affirmed by natural theology was also affirmed and supplemented by supernatural theology.[24]

Given this, we would need to make the point that if one is going to argue against the God of Western theism, as that God is described by Thomas and others, a *full-orbed* picture of this God can only be had by way of God's supernatural revelation. This Kenny could not dispute without himself being out of accord with the substance of Western theism.

So, with respect to this Christian God, central to his identity is that he is triune, and that the second person of the Trinity came down, taking on a human nature, and lived in space and time.[25] And central to *that* claim is the further claim that he did this without in any way sacrificing his essential deity (i.e., his omniscience, omnipotence, aseity, immutability, etc.). Here we could point Kenny to the biblical texts that affirm this and to the ecumenical creeds that have been affirmed by Christians—both Romanist and Protestant—for centuries.

Take the Chalcedonian Creed (AD 451), for example. That creed affirms, in part, that the second person of the Trinity is "one and the

---

from reason alone, and since he is convinced that God's existence is *not* self-evident to us (see *Summa theologica* 1.2.1), whatever role Scripture played for Thomas was *not* one of a foundational *principium*.

[24] The point here is not whether Thomas's method was correct. I would hold that it was not. Rather, the point is to move Kenny to the reality of revelation as the true ground for knowledge of God.

[25] It is vitally important at this point to recognize that any discussion of the incarnation or of Christ presupposes the triunity of God (tenet 1). As is clear, for example, in Christ's baptism, in order for him to be the Son, there must be a Father; and Christ's conception—that which brought about the union of the divine and human natures in him—was accomplished by the Holy Spirit (cf. Luke 1:35).

same Christ, Son, Lord, only begotten, to be acknowledged in two na-tures, inconfusedly, unchangeably, indivisibly, inseparably . . ." Thus, the second person of the Trinity, who himself is fully God, in taking on a human nature, became the Lord Jesus Christ. This Christ is One who, in taking on a human nature, now has two natures. But it is ab-solutely essential to notice that in this one person with two natures, those natures were in no way confused (such that the divine became the human), changed (such that the divine or the human became something else), divided (such that the one nature could, in Christ, be removed from him), or separated (such that the two natures required two persons). In other words, Christianity has historically affirmed that there are properties that only God has and that are essential to him, and there are properties of creation, both of which themselves can be unified in one person without either "side" of those properties losing what it is essentially. The divine remains divine and the human remains human. And yet they are unified in one person. The person who became man remained fully God.

The creed goes on to affirm that "the distinction of natures [was] by no means taken away by the union, but rather the property of each nature [was] preserved, and concurring in one Person and one Subsis-tence, not parted or divided into two persons, but one and the same Son, and only begotten God, the Word, the Lord Jesus Christ."

In historic Christianity, therefore, we do not affirm that there is a god who is simple, immutable, omniscient, and so on *simpliciter*. Rather, Christian theism affirms that there is one God in three per-sons, each of whom is fully God and therefore partakes of all of God's essential attributes. But we also affirm that this God, in the person of his Son, took on the characteristics and properties of creation without in any way undermining, subverting, denying, or impugning his es-sential character as God.

If this is the case, then it is no stretch, theologically and in terms of historic Christianity, to affirm both that God remains immutable and omniscient, essentially and eternally knowing all things through himself, and that he is fully cognizant of each and every temporal fact of creation. His being aware of what is happening *now*, in other words, is no threat to his essential character—neither his immutability nor his omniscience—since the church has affirmed as one of its central teachings that this is exactly what takes place in the Son of God as the God-man.

We might anticipate a couple of objections from Kenny (et al.) at this point. Kenny might argue that the incarnation of the Son of God is a unique occurrence in Christianity and cannot be applied more generally to an understanding of God. To this objection we might offer the following retort: True it is that the incarnation is *sui generis*; there is nothing identical to it in history. Having said that, however, we will remember that one of our basic, guiding principles is, as the Westminster Confession 7.1 says, that God has voluntarily condescended to and in his creation, and that his condescension is expressed by way of covenant.

In other words, the only reason that any of us, Kenny included, can have any knowledge of God is that he has seen fit to "condescend" to us. Now what might this condescension mean? As we have seen, it surely does not mean that he determined to occupy a place, or space, in which he was initially absent. Instead, it means that God expressed himself by "stooping" to use aspects of creation in order to interact with that which he had made. That interaction was a free activity that he determined to do, because he did not have to create. This is what "voluntary" means.

So given his determination to create, and because his character is so "wholly other" than creation (in that he is immutable, infinite, eternal, etc.), he "stoops down" (as Calvin put it) by relating himself to that creation and to us. And that "stoop" requires that we be able to relate to him, to know him, to interact with him, and he with us. This interaction is a covenant interaction. It places obligations on us as people made in his image. But in no way, or at any moment, or on any occasion does it change who God is as God. He does not stoop down simply by becoming one of us. He stoops down by remaining who he is, even while he reveals himself in and through his activity in creation.

So in answer to Kenny, from the beginning, God has been able to remain who he is essentially, all the while really and truly interacting with every aspect of his creation. We see it preeminently in Christ, but it has been there, in various forms and contexts, from the beginning of time.[26]

The second objection that Kenny might want to lodge against us is what he would perhaps judge to be the absurdity of thinking in this way. "How," he might ask, "am I supposed to believe or understand that God unites himself to aspects of creation all the while never changing his essential character?"

The first and most obvious response to this would be to point to the historic doctrine of the incarnation. What cannot be denied is that the church has always affirmed that God, in the second person of the Trinity, was conceived by the Holy Spirit, was born of the Virgin Mary, suffered under Pontius Pilate, was crucified, died, and was buried. Even as these truths are affirmed, the church has also recognized that none of this in any way undermined, denied, subverted, or diminished the full deity of the Son. Thus, as far back as the third century, the church father Athanasius wrote:

> The Word was not hedged in by His body, nor did His presence in the body prevent His being present elsewhere as well. When He moved His body He did not cease also to direct the universe by His Mind and might. No. The marvelous truth is, that being the Word, so far from being Himself contained by anything, He actually contained all things Himself. In creation He is present everywhere, yet is distinct in being from it; ordering, directing, giving life to all, containing all, yet is He Himself the Uncontained, existing solely in His Father. . . . Existing in a human body, to which He Himself gives life, He is still Source of life to all the universe, present in every part of it, yet outside the whole; and He is revealed both through the works of His body and through His activity in the world. . . . His body was for Him not a limitation, but an instrument, so that He was both in it and in all things, and outside all things, resting in the Father alone. At one and the same time—this is the wonder—as Man He was living a human life, and as Word He was sustaining the life of the universe, and as Son He was in constant union with the Father. Not even His birth from a virgin, therefore, changed Him in any way, nor was He defiled by being in the body.[27]

---

[26] These points are developed as well in Oliphint, *The Majesty of Mystery*.

[27] Athanasius, *The Incarnation of the Word, Being the Treatise of St. Athanasius (De Incarnatione Verbi Dei)*, trans. C.S.M.V. St. Th. (London: Geoffrey Bles: Centenary, 1944), 45–46.

What Kenny, therefore, has to recognize is that the truth of the incarnation requires that "absurdity" take on a different meaning than the one he likely intends. That which is *truly* absurd is whatever is in opposition to God; and surely the incarnation is not. Absurdity, therefore, has to be measured not in terms of what *we* can comprehend, but in terms of what God has said to us.

This brings us to the second response we could make to Kenny's possible objection. Following on the first, the objection might be that the notion of absurdity itself has a host of assumptions behind it, which themselves point either to an assumed autonomy or to the Christian context. Perhaps Kenny would think such things absurd because he has concluded that whatever is difficult to understand cannot be true. More specifically, perhaps his notion of absurdity would include that (what he deems to be) incompatible properties could never, by definition, become compatible.

But this notion of absurdity simply runs in a circle. Anyone who thinks absurdity is defined by certain incompatibilities must also make a case for those incompatibilities being such that they could *never*, in any way, come together. And the case that would be made for such an idea would itself assume an autonomous notion of our laws of thought and of being.

On Christian assumptions, however, God is able to bring together things that might appear to be incompatible because he is sovereign over those things, meticulously so, and thus his actions can and will supersede our ability completely to comprehend them. If God can come down and relate himself to his creation, and do so for eternity, without in any way denying his deity, then surely what looks absurd to some is actually the very wisdom of God.

What we are saying, in other words, is that the notion of absurdity itself is loaded with assumptions and cannot be taken at face value when lodged against the Christian position. That which is foolish to those who are perishing is, in reality, the very power of God himself (see 1 Cor. 1:18–25).

So there can be no real objections to any position that has at its root the truth of God. Any unbelieving objections that come our way come because it is the truth of God that is being opposed. The only real and lasting solution to those objections is that they be exposed in the light of God's revelation. The only real remedy to such objections is that those who lodge them bow the knee to Christ and thus begin to see light by his light.

The above examples were intended to show how a covenantal apologetic might argue from the perspective of the other position itself. I have tried to show two different attempts at reasoning that are, *on their own terms*, fallacious. I have introduced the Quicksand Quotient—an approach that tries to ferret out the presuppositions of an opposing viewpoint in order to show its internal inconsistency. But we have also seen that the same Quotient can and will be lodged against us, so that we must be prepared to show its fallacies as well.

In all of this, I have pointed to the reality of Christ the Lord and his Word. This must be our ultimate aim. Only in that reality will it ever be possible for one who opposes Christianity to see the truth for what it is. And it is only as the truth (who is Christ—John 14:6) is presented that one who is trapped in unbelief will have the opportunity for his chains to be broken, his mind to be renewed and transformed, so that what initially appeared to be a problem becomes that in which the very glory of God is revealed.

Unto my Lord Jehovah said,
"At My right hand I throne Thee,
Till at Thy feet, in triumph laid,
Thy foes their Ruler crown Thee."
From Zion shall Jehovah send
Thy scepter, till before Thee bend
The knees of proud rebellion.[28]

---

[28] "Unto My Lord Jehovah Said," Irish Psalter, 1898.

3

Proof to All Men

In order not to create an infinite regression, the proofs themselves must proceed from the kind of propositions that, being immediately certain, are not capable of proof or do not need it.[1]

Christian apologetics has a long and disparate history.[2] Especially since the Middle Ages and into the time of the Reformation, debates raged about the place, method, and means of apologetics itself. Those debates will not be resolved here. In light of those debates, and consistent with the theology of the Reformation, we are attempting to lay out some of the main and central contours (including the ten tenets) that a Reformed, covenantal apologetic should embrace.

What we hope to accomplish in this chapter is to clarify ways in which our basic principles (the ten tenets) relate to the notion of proof in apologetics. In order to do that, we will need to elaborate on some of those principles and try to situate them properly in light of (some of the) historical discussions and debates in and about the use and place of apologetics itself. This chapter, therefore, will take on a more polemical tone, but always with a view toward clarification of a covenantal apologetic approach.

Paul at Athens

When Paul addressed the philosophers and citizens of Athens in Acts 17, he concluded his address with the following: "The times of ignorance

---

[1] Herman Bavinck, *Reformed Dogmatics*, vol. 1, *Prolegomena*, ed. John Bolt, trans. John Vriend (Grand Rapids: Baker Academic, 2003), 211.
[2] As far as I know, the only volumes that attempt to display that history in a collection of the apologists' own texts are William Edgar and K. Scott Oliphint, eds., *Christian Apologetics Past and Present: A Primary Source Reader*, vol. 1, *To 1500*, and vol. 2, *From 1500* (Wheaton, IL: Crossway, 2009, 2011).

God overlooked, but now he commands all people everywhere to repent, because he has fixed a day on which he will judge the world in righteousness by a man whom he has appointed; and of this he has given assurance to all by raising him from the dead" (Acts 17:30–31). We will look again at Paul's address later. For now, we will focus on Paul's conclusion.[3]

Luke tells us that Paul's spirit was provoked within him as he waited in Athens. It was provoked because of the rampant idolatry there (Acts 17:16). Paul understood the idolatry in Athens as an expression of the suppression of the truth in unrighteousness (Rom. 1:18ff.; tenet 5). What must have moved Paul was not that the religions in Athens were expressions of honest seekers. Rather, what provoked him was his knowledge that the plethora of idols all around him were evidence of rebellion against the true and triune God. And the only remedy for that rebellion was the gospel of Jesus Christ.

So in the synagogue and in the marketplace, Paul began to preach. It is instructive for us to recognize that Paul's preaching did not appear to take one form in the synagogue and another in the marketplace. He did not speak of "Judeo-Christian" truths in the synagogue only and then of generic theism in the marketplace. What provoked the request for Paul to address the council and citizens at the Areopagus was his preaching of Christ's resurrection in the marketplace. It was the Epicurean and Stoic philosophers who "invited" Paul to an official gathering. They did so, Luke tells us, because the philosophers thought Paul seemed "'to be a preacher of foreign divinities'—in that he was preaching Jesus and the resurrection" (Acts 17:18).

We should not miss the point that Luke makes here. It was Paul's preaching of Jesus and the resurrection that provoked the response that Paul was a preacher of "foreign *divinities*." Surely this would include the fact that whatever else Paul was saying, it was clear to his listeners that Christ was himself a "divinity" and not a mere man.

A brief excursus might be helpful here, by way of clarification. We should not draw too hard a line between preaching, on the one hand, and apologetics, on the other. As we have been at pains thus far to say,

---

[3]For a discussion of the redemptive-historical content of Paul's address, see Lane G. Tipton, "Resurrection, Proof, and Presuppositionalism," in *Revelation and Reason: New Essays in Reformed Apologetics*, ed. K. Scott Oliphint and Lane G. Tipton (Phillipsburg, NJ: P&R, 2007).

apologetics is a defense of the *Christian* faith. As a Christian defense, we should expect that the *content* of apologetics can substantially overlap with the content of preaching and evangelism. In whatever *mode* of communication, whether preaching, evangelism, or apologetics, it is the gospel of Jesus Christ that has to be our focus.

So even when Paul was in the marketplace, speaking in the presence of the philosophers, he was intent that his listeners understood the import and centrality of Christ and his resurrection. Of course, because Paul knew his audience, he was wise in his choice of topics and ideas to present. A sermon in a Christian church, for example, could take into account much more specific biblical content and context than an address to those who have little to no knowledge of Scripture. But in any case, what was needed was an understanding of who God in Christ is, what he requires of us, and what he has accomplished for his people. The apostle Paul wanted to make sure that his Areopagus audience heard of Christ and his work, and he wanted them to recognize that, because of that work, it was their obligation, as God's covenant creatures, to repent and believe.

In verse 31, Paul links together the end of history, the reality of judgment, and the resurrection of Christ. It is difficult to know exactly what these particular Epicureans and Stoics believed. By the time of Paul's stint in Athens, both philosophies had been around for four hundred years or so. Like all other philosophies, changes and mutations had certainly occurred since their inception. But it was quite likely that, whatever they believed specifically, these philosophers held to a polytheistic philosophy in which the gods were unconcerned for the lives of mere mortals. Death was glossed as irrelevant, since it was, quite literally, a passage into nothing.

Paul's choice of topics and truths to discuss at the Areopagus took these philosophies into account. He assured his listeners that it was certainly not the case that God was uninvolved in their lives. As a matter of fact, God was as close to them as their own individual lives; they all lived, moved, and existed in the true God (17:28).

This "closeness" of God entailed obligations for them, as Paul made clear. Because God is the sovereign One, independent of anything we could contribute (17:24–26), and yet requires us to relate favorably to him, we are in dire straits. Any philosophy or idea that tries to brush away a fear of God or of death is merely an illusion. Death will come, Paul made clear, and so will judgment. And it just so happens, said Paul, that this God has appointed Christ to judge each and every person. The assurance of that judgment is that God raised Christ from the dead.

All of this is covenantal language. God's creation, his appointing the boundaries for all men, his independence together with his exhaustive presence with each of us—these signify nothing other than God's sovereign initiation of a relationship with all of his human creatures, a relationship that places obligations on us.

Some of our English translations render the word "assurance" in verse 31 as "proof" (see, for example, the New American Standard Bible). The word used in the Greek can carry either connotation (more on this in the next chapter). The point that Paul was making to his listeners was that they could be assured, because God had proved, that judgment will come. They could be assured, and they had proof, because death has been conquered in the man whom God appointed; he has raised him from the dead.

Death, therefore, in contrast to Epicurean and Stoic philosophy, is not the end. It is rather the beginning of another mode of existence. And that mode of existence is consummated at the judgment, which will be carried out by the One whom God has raised. He raised him and he gave him authority to judge all mankind. In other words, the logic of Paul's argument is that because God has raised Christ, and because Christ now lives as risen from the dead, he has authority to judge everyone else who dies. And everyone dies.

As mentioned, more will be said later about Paul's Areopagus address. The two points we want to see at this juncture are that (1) Paul's message to the pagan philosophers and citizens of Athens is replete with covenantal language, and (2) a part of that language includes the statement that God, by raising Christ from the dead, has proved that Christ will judge the dead. Paul was not content merely to get their notion of God adjusted. He was not attempting to change their polytheism into mere monotheism. Neither was he interested in giving them a generic or abstract description of God's attributes. The attributes that he does give them (e.g., sovereignty, aseity, omnipresence, etc.) are all charged with covenantal meaning and obligations. And they all find their true reference point in Christ's authority and resurrection.

But, we could ask, what made Paul think that he could reach his listeners in this way? Was he not simply, and in confrontational fashion, setting his own beliefs over against theirs? Wasn't Paul's address at the Areopagus nothing more than a shouting match between different worldviews? In order to answer these questions, and to set up for further discussion, we need to take a closer look at the substance of a couple of our tenets.

Where Shall I Flee?

As we saw in chapter 1, once sin entered the world, the very first human response to the presence of God was to attempt to hide (Gen. 3:8). It was a response of desperation—a vain and futile activity. But the shame and guilt that disobedience brought to Adam and Eve motivated their self-deception. They acted as though they could hide from the One who had created them and everything around them. They pretended that the very creation God had made could shield them from their Maker and Lord.

Since that fateful day, man has continued to pretend that he can hide from God (cf. Jonah 1:1–10). In perpetual and culpable acts of self-deception, we continually in Adam embrace the irrational supposition that God cannot find or see us.

In a moment of praise for God's merciful redemption, David recognized the scope of God's sovereignty, omniscience, and omnipresence:

> You know when I sit down and when I rise up;
>   you discern my thoughts from afar.
> You search out my path and my lying down
>   and are acquainted with all my ways.
> Even before a word is on my tongue,
>   behold, O Lord, you know it altogether.
> You hem me in, behind and before,
>   and lay your hand upon me.
> Such knowledge is too wonderful for me;
>   it is high; I cannot attain it.

Where shall I go from your Spirit?
   Or where shall I flee from your presence? . . .
If I say, "Surely the darkness shall cover me,
   and the light about me be night,"
even the darkness is not dark to you;
   the night is bright as the day,
   for darkness is as light with you.

For you formed my inward parts;
   you knitted me together in my mother's womb. . . .
My frame was not hidden from you,
when I was being made in secret,
   intricately woven in the depths of the earth.
Your eyes saw my unformed substance;
in your book were written, every one of them,
   the days that were formed for me,
   when as yet there was none of them. (Ps. 139:2–7; 11–13; 15–16)

David is not only expounding personal truths in this psalm. He is recognizing the sheer magnitude of God's covenantal character over all of creation. This knowledge is "too wonderful," says David, even unattainable (v. 6). The fact of the matter is that God is present with and sovereign over all his creation. That presence includes his exhaustive knowledge of all that takes place in all of creation, including all that every person is, does, and says. As we have said, every person lives, moves, and exists in God. This includes God's meticulous sovereignty over every single detail of our lives, from conception and into eternity. At every step, with every heartbeat, God is sovereignly present.

This is good news for David because he has put his faith in this God. But it is anything but good news for those who continue to rebel against him. That rebellion does nothing to hinder God's sovereign presence or knowledge. It is not as though David is saying that God knows the "frame" of those who love him, but is ignorant of those who rebel against him. The only difference with respect to these characteristics of God is how we respond to them. Either we can, like David, praise God for who he is, or we can deceive ourselves into thinking that we can hide from him. These two options, we should recognize, are the only two available for man (tenet 7).

When Paul addressed the Athenians at the Areopagus, he was addressing, as Francis Schaeffer once put it, "men without the Bible."[4] As such, there were (at least) two universal truths—truths that are applicable to all people everywhere and at all times—that lay behind his address. These truths have been broached already, especially in our tenets, but need to be expounded a bit here since they will become a central focus of our discussion of apologetic method and proofs below. Specifically, we need to add important biblical details to tenets 4, 5, and 6.

God's Inescapable Image

First, Paul made clear to the Athenians and their philosophers that they were all responsible creatures of God, and that they owed their very existence to him (Acts 17:28–29). He made clear to them, in other words, that they were all covenant creatures made in God's image. It is this image of God that is the presupposition behind everything else that we *are*.

If we remain in our sins, in Adam, we are judged and condemned *because we are God's image*. If we come to Christ, by grace through faith, there is no condemnation *because, in Christ, the image of God which we are is being renewed* (cf. Eph. 4:24; Col. 3:10). Being "image of God," therefore, is one of the most basic covenantal categories for us (tenet 4). It is a universal truth about us, from the beginning of creation and into eternity future.

At the point of creation, God condescends in order to relate to his creatures on their level. As we have seen (WCF 7.1), this voluntary condescension is called God's covenant. It entails that God is our ultimate environment. But what does it mean that God is our ultimate environment? Two emphases can be given here, the first dealing with who we are and the second, implied in the first, with what we know.

When God condescends to his creation, he does so in order to relate to that creation, to be involved in it (all the while remaining who he essentially is). More specifically, he creates man (both male and female) in his own image. This means that we are, originally, fundamentally, and eternally, image. This truth goes hand in

---

[4] Francis A. Schaeffer, *Death in the City* (Downers Grove, IL: InterVarsity, 1969), 93.

hand with the fact that God is our ultimate environment. We all, as human beings, live *coram Deo*, in the presence of him in whose image we are.

This is one reason it might be helpful to remember the analogy of a mirror image. If the image of God is analogous to an image in a mirror, then we realize that the original must be at all times present, in front of the mirror, in order for there to be an image at all. But we also see that the image, as image, while reflecting the original, depends at every second on the presence of the original for its very existence. If the original is no longer present, the image is gone. Image is essentially dependent, for its existence and every one of its characteristics, on the original. The original, however, is in no way dependent on that image in order to be what it is. Furthermore, the image is of a completely different character than its original.

The Lord God who made us as image gave us responsibilities with respect to his creation, responsibilities that presuppose our inextricable (universal) bond with creation. Given that he is Lord, he gave us the responsibility to be "under-lords" over his creation; he gave us dominion over what he had made. This dominion includes (though it does not exhaust) the fact that there is a "lordship" relationship between man, as male and female, and the rest of creation. In order to understand just what this lordship relationship is, we look, in the first place, to God who is the Lord. Two aspects of lordship should be highlighted here.

1. As Lord, God has committed himself, for eternity, to his creation. He has promised not to annihilate what he has made, but rather to keep it for himself forever. This covenant commitment of God the Lord to tie himself to what he has made will go on without end.

2. Because he is Lord, the relationship that obtains between us and him is not one of equality. God's commitment to us does not entail that he has become an equal partner in this relationship. He is and remains God, and we are and will remain his creatures. He neither depends on us nor owes us anything (Rom. 11:33–36). We owe him everything, including allegiance and worship, and we owe it to him for eternity. He rules over us—lovingly, sovereignly, wisely—and we submit to that rule (either now or in the future—cf. Phil. 2:9–11).

When God created us in his own image, he intended for us to be lords, *under him*, over everything else that he made. Our lordship over creation carries the same two implications, noted above, of God's lordship over us.

1. God has committed us to creation in such a way that we are inextricably linked to it. For example, it is instructive to notice that in creating the animal world God used the same "dust" that he used in creating Adam (we will return to the importance of this in chapter 6). In creating Adam, "the Lord God formed the man of dust from the ground" (Gen. 2:7; cf. Eccles. 3:20). This is intended to show us, at least, that we, like the beasts, are children of dust (Gen. 3:19). Adam (and, indirectly, Eve, since she came from Adam) came from the same "stuff" as the beasts (2:19). Thus we are linked with the dust of creation, in one sense, because, like the animals, we are taken from it; we are quite literally a part of it.

But there is a significant difference in the creation of Adam, a difference, we could say, that marks us off from everything else created: "Then the Lord God formed the man of dust from the ground and breathed into his nostrils the breath of life, and the man became a living creature" (2:7). Of course, the beasts of the earth were living creatures of God as well. But *our* living is the result of an entirely different, God-originating and -animating activity. The act of God that constituted man as a "living soul" was a result of God's own inbreathing. It was that inbreathing, the imparting of the very breath of God in us, that made us "image of God."[5]

The point to be recognized here is that, in creating us as image, God bound us together not only with himself, but with creation as well. There is a bond of humanity with (the rest of) creation such that one will not and cannot exist without the other.

It is for this reason that Paul, in speaking of what is sometimes called the problem of evil in Romans 8 can say confidently that, as a result of our sin, the whole creation groans and itself was subjected to futility (Rom. 8:19–20). It does not groan because of its own inherent deficiencies, but because, in our sinning, we subjected it to

---

[5] This should not be read dichotomistically, as if the image of God in us resides only in the spiritual, or "soul-ish," aspect of man. The point to be made in the text is that God constituted us, both body and soul, as image by virtue of his breathing into what was otherwise nonimage.

futility (cf. Gen. 3:16–19). Creation, in covenant with man, fell because we fell.

2. As with God's lordship over us, our lordship over creation is not one of equals. We were meant to rule over—lovingly and wisely—all that God made. Because of the entrance of sin, matters have become complicated (to say the least) and our ruling sometimes causes harm rather than good. I remember reading somewhere the question and answer of George Whitefield, "Do you know why the cats hiss and the dogs bark when you walk by? They know you have a quarrel with your Maker."

The point to be made here, however, is that there is an inseparable and ineluctable link between ourselves and the world, a link that is both established by God and intended to reflect his character. Because of that, we are people created to know and to interact with our world, all to the glory of the triune God, our Creator. It is this crucial but (almost) universally neglected truth—that our covenantal connection with the world is initiated, constituted, orchestrated, and sustained by the triune God—that is the theological key to a Christian understanding of our "situated-ness" in the world and our access (and knowledge of that access) to reality.

One other theological point, a point we need to continue to set forth throughout this book, must be mentioned again in this context. Because God is who he is, all of his dealings with us and with creation presuppose his voluntary condescension. In John Calvin's words:

> For who even of slight intelligence does not understand that, as nurses commonly do with infants, God is wont in a measure to "lisp" in speaking to us? Thus such forms of speaking do not so much express clearly what God is like as accommodate the knowledge of him to our slight capacity. To do this he must descend far beneath his loftiness.[6]

In relating himself to us, the triune God creates the means by which he condescends to us. He reveals himself via human language, meaning, experience, and even flesh (supremely in Christ) in order to faithfully maintain his covenant with us; and he does all of this while remaining fully and completely God.

---

[6]John Calvin, *Institutes of the Christian Religion*, ed. John T. McNeill, trans. Ford Lewis Battles, 2 vols., The Library of Christian Classics (Philadelphia: Westminster Press, 1960), 1.13.1.

As human beings, therefore, we are situated within the context of God's presence and are, by virtue of that situated-ness, images of him. We live and move and have our being in him. This is true whether we are covenant keepers (in Christ) or covenant breakers (in Adam). In either case, we are covenant creatures with God as our ultimate environment, responsible to image him in all our living, thinking, and doing. This is who we are by virtue of God's creation.

Unfortunately, the story of creation is not the whole story. As we have seen, something went wrong, terribly wrong. God's fellowship with Adam and Eve that was a natural part of the created order was radically and decisively disrupted. The image of God as male and female, fully and completely revealed in the garden prior to sin, became a source of shame after the fall (Gen. 3:7). Though God graciously clothed Adam and Eve after their rebellion, their need itself for clothing, though a genuine necessity subsequent to their sin, was nevertheless fundamentally unnatural and not a part of the created design or order. What was true physically was just as true spiritually; the image of God that Adam and Eve fully exhibited prior to sin was now a source of shame owing to their real guilt, and was covered up because of sin.

This, then, is the serious problem, even the terminal condition, that confronts us. After the fall, the image of God becomes a source of shame; our visceral reaction to who we are as image (including the presence of God ever before us) is to hide and suppress whatever we can of that image (Gen. 3:8–10). Though the image itself remains (because that is who we essentially *are*), it has been fractured and broken because of sin. Thus, we would, if we could, hide from God, and we make it our goal to construe the world in such a way that we would not have to face him. We would pretend that access to God by way of his revelation (both in the world and in his Word) is impossible. We might even come to think that it is our very environment or context that is a barrier to a sure and certain knowledge of God.

God's Unabated Revelation

But the second theological truth that informs Paul's Areopagus address is that God is not hindered by our pretended contexts and supposed barriers. His revelation comes through; it bombards us externally and internally. He continues, always and everywhere, to reveal himself to those who are his image. And that revelation always and everywhere meets its mark and accomplishes its goal. As image, we *know* him, and that knowledge makes us covenantally accountable to him (tenet 5).

In Romans 1:18ff., according to Calvin, there is a universal application of the image of God, relative to sin, given by the apostle Paul. "Paul shows that the whole world is deserving of eternal death. It hence follows, that life is to be recovered in some other way, since we are all lost in ourselves."[7] Paul's point, in other words, is initially to show that we are all under the grip of sin and that the way out of that condition requires something outside of us. It is crucial to note here, as we have said, that Paul's purview in this passage is universal; he is not attempting to describe the way things are or have been in particular circumstances or with particular people only. He is not saying that only some know God and others are ignorant.

All people have (what Calvin called) a *sensus divinitatis* (about which I will say more below), which simply is the true knowledge of God, and all are therefore rendered without excuse. All people are covenantally bound to be judged by God. Paul's point in Romans 1 and 2 is to argue that we all are in the same depraved boat. Since we all are under the same curse of sin, the gospel and its truth is for every person as well—to the Jew first, and also to the Greek (Rom. 1:16).

Beginning in Romans 1 and into Romans 2, Paul's particular purpose is to describe just what the image of God looks like even while we remain in our sins (in Adam). He wants to show us how that image works in light of our rebellion, and what processes it engages in while we remain in our sinful state. Because of the central and important truths that Paul elaborates in this passage, we need to linger here for a few minutes. These truths will become important as we move forward.

For our purposes, however, we will confine our discussion of this passage to elements germane to the *sensus divinitatis*, or the *sensus*, for short. Some of these truths have already been affirmed in previous chapters. I reiterate them here in light of our discussion of theistic

---

[7] John Calvin, *Commentaries on the Epistle of Paul, the Apostle, to the Romans* (Edinburgh: Calvin Translation Society, 1849).

proofs in this chapter and given the importance and application of the *sensus* in future chapters.

Let's frame Paul's affirmation of the *sensus* in terms of a threefold and mutually related truth: (1) The *sensus*, as a central aspect of our being made in God's image, is God's revelation to us. (2) As revelation it is implanted in us by God himself. (3) Given (1) and (2), as Paul makes clear, the *sensus* is knowledge of God, a knowledge that is universal and infallible. We will take these three in reverse order.

Notice, first of all, that born as we are into our sinful state and continuing in that state by virtue of our wickedness, we all nevertheless know God. The way in which Paul introduces this notion in Romans 1:18 is not to tell us first about our knowledge of God. His initial concern is the revelation of God's wrath and the reason for it. And the reason for such an expression of wrath by God lies in that we all, in our sins, suppress the truth. But Paul immediately realizes, as he writes, that he should explain what he means by "suppress" and "truth." He takes up the latter first.

He affirms, beginning in verse 19, that there is a knowledge of God in every man. He affirms that in the context of elaborating on our suppression of the truth (v. 18), and then by explaining what that truth is that we suppress. In sum, the truth that we suppress is not truth, first of all, about nature or about aspects of this world. The truth that we suppress in unrighteousness is simply this: the "clearly perceived" (v. 20) and "understood" (v. 20, NASB) knowledge of God. This is no obscure knowledge; nor is it knowledge that is beyond our capacity to understand. This knowledge that we have is both perceived—clearly perceived—and something that we somehow understand.

This knowledge of God that we all have is knowledge with significant and substantial content. Universally, clearly, and infallibly, we know much about God by virtue of this clearly perceived and understood revelation of God to us. We know his invisible nature, namely, his eternal power and deity (or "God-ness"). We know these things to such an extent that Paul can pronounce in verse 21 that since the creation of the world to the present, human beings are and have always been creatures who "knew God."

This is strong (and clear) language. It explicitly states that all of us, "since the creation of the world," are characterized as those who knew (and know) God; we know his deity and his power—in short, all those things that are a part of his invisible nature. And what are those things? Charles Hodge, in his commentary on Romans, says that Paul means to delineate here "all the divine perfections"[8] in his affirmation of those things which we know about God. Presumably, then, human beings are created such that we know God to be "a Spirit, infinite, eternal, and unchangeable, in his being, wisdom, power, holiness, justice, goodness, and truth."[9] Important truths such as these (and we could say these truths are really the most important ones) God has seen fit not to leave to our own reasoning process to discover; they are not left to the schools or seminaries; they are not in any way dependent on the capacities of human creatures themselves for the process of knowing. They are given to us, revealed to and in us, implanted in us, by the creative power and providence of almighty God the Creator.

This seems altogether consistent with God's character. There would be something amiss if God chose to create us but then to hide himself from us, either leaving us without a witness to himself or, perhaps worse, leaving us to ourselves to try to figure out what he is like.[10]

Just what kind of knowledge God has given and how it might function is another question, but the import of Paul's pronouncement here should not be lost. He is affirming that human beings, all human beings "since the creation of the world," know and have always known the character and attributes of the true God. This would indicate in fairly strong terms that, whatever else we might want to say about the *sensus*, it is in fact *knowledge* (*notitia*).[11]

The second aspect of the *sensus* is God's internal implanting of this knowledge in us. Notice, again, how Calvin describes it:

---

[8] Charles Hodge, *A Commentary on the Epistle to the Romans*, rev. ed. (Philadelphia: Claxton, 1866), 37. Hodge likely got this from Calvin; see Calvin, *Institutes*, 1.5.11.

[9] Westminster Shorter Catechism, answer 4.

[10] Recall that the Westminster Confession rightly attributes our inability to know and serve God not, in the first place, to our sinfulness, but to our constitution as creatures. We are, as created, inherently limited in our ability to understand and to worship God. Thus, God's revelation of himself to us, as Paul notes, was necessary not simply because of or after the fall of man into sin, but at creation's inception.

[11] Given our discussion of Kant above, we can also see that Kant's attempted divorce of faith and knowledge is, at bottom, anti-Christian.

To prevent anyone from taking refuge in the pretense of ignorance, God himself has implanted in all men a certain understanding of his divine majesty. Ever renewing its memory, he repeatedly sheds fresh drops. Since, therefore, men one and all perceive that there is a God and that he is their Maker, they are condemned by their own testimony because they have failed to honor him and to consecrate their lives to his will.[12]

And further:

Men of sound judgment will always be sure that a sense of divinity which can never be effaced is engraven upon men's minds. Indeed, the perversity of the impious, who though they struggle furiously are unable to extricate themselves from the fear of God, is abundant testimony that this conviction, namely, that there is some God, is naturally inborn in all, and is fixed deep within, as it were in the very marrow. . . . For the world . . . tries as far as it is able to cast away all knowledge of God, and by every means to corrupt the worship of him. I only say that though the stupid hardness in their minds, which the impious eagerly conjure up to reject God, wastes away, yet the sense of divinity, which they greatly wished to have extinguished, thrives and presently burgeons. From this we conclude that it is not a doctrine that must first be learned in school, but one of which each of us is master from his mother's womb and which nature itself permits none to forget, although many strive with every nerve to this end.[13]

We know God not because we have reasoned our way to him, or have worked through the necessary scientific procedures, or have inferred his existence from other things that we know; rather, we know him by way of his revelation. We know what God is like "because God has shown it" to us.

The knowledge we have of God is knowledge that he has given to us. It is "implanted" in us, "engraven" in our minds, "naturally inborn" in all of us, "fixed deep within" us, a knowledge "which nature permits none to forget." As Creator, God has guaranteed that he will never be without witness to the creatures who have been made in his image. He has ensured that all of his human creatures will, and will always, know him.

---

[12] Calvin, *Institutes*, 1.3.1.
[13] Calvin, *Institutes*, 1.3.3.

The *sensus*, then, is not a doctrine or teaching that is learned, but rather something that is present within us "from our mother's womb." Such is the case because this knowledge is not dependent on us to be acquired; it is *given* by God. So we have the *sensus* because we are God's image and God implants the knowledge of himself within each of us as his image. And this knowledge is, *ipso facto*, universal and infallible; to say otherwise would render those in Adam excused before God (cf. Rom. 1:20).

But how could that be the case? How could it be that something within us flawed and imperfect human beings could be such that its content is always and everywhere infallible? This brings us to the third element of the *sensus*—revelation.

Traditionally, this section of the book of Romans has been understood to be discussing the topic of natural, or general, revelation. The knowledge of God that human beings possess is not a knowledge that depends for its acquisition and content on something within us. It is a knowledge that is given, and it is given by God himself. It is the revelation of the character of God given to man in and through the things that are made. Thus, the *sensus* is regarded by Paul as knowledge itself that comes directly and repeatedly from God himself through the things that God made and sustains. This, of course, is consistent with the Old Testament understanding of natural revelation as well. The psalmist, therefore, can say:

> The heavens are telling the glory of God;
>   and the firmament proclaims his handiwork.
> Day to day pours forth speech,
>   and night to night declares knowledge. (Ps. 19:1–2, RSV)

Of course, it is not, strictly speaking, the heavens that are declaring God's glory, but it is God declaring his glory "through the things that are made" (the heavens). The *sensus* itself, then, is revelation from God, implanted in us by God, and is true knowledge of God, the true God, that is clearly perceived and understood by us.

There is another factor that we need to see from Paul's discussion in this passage. We should remember that Paul began his discussion of the *sensus* not directly but indirectly, as an elaboration of the notion of "truth," which truth we all, in our sins, suppress. Specifically, the truth suppressed is the subject of Paul's description of the *sensus*. We should note that the suppression is not a part of the *sensus*, but the truth suppressed is. The suppression itself is, rather, an elaboration of what it means to be ungodly and wicked (cf. Rom. 1:18).

We must acknowledge, therefore, that the context, the situation, the environment, for all men everywhere, no matter what the language or custom, is the presence and knowledge of the true God, a knowledge that comes by way of God's self-attesting natural revelation. The implications of this for Christian epistemology (theory of knowledge), and for Christian apologetics and philosophy generally, are multifold and abundant, exciting and stimulating, but we cannot pursue them here.[14]

As was said above, it seems to be altogether true and right that man (male and female), by virtue of being created in the image of God, always and everywhere carries the knowledge of God with him. This knowledge does not come by the proper and diligent exercise of our cognitive, emotive, or volitional capacities; it rather comes by God's own revelatory activity within us.[15] Thus we could say that what Paul is affirming here is the basic, foundational reality of universal theism. This is not a "bare" theism, in which we might believe that something, somewhere, somehow bigger than us exists. Rather, it is true and universal knowledge of the true God that is ours as his image.

One important qualifier needs to be added here and should be developed, but cannot be elaborated. Since this knowledge of God that all people have is implanted by God through the dynamic of his revelatory activity, it is a knowledge in many ways quite different from most (if not all) other kinds of knowledge that we acquire. It is a knowledge, we could say, that is presupposed by any (perhaps all) other knowledge. For this reason, it may be best to think of it as more psychological than epistemological.[16] It is a knowledge that God infuses into his human

---

[14] For an exegetical discussion of the *sensus*, see K. Scott Oliphint, "The Irrationality of Unbelief," in *Revelation and Reason*, ed. K. Scott Oliphint and Lane G. Tipton (Phillipsburg, NJ: P&R, 2007).

[15] Notice Paul's point that what is known about God is made manifest within us, and Calvin's that "God himself has implanted in all men a certain understanding of his divine majesty" (*Institutes*, 1.3.1). The actor, clearly, according to both Paul and Calvin, with respect to the acquisition of any knowledge of God, which is the *sensus*, is God, not us; we are the (unwilling?) patients.

[16] That is, knowledge that is initially and centrally focused in the soul (*psyche*), rather than centrally focused in the mind.

creatures, and continues to infuse into them, even as they continue to live out their days denying or ignoring him (in Adam).

We should also note that this knowledge of God is implanted "through the things that are made." Thus, it comes, always and anon, whether or not the human creature claims to know God or to have reason for not knowing. This means that entailed in our condition as human beings is access to the world as created. Behind every culture, behind any context or conditioning, behind any linguistic construct is the world known, and known as created by the true God who is known. As God reveals himself through the universe, the universe is known to us even as God is known to us.

To put the matter theologically, we must know the world in order to know God, and we must know God because we are his image. There is, therefore, a universal and necessary access to the world in such a way that we know God through knowing it.

Another implication of this formulation of the *sensus* is that true theistic belief of this kind always and everywhere is infallible. That is, there can be no situation in which God implants the knowledge of himself and in which the person to whom this knowledge is given fails to know God. This does not mean that our knowledge of the world is infallible, however, since all that is required for an infallible knowledge of God is his implanting that knowledge in us through the things he has made. Not required is that we infallibly know the things that are made, but only that we do know them by virtue of being inextricably tied to them covenantally.

The universal truths of our being image of God and, thus, of knowing God inform Paul's address at the Areopagus. More generally, they must inform any and every attempt to defend the Christian faith. It is our covenant relation with God that defines every person, and it is the substance of that relationship that provides the backdrop, and access, to every person to whom we speak.

How, then, should we think about what it means to "prove" the existence of God?[17]

---

[17] For a much more technical survey and analysis of Reformed responses to the proofs of natural theology, see Michael Sudduth, *The Reformed Objection to Natural Theology*, Ashgate Philosophy of Religion Series (Burlington, VT: Ashgate, 2009); and K. Scott Oliphint, "Is There a Reformed Objection to Natural Theology?," *Westminster Theological Journal* 74, no. 1 (2012): 169–204.

Proving the Proofs

The notion of proof is multifaceted. It is often assumed that it is illegitimate to assert anything not susceptible to a strict proof. We should notice, first of all, that the idea that any and every assertion must be proved before believed or asserted is necessarily impossible. For example, take a standard, simple syllogism:

(P1) All men are mortal.
(P2) Socrates is a man.
(C) Socrates is mortal.

This syllogistic proof is an argument, with three propositions: two premises (P) and a conclusion (C). Now, what do we want to say about this argument? Is it *valid*? Yes, it is, but a valid argument makes no pronouncement on its *truth*. Why not? Because the definition of a valid argument is that the conclusion necessarily follows from the premises, whatever they say. An argument can be valid without considering the "truth question." So we could agree that the above argument is valid, but we have yet to say anything about its truth.

So the next question that can be asked is whether this argument is *sound*. A sound argument is a valid argument in which the premises are true. A sound argument *does* broach the truth question. But how do we go about moving from a valid argument to one that is sound? How do we get at the notion of truth in an argument? One way would be to ask, is P1 true? Our initial inclination would be to respond, "Yes, of course it is." But then we might ask, how would we know such a thing? How, in other words, would we gain the knowledge (if it is true) that *all men* are mortal? Suppose someone demanded that we prove P1. How would we go about doing *that*?

In order to delve into this latter question, we need to recognize that there are at least two significant and global limitations to the notion of proof. First, absolutely conclusive proofs are hard to come by. This is the case for a number of reasons. One of the reasons is that there are divergent opinions on what constitutes an absolutely conclusive proof. Is it a proof that is objectively sound whether or not someone accepts it? Does it have to be accepted by a person in order to be *proved* as absolutely conclusive? If not, then how do we understand the notion of conclusive? That is one limitation.[18]

The other limitation, which goes back at least as far as Aristotle, is that we cannot operate or even think in a context in which every assertion *requires* a demonstrative proof. For example, one of the most stimulating arguments presented over the past few decades has been Alvin Plantinga's assertion that there really is no successful case for the existence of "other minds" (i.e., other people). No philosopher has successfully argued for that existence, since it cannot be established on an empirical or a nonempirical basis.

Plantinga, however, does not conclude that it is irrational to believe in other minds just because a successful argument has yet to be given for them. Rather, he contends that it is entirely rational to believe in other minds and that, as a matter of fact, all of us *do* believe such things. So the impetus behind his argument is that belief in other minds is rational, even though not (yet) proven.

When logicians speak of proofs, they oftentimes categorize them into two different sets—empirical and nonempirical. These categories, however, are themselves not as clear as they might first appear. Empirical proofs, obviously, are proofs whose statements rest on empirical evidence. If I say to you, "I have a red car," that is a statement that can be empirically verified. It can be shown via the senses to be true or false. You can look at the car. When we deal with more complex empirical statements, the verification must necessarily take on layers of justification that can make the proof itself more complex.

If I say to you, "Caesar crossed the Rubicon in 44 BC," that statement is still an empirical one, but because of its location in history, it now must be verified by appeals to certain other kinds of legitimate authority. That is not a deficiency of the proof, because it is necessary for its verification, but it should be seen as increasing the complexity of what an empirical proof is.

Other empirical statements, like "All men are mortal," are inductive generalizations that should be seen not always as conclusive but as having their legitimacy—provided they do—within a certain context.

---

[18] Included in this discussion might also be the notion of epistemic certainty. This is a more technical point, but if we define epistemic certainty (roughly) as accruing to a proposition whose warrant cannot be superseded, then that kind of certainty will have, by definition, a significant subjective component.

Statements like this one, and like "Every effect must have a cause," are empirical statements, sometimes called evidential statements, because they are general principles derived from experience. More on this below.

But there are also nonempirical statements, thus nonempirical proofs. If I say to you, "All people should respect the property rights of others," it is difficult to see how this statement could be empirically verified. As is the case with many moral statements, these kinds of statements will necessarily rely more on some other kind of justification rather than one that is empirically verified. That is, in nonempirical kinds of proofs, the strength of the proof depends more on the kind and merit of the justification given for the premises offered in the proof.[19]

Now we should note that even with nonempirical proofs, there can be, and often must be, appeals made to empirical evidence. That evidence can serve as part of the justifying reason for the statements made. For example, in order to justify the statement above on property rights, you might point to examples in which those rights have not been respected, and the unwanted results of those examples. Or you might point to laws in which those rights have been granted, and the desirable outcome of those laws. These are empirical scenarios that provide elements of justification for the nonempirical claim made.

But what about statements about God? Do they belong to empirical proofs or to nonempirical proofs? That depends on the particular statements. If I want to make the claim that "God is eternal," it will be difficult to point to empirical evidence to justify that claim. At that point, we will likely need to access a legitimate appeal to authority in order to argue for or support that claim.

But if I make the statement, "God exists," there may be, along with nonempirical justifying reasons, empirical evidence to justify such a statement. So whether or not we can prove God's existence depends on what we mean by proof.

Merriam-Webster's Collegiate Dictionary includes this definition of *proof*:

la: he cogency of evidence that compels acceptance by the mind of a truth or a fact.[20]

---

[19] This kind of nonempirical "ought" statement was what, in part, caused trouble for Dawkins and the Skepchick, as we saw in chap. 2.

[20] *Merriam-Webster's Collegiate Dictionary*, 11th ed. (Springfield, MA: Merriam-Webster, 2003).

Using this definition, we might want to say that, strictly speaking, the existence of God cannot be proved. However compelling the evidence, it is not its cogency that compels acceptance; rather, it is the Holy Spirit alone who can compel agreement.

A second definition is this:

> b: The process or an instance of establishing the validity of a statement esp. by derivation from other statements in accordance with principles of reasoning.[21]

Given this definition, we might want to say that what we are after is *more than* proof, since, given what we have said above, we want not simply a valid argument, but a sound argument as well. And if soundness is what we are after, again the Holy Spirit is the One who compels agreement to the truth.

So the notion of proof is complicated. And notice that we have not even begun to discuss the complexities of sin's effects on the mind and the radical changes that are caused by regeneration. Those truths play a major role in a discussion of proofs for God's existence, so that the complexity is made more obvious, and is increased, for those who trust in Christ.

The point we need to recognize here is that a "proof," as discussed above, is really only a subset of a larger set. Once we think carefully about the *truth* of a given premise, we are into the assumptions and ideas that must be (often unspoken) aspects of the premise itself. That is, there are a host of things surrounding a proof that are and must be taken for granted in order for the proof to be conclusive. "All men are mortal" has behind it a host of assumptions and ideas that might need to be pursued. Pursuing those ideas will take us beyond the strict syllogism itself and into areas of epistemology (i.e., how we *know* such things). It is this "larger set" of truths, concepts, assumptions, and ideas surrounding proofs that we are concerned to articulate and to make clear in the context of a covenantal apologetic.

So it is crucial to recognize the severe limitations of even the best proofs and thus seek to provide justifying reasons, both empirical and nonempirical, for the "larger set" that surrounds any proof.

---

[21] *Merriam-Webster's Collegiate Dictionary.*

What a Burden

This might be a good place briefly to mention the notion of "burden of proof" (*onus probandi*) as it applies to argumentation. The primary thing to keep in mind in this regard is that the burden of proof is a loose and ever-shifting concept, not as concrete as some would like to think.

One book on critical thinking defines the "burden of proof" in this way: "The burden of proof rests most heavily on the side of the issue that, from the point of view of educated common sense, is most implausible or unusual or unbelievable."[22] If we are used to reading with a biblically critical eye, a number of questions will immediately come to mind with respect to this definition. What, we could ask, *is* "the point of view of educated common sense"? This phrase can be taken generally, of course, so that we can affirm much that is "common" to our experience. The problem, however, is that what is "common" is also fraught with sin and confusion, so that "common sense," from the point of view of the *actual* world that God created and controls, is often sense*less*.

We could ask the same question of the adjectives used. As we will see in chapter 6, what is plausible or implausible with respect to foundational questions about Christianity and its objectors is, more often than not, in the eye of the beholder. So also for what is "unusual" or "unbelievable."

All of this said, however, we should not shirk from taking on the burden of proof when appropriate. We should expect that for anyone "in Adam," the Christian truths that we propose will seem to be implausible or unusual; indeed, many of those truths *are* unusual for those whose lives are characterized by a constant suppression of the truth. Not only should we be anxious to take on the burden of proof; we also recognize that there are evidential and rational "proofs" for God's existence in every fact of the world, both within us and outside of us.[23] The opportunity to point out those facts is something for which we hope in our discussions, so we will gladly assume the burden of proof when we can.

---

[22] Brooke Noel Moore, *Making Your Case: Critical Thinking and the Argumentative Essay* (Mountain View, CA: Mayfield, 1995), 11.
[23] Recall tenet 10.

But we can also legitimately ask our interlocutors to make sense of their own positions in the context of their arguments. As we will see in chapter 6, evolutionary arguments tend to shy away from the clear and obvious fact that human beings have minds that are vastly superior to anything that exists in the animal kingdom. And given a standard notion of causality and its interconnection to its effects, it would be highly unusual if that which is mindless caused people with highly developed, even *uniquely* developed, minds. The burden rests legitimately on the one who thinks such things have occurred, given that there are no evidential examples of such occurrences.

We should not be frightened, then, or unduly offended or defensive if those to whom we speak thrust the burden of proof on us. We should happily accept it and then proceed to explain just how all that is has its final, foundational, and comprehensive explanation in the triune God who created it.

The notion of "burden of proof" also implies that the one on whom the burden rests will be able to give an *argument* for his position. This, too, we should welcome, as long as we understand what we have previously noted and what we will discuss in coming chapters.

We need to make clear that the arguments we give will be in support of what we know to be the case, and will not, because they cannot, proceed on the basis of some kind of neutral notion of rationality or evidence. If what our opponents are clamoring for, in requiring that the burden of proof be ours, is a consent-compelling syllogism, therefore, we can remind them that there are arguments in abundance that move beyond a mere syllogism. We can help them to see that some "proofs" operate more in the context of persuasion than of demonstration. This is nothing new; it is part of the warp and woof of argumentation. More on that in chapter 6.

How Do You Know?

In keeping with the design of this book, I want to provide an example of how this discussion of proofs might actually look. In order to do that, a brief mention of some of the "common" theistic proofs is necessary.

Thomas Aquinas (1225–1274) is arguably the best intellect that the church has ever produced. Because of the sheer magnitude of his writing, discussions about what Thomas believed and how to understand him continue unabated. Whatever Thomas himself understood and believed, however, there is little question that his followers have been (mostly) uniform in their ascription and analysis of his theistic proofs.[24] Our concern here, therefore, will be with the way in which Thomas's proofs have been applied to apologetics.

We need not venture, at this point, into the nitty-gritty of Thomas's "five ways."[25] We can instead constrain our analysis to a specific application of Thomas's second way, the way of causality. In order to do that, we will use an actual transcript of that argument as it was presented in a discussion between a Christian (C) and a humanist (H). Because the dialog below is from an actual transcript, the statements will betray a conversational, rather than written, tone. That, however, should not keep us from picking up the problems inherent in the argument. I have edited the discussion in order to focus on the salient points of our analysis of proofs.

The conversation begins:[26]

H: So humanism, I think, is the best expression of modern science. It's the scientific outlook, using the rigorous methods of the scientific inquiry in order to test hypotheses about nature.

C: Well, I agree . . . that we need to be rational; we need to be scientific. . . . Now one of the fundamental, rational laws of all thought . . . is that every event, everything that comes to be, has a cause.

H: Well, you said that every event has a cause. You maintain that every event has a cause. Is that what you said?

C: That's exactly right. Everything that comes to be has a cause.

---

[24] Note also: "The form and the function of the proofs of God's existence in the Reformed orthodox systems, thus, also provide evidence against the claim that this theology is a form of rationalism. On the one hand, these proofs do not function as the necessary and proper foundation of the doctrine of God. They do not typically serve, as they did in Aquinas's *Summa*, as a demonstration of the ability of reason to point toward the same conclusion as is given by revelation, and therefore of the ability of reason to venture into theological discussion." Richard A. Muller, *Post-Reformation Reformed Dogmatics: The Rise and Development of Reformed Orthodoxy, ca. 1520 to ca. 1725*, vol. 3, *The Divine Essence and Attributes*, 2nd ed. (Grand Rapids: Baker Academic, 2003), 192.

[25] The "five ways" of Thomas are those five proofs for God's existence spelled out, in different ways, in a number of his writings. They include arguments (1) from motion, (2) from cause/effect, (3) from contingency/necessity, (4) from gradations of being, and (5) from design.

[26] What follows is an edited version of "Secular Humanism," *The John Ankerberg Show*, complete program transcripts (Chattanooga, TN: John Ankerberg Evangelistic Ministries, 1986), 3–7. The names of the two interlocutors are not important here and will remain anonymous in order to highlight the method itself.

H: Okay. Then you say, "The universe has a cause," and I take it that you would say that God caused the universe. My question then is, "If every event has a cause, what caused God?"

C: You see, you just confused the statement. "Everything that comes to be has a cause." God didn't come to be, so He doesn't need a cause. Just as the atheist believes . . .

H: You contradicted your notion that everything has a cause.

C: No I didn't. Let me finish. Just as the atheist believes that the universe is eternal . . . and therefore didn't need a cause, if you can have an uncaused universe, we can have an uncaused God. What's sauce for the goose is sauce for the gander.

Later in the conversation:

H: You're only pushing your ignorance one step back.

C: No, no, you're missing the point. You're not listening to it.

H: I'm listening to everything.

C: Everything that comes to be has a cause . . . that's the principle. The universe came to be, therefore the universe has a cause. Now, if God always existed, He didn't "come to be" . . .

H: He did not come to be. I see . . .

C: . . . He doesn't need a cause.

H: . . . Well, you're defining the situation. You're assuming your case by definition.

C: Not at all. The rational person . . .

H: . . . How did you know that God did not come to be? How do you know that?

C: We know that the universe came to be . . .

H: But how do you know that God did not come to be?

C: . . . and we know that everything that comes to be had a cause.

H: But how did you know that God did not come to be?

C: Because everything that comes to be has a cause, and if he caused the universe to come to be, he couldn't have come to be.

H: By definition you're defining . . . you're trying to define what you want to prove. How do you know?

Still later:

H: . . . And now you're leaping beyond the range of observation. You're only pushing your ignorance back one step.

Then, finally:

> C: Well, why is it rational for you to believe that the universe is un-
> caused, and irrational for me to believe that God is uncaused?

Before we look more specifically at this proof, a couple of general comments are in order. The context in which most theistic proofs have been developed and offered is a context of so-called evidentialism. Using very broad strokes, evidentialism can perhaps best be summed up in a now-famous quote from the nineteenth-century ethicist-philosopher W. K. Clifford. In his essay "The Ethics of Belief," Clifford stated that "it is wrong always, everywhere, and for anyone, to believe anything upon insufficient evidence."[27]

This statement by Clifford is not referring to something that he invented (i.e., evidentialism); he is simply articulating a mindset that has been prevalent throughout history. It is a mindset that attempts to formulate what has been dubbed the "ethics" of belief; that is, a discipline that sets the parameters for what one *ought* to believe and what one *ought not* to believe. And clearly, according to Clifford's description, one ought not believe anything that is not supported, or supportable, by sufficient evidence.

The apologetic response to this mindset has been, in the main, to try to provide sufficient evidence for one's belief in God. So, for example, in all of Aquinas's proofs, he works from the evidence he thinks is available to all men and attempts to move from that evidence to (evidentially supported) knowledge of God. In that way, he wants to show that our knowledge of God is rational; it has the evidential support that is required for rationality.

Part of the problem with this evidential response (and any of its ilk) is that it seems to assume there are evidences that all of us will "read" in the same way. It presupposes that "evidences" are merely and only objective and taken in some neutral fashion, by us or by anyone else who has access to them. In responses like Aquinas's, no question is put forth as to a possible interpretive problem with respect to the evidences. They are what they are, we all universally understand them

---

[27] W. K. Clifford, "The Ethics of Belief," in *Philosophy of Religion: An Anthology*, ed. Charles Taliaferro and Paul J. Griffiths, Blackwell Philosophy Anthologies (Oxford: Blackwell, 2003), 77.

in the same way, and whatever we propose to believe must simply comport with them.

This attitude is illustrated well in the purported response of atheist Bertrand Russell when asked what he would do if, at his death, he were confronted with God. His response to God, Russell surmised, would be, "Not enough evidence! Not enough evidence."[28] In other words, Russell was convinced that God had not provided enough evidence for him to believe in God. The problem, from Russell's perspective, was clearly God's and not his.[29]

The problem with an evidential approach of this kind, however, can be seen in tenets 5, 6, and 10. If all people know God by virtue of *everything* that he has made (and thus *everything* that confronts them, both internally and externally), then the problem is not with the evidences. *Everything evidences God's character.* There is no spot in the universe that does not reveal the true God. The problem, *contra* Russell, is not with God; the problem is with us.

Now perhaps we can begin to see why the dialog above took the direction that it did. There are a number of things one could say about that dialog, but we will be content here to note two of the most serious problems.

First, notice again how the dialog begins:

H: So humanism, I think, is the best expression of modern science. It's the scientific outlook, using the rigorous methods of the scientific inquiry in order to test hypotheses about nature.

　C: Well, I agree . . . that we need to be rational; we need to be scientific. . . . Now one of the fundamental, rational laws of all thought . . . is that every event, everything that comes to be, has a cause.

The humanist sets the stage by affirming his allegiance to "scientific inquiry," by which he means, in part, empirical investigation. This is, we should note, to be expected.

But the Christian then attempts to stand on the humanist's ground. He sets his own argument within the context of a supposedly neutral rationality, including a supposedly neutral "fundamental, rational" law

---

[28] As quoted in Richard Dawkins, *The God Delusion* (New York: Houghton Mifflin, 2008), 104.
[29] On the evidential problem, see K. Scott Oliphint, *Thomas Aquinas* (Phillipsburg, NJ: P&R, 2017), chap. 2.

of "all thought." By this point, our discussion of covenantal apologetics should cause us to raise some bright red flags over this concession by the Christian. He has just conceded that his discussion can proceed apace on exactly the same ground that the humanist affirms.

We have already seen that the ground on which any unbelieving position stands is quicksand (tenet 7). This does not mean that scientific inquiry is useless and always in error. What it does mean is that, when it comes to questions of truth, of the origin of the universe, of evidence for that origin, what the humanist means by "scientific inquiry" will suppress what is obvious (tenet 6) and will not see the very facts of inquiry as *God's facts* in the first place (tenet 10). To concede the starting point to the humanist is to concede the argument altogether (a concession that is obvious in the argument's conclusion).

This leads to our second concern. Notice again what happens toward the end of the discussion. As the Christian moves to the fact of God's uncaused existence, the conversation takes this turn:

> H: . . . How did you know that God did not come to be? How do you know that?
>
> C: We know that the universe came to be . . .
>
> H: But how do you know that God did not come to be?
>
> C: . . . and we know that everything that comes to be had a cause.
>
> H: But how did you know that God did not come to be?
>
> C: Because everything that comes to be has a cause, and if he caused the universe to come to be, he couldn't have come to be.
>
> H: By definition you're defining . . . you're trying to define what you want to prove. How do you know?

Five times in this snippet of the dialog, the humanist asks the epistemological question. He wants to know how it is that the Christian knows that God did not come to be. Notice the way the Christian answers the repeated "How do you know?" question. His responses are: "We know that the universe came to be," "and we know that everything that comes to be had a cause," "Because everything that comes to be has a cause, and if he caused the universe to come to be, he couldn't have come to be." The response of the Christian, in other words, is simply to repeat the argument over and over again.

But the question being asked by the humanist is a good one and to the point. It is not a question about the statements already contained in the argument itself. The humanist's question, "How do you know?," relates to the *ground* of the Christian's knowledge *about God*. But because the Christian began his discussion by conceding the humanist's starting point—i.e., by supposing that "scientific inquiry" carries the same presuppositions for both of them—there is no way for him, now, to move the discussion in the proper direction.

Not only so, but when the Christian says, "if he caused the universe to come to be, he couldn't have come to be," he is assuming, illegitimately, given his admitted ground of "scientific inquiry," that the only options available to him and the humanist are either the existence of God as uncaused or the universe as caused. But why, we could ask, given "scientific inquiry," are these the only two options available? What *scientific* principle requires that these be the only options?[30] We can sense the struggle of the Christian in this discussion: he wants to affirm Christian principles, but has no access to the only means by which such can be affirmed—God's revelation.

Before reorienting and reworking the discussion above, let's affirm what we can about this argument. We certainly don't want to argue with the notion that everything that comes to be has a cause. That is about as analytic a statement as one can get; the subject is contained in the predicate. And we have no quarrel with the supposition that everything that exists can be summed up in terms of God, as Creator, and creation—the notion of existence is exhausted in both. So it might be useful, depending on the occasion, to employ an argument similar to this one. What cannot be employed, however, are the presuppositions behind the Christian's method. We cannot, for example, concede the starting point of the discussion.

---

[30] Worth noting in this regard is Plantinga's discussion of the conflict between science and religious belief. Speaking of a purported "deep difference" between science and religion, Plantinga says, "That difference indicates a science religion conflict only if *science* tells us that beliefs in all the areas of our epistemic life ought to be formed and held in the same way as scientific beliefs typically are. But of course that isn't a scientific claim at all; it is rather a normative epistemological claim, and a quixotic one at that." Alvin Plantinga, *Where the Conflict Really Lies: Science, Religion, and Naturalism* (New York: Oxford University Press, 2011), 123–24. Plantinga's discussion is well worth reading. The problem in the premise to his entire argument, however, is that science and religion are reconciled *only if* one takes a theistic-evolutionary position. This supposition is significantly detrimental to the positive contribution of the book. For more on this book by Plantinga, see my review in the *Westminster Theological Journal* 75, no. 1 (2013): 205–9.

So how might this discussion go for a covenantal apologist? We can only attempt a possible way forward here, but even that attempt can hopefully be instructive if an argument of this sort is going to be employed covenantally. Let's try to reconstrue the argument as between a humanist (H) and a covenantal apologist (CA):[31]

H: So humanism, I think, is the best expression of modern science. It's the scientific outlook, using the rigorous methods of the scientific inquiry in order to test hypotheses about nature.

CA: Well, I agree that scientific inquiry is important. Science depends on certain universal laws. One of those laws is that every event, everything that comes to be, has a cause.

H: Okay. Then I suspect you want to say, "The universe has a cause," and I take it that you would say that God caused the universe. My question then is, if every event has a cause, what caused God?

CA: The problem with that question is that it seeks to turn a scientific law into one that must be universally applied to all that exists. That use of the law is no part of what I have affirmed. I have affirmed the law of causality as a scientific law, not as a law that applies to all that exists. Everything that comes to be has a cause . . . that's the principle. The universe came to be, and therefore the universe has a cause. Now, if God always existed, he didn't "come to be" . . .

H: He did not come to be. I see . . .

CA: . . . He doesn't need a cause.

H: . . . Well, you're defining the situation. You're assuming your case by definition. How do you know that God did not come to be? How do you know that?

CA: I know that in the same way that I know that the law of cause and effect, with all of its regularity, itself presupposes a God who is faithful to his covenant promises. This God has made clear, since the time of Noah, that "seedtime and harvest, summer and winter" will continue until history is no more. It is only on that basis that you can engage in the "scientific inquiry" that you so cherish.

H: But how do you know that God did not come to be?

CA: I know that in the same way that I know that the law of cause and effect obtains in this world. Because Christian theism alone can account for such things by way of what God has revealed to me in his infallible revelation.

---

[31] As in all arguments of this sort, there are a multitude of ways the argument *could* go rather than the way I imagine it here. Whichever way(s) it goes, however, the ten tenets of a covenantal apologetic will always be in some way(s) applicable.

H: Wait a minute. I thought we were discussing science here. On what basis do you purport to bring into our discussion a reference to God's revelation? By definition you're defining . . . you're trying to define what you want to prove.

CA: The "on what basis" question is a good one, and one that we both should address. Let's think of it this way. Suppose we agree that the universe includes the totality of what we are able to sense. Included in that totality would be time and space.

But now what has to be the case if we are going to posit a "cause" of the universe? That "cause" could not be in time and space, because then it would be as much a part of the universe as you and I are, and could not then cause it to be. So whatever "cause" of the universe there is would have to transcend the universe itself, including time and space.

So if there is a cause to the universe, it cannot be bound by time or space. It must, in that case, be both eternal and infinite.

H: Okay. I'll grant your point.[32] If there is a cause to the universe, it must transcend time and space and therefore not be temporal or bound by space, but must be both eternal and infinite.

But now, I must say, you've backed yourself into an inescapable and irrational corner. You want to posit one that is not bound by time or space—one who is both eternal and infinite. But there can be no explanation given for something such as an "eternal" cause or an "infinite" beginning. How can it be that the One that you want to posit as the first cause is eternal, when the very definition of a cause-effect relationship necessarily includes a temporal sequence of cause and effect?

By definition, the effect must come after the cause; the universe is the effect, you say, but that effect is temporal and finite, while the cause is supposed to transcend both categories. You have no way to relate your eternal and infinite cause to the temporal and finite universe. By definition, there can be no connection between the two if it is *knowledge* we're after; there is no bridge between the eternal and the temporal. Surely Immanuel Kant has taught us at least this much, hasn't he?

One more point of irrationality before you respond. You tell me that this first cause that you think exists has revealed things to you. By definition that means that he (or it) is active in time and space. He speaks, which implies a temporal sequence. He speaks to you (and I suppose you would say to Moses, to Paul, et al.) and that requires that he be located somewhere.

---

[32] As we will see in chap. 7, this point *need not* and *may not* be granted. It presupposes the *sensus divinitatis*. We are granting the point here in order to move the discussion forward as an example.

And now we're back to the same problem. The One that you think caused the universe is actually active in the temporal and finite universe. He is a part of the contingencies for which you posit an explanation. This surely makes no rational sense.

CA: You are right to challenge me on the relationship of the universe (time and space) to eternity. And you are correct to note that the One that I claim to be eternal actually reveals himself in space and time.

In response to these objections, we need to think about the crux of Christianity itself. You surely know that Christianity is called Christianity because it has its focus in Jesus Christ. Perhaps unknown to you is the fact that the church, both Roman and Protestant, on the basis of God's revelation, has affirmed, since Christ came, that he is one person, the second person of the Trinity, and that he took on a human nature even while he remained who he is—the eternal Son of God.

In response to your objection, then, Christianity has always held that God, since he freely chose to create, condescended to his creation, supremely in the person of his Son. In that condescension, God remains who he is as eternal and infinite, even while he reveals his character by interacting, in time and space, with us.

This is the warp and woof of God's entire interaction with his creation in history. It is an interaction with the eternal, infinite God, but a God who has come down to relate to his human creatures. That relationship places obligations on us all. We are to repent of our blindness and believe in Christ.

H: Hold it! Now you've really crossed the boundary of our purported scientific discussion. You've come squarely and explicitly to the topic of your own religious commitment. And whatever else you want to say about it, *that is not science!* Not only that, but you are asking me to believe something—that Christ was both God and man—that is impossible for me to categorize in my own mind, as I suspect it's impossible for you or anyone else. How can I believe in such an absurdity?

CA: Let me address your second point first. If I have as my basic foundation for knowledge the truth that is given in God's revelation, then that revelation controls what and how I think about things. It controls the fact that God's command to "subdue the earth," given at creation, assumes that human beings can know and develop the myriad aspects and potentialities of the world.

It also controls how I must think about God and about his relation to creation. What that means, in part, is that, since I am a creature, I will never have exhaustive knowledge of anything—not of creation or any part of it, and certainly not of God. So since my knowledge will always be limited, and since it is based on God's own revelation, I can both trust all that God says, and also realize that my knowledge and understanding are limited by my own creaturely and sinful status.

Your first point, however, brings up an interesting discussion. You have claimed, throughout our dialog, to be "scientific," adhering only to "scientific inquiry" in what you affirm. And yet, you also want to claim that everything around us came about by some unguided, random process of evolution. My question to you is this: What scientific inquiry have you engaged in that has affirmed, empirically, that there is no one guiding the processes of the universe? Can you show me the evidential foundation for random, unguided evolution?

You cannot, of course. And the reason you cannot is because your commitment to an unguided process of evolution is every bit as "religious" as my commitment to Christ. It is an attitude not of science, but of faith that causes you to affirm that the universe is unguided. Not only so, but the faith that affirms such things is itself blind and unguided. It has no foundation, and it contains no knowledge. It is simply posited.

But now *you* have an irrationality problem. You commit to a discipline—science—that itself cannot move one inch toward progress unless it depends on and trusts universal laws. The very foundation of experiments and the testing of hypotheses assumes these laws. Without them, anything you inspect and any context in which it is inspected would be chaos. The germ might mutate immediately into a car, or the planet in the telescope might suddenly turn into a cosmic candy bar. If the world is, as you want to assume, unguided, then there is no foundation left for your "scientific inquiry" to be conducted.[33] It can only be conducted because of the Christian theistic principles that I hold.

Your scientific theory is in deep need of something that will guarantee the presence and predictability of events in the world. Christianity provides that guarantee. Your unguided naturalism has no way to do that.

H: I'm afraid you've gotten me all wrong. I don't believe for a minute that the events in the universe are all unguided. As a matter of fact, I am committed to the opposite conclusion. My friend Sam Harris has written a masterful exposition of the myth of free will.[34] And the

---

[33] This is an example of the *ad hominem* approach that we discussed earlier.
[34] Sam Harris, *Free Will* (New York: Free Press, 2012).

reason that free will is a myth, Harris and I understand as committed scientists, is that all that happens is the product of a materially determined process. Since everything that happens, happens according to that process, there can be no real choice for human beings. We, too, are simply products of the processes of our material make-up. Science can continue apace because reality is so marvelously and determinatively predictable. It moves inexorably as it is materially determined to move.

CA: Well, my scientific friend, it appears that you and I have just engaged in a monumental waste of time and resources. Let me apologize for that.

H: What do you mean "waste of time"? I have been busy trying to convince you to see things my way, and you have been busy doing the opposite. I thought, at least, that our debate was worthwhile.

CA: Worthwhile? How could that be? If I am materially predetermined to believe what I believe, and you are as well, then what we believe is simply a product of our material selves. We have no choice at all about what we believe; and why we believe what we do makes no sense to discuss at all, since the "why" is embedded in our predetermined matter.

It seems to me that you have gotten yourself into an intellectual bind. If the universe is unguided, then what you think about science is nothing more than a random figment of your own imagination. In that case, science cannot ground or found its own enterprise; the best it can do, as David Hume showed us centuries ago, is depend on some kind of subjective "habit." And a habit is no way to try to uncover the mysteries of the universe; because it is subjective, it has no bearing on whether or not the universe is knowable or predictable. For that, something much stronger is needed. What's needed is actual predictability. And that comes only in Christian theism.

If, on the other hand, your friend Sam Harris is right, then all the things you and I have discussed—science, religion, predictability, etc.—are also just figments of our imagination. They are not in any way the products of our own decision making. Your humanism is exactly the same as my Christian theism. They both are produced by our material composition. And if that is the case, there is nothing left for us to talk about. Our respective beliefs are little different than the fizzy head of a draught beer; they're just a matter of materially determined characteristics.

So, I leave you with this thought. Neither unguided naturalism nor predetermined physicalism can give you what you want; neither can give you a way to be committed, as you are, to "scientific inquiry" as your starting point for knowledge. Only Christian theism can give you that. Only in Christian theism can science begin and thrive. Without Christian theism, your commitment to science is nothing more than a meaningless, purposeless noise. Like your own existence, it makes no sense whatsoever; either it is an unguided, chaotic datum, or it does what it was predetermined to do. In either case, there can be no real meaning ascribed to it.

But if God has created the universe and has come down to act in and for his creation, and if he has condescended in his Son to remedy the problem of those who are committed to opposing him, then it will only be repentance and trust in Christ that will allow for a proper view of the world, "scientific inquiry," and ourselves.

Obviously, this discussion could have gone in any number of directions and could have taken turns and twists that were not explored here. That is to be expected. There is not one, or one kind, of way to respond to this kind of objection. Hopefully, however, enough has been given to show a possible way in which a proper, covenantal response could be employed, a way in which the gospel becomes a central part of an apologetic response.

We have attempted to show in this chapter how and why the notion of proof is, at best, tenuous. It is not a useful way to discuss apologetics if our goal in a Christian defense is to set *Christianity* forth as the only viable option. But we dare not simply end with a negative "not proof" conclusion. In the next chapter, we will present the positive case for *persuasion* as the proper mode of a covenantal apologetic. That chapter, then, is central to all that we have thus far argued and will be crucial for what we discuss in chapters 5–7.

O wherefore do the nations rage,
And kings and rulers strive in vain,
Against the Lord of earth and heav'n
To overthrow Messiah's reign?[35]

---

[35] "O Wherefore Do the Nations Rage," *The Psalter*, 1912, from Psalm 2.

4

We Persuade Others

Therefore, knowing the fear of the Lord, we persuade others (2 Cor. 5:11).

In neither the early nor the high orthodox eras do we find the proofs stated as a basis in rational philosophy or natural theology upon which the system of revealed doctrine can build. In relation to these issues, even the Thomistic "five ways" take on a character not at all familiar to their famous author: they are now rhetorically, not demonstratively, framed.[1]

"Trivial" Matters

The *Trivium*

In Plato's *Phaedrus*, Socrates and Phaedrus discuss the pros and cons of the written word as over against oratory, the spoken word. Socrates was convinced that a move from oratory to the written word would produce a shallow people, people who were no longer able to speak and argue from the capacity of their own minds. Socrates was a champion of the "oral state of mind." He was convinced that only through hearing and remembering the spoken word could truths be deeply and permanently engraved on the soul. Any truths gained through writing could not pierce the inner chamber of the mind; they could only lie on the surface.

Socrates, a defender of oration, fought and eventually lost this battle against his student Plato, who was convinced of the advantages of the written word. There can be little doubt that Plato was right in his allegiance to the written word. The dissemination of knowledge

[1] Richard A. Muller, *Post-Reformation Reformed Dogmatics: The Rise and Development of Reformed Orthodoxy, ca. 1520 to ca. 1725*, vol. 3, *The Divine Essence and Attributes*, 2nd ed. (Grand Rapids: Baker Academic, 2003), 170, 193.

and information is an invaluable tool for the masses; a primarily oral culture could thrive only with those who had the time and education necessary—in other words, with the elites. The downside, however, to the transition from the oral to the written word has been an ever-so-slow but unrelenting neglect of the importance of rhetoric and persuasion.

Historically, in the West it was thought that the best foundation for education was in the so-called liberal arts. "Liberal" arts were so named because they were meant to apply to free citizens. They were also meant to provide for free citizens an education that would prepare students for a robust and productive life in society.

It would be useful, perhaps, to trace this initial emphasis on the liberal arts to current-day trends in education. Anecdotally, at least, there seems to be far less emphasis on the liberal arts and much more emphasis on practical arts—arts designed to enhance the possibility of employment. This practical emphasis is understandable, even commendable. But one of the negative consequences of a practical emphasis is that one can proceed apace through every program of education, including a doctorate, and never undertake the type of study that used to be touted as foundational for any true, meaningful, and lasting education.

The current practical bent, it seems, does not bode well for any discipline, theology included, in which a premium is placed on the value of the word and of thinking. An education that is focused on practice may produce employment, but it may also produce a society wherein reading, thinking, studying, meditating, synthesizing, and persuading are virtually absent. Witness, for example, any televised political debate. No matter which side of the political spectrum one is on, to call what happens on television within an hour or two a debate is, from the perspective of history, laughable.[2]

In the "old days" (and by that I mean a few thousand years ago), a student's curriculum would initially consist of three subjects, called the *trivium*. These three needed to be learned in their particular order, as each would build on the one prior to it. The first thing a student

---

[2] Still unmatched for its penetrating analysis in this regard is Neil Postman, *Amusing Ourselves to Death: Public Discourse in the Age of Show Business* (London: Methuen, 1987).

would be required to learn is *grammar*. In this discipline, students learned the proper way to understand languages (as well as other disciplines). Because there are rules to every language, it is important to understand and apply those rules in order to grasp and apply the basics of communication.

For example, in some parts of the United States, someone might say, "I ain't got no gas in my car." Because language also has a contextual component, most listeners will understand what the person is communicating. He is communicating that there is no gasoline in his car. But what he is actually *saying*, according to the rules of grammar, is the opposite of what he wants to communicate. What he is saying is that his car does, in fact, have gasoline (as in mathematics, so also in grammar, two negatives make a positive). To say, "I ain't got no gas in my car," is the same as saying, "I have gas in my car." In other words, to "don't have no" is the same as "having some."

Again, because language has a contextual component, proper communication can take place without meticulous rules of grammar being applied, or even when such rules are transgressed. But if what one is concerned about initially is clarity of communication (as is *supposed* to be the case, for example, in a sermon), then the rules of grammar are essential, *both* for listening *and* for meaningful communication.

The second subject matter that students would take up was called *dialectic* or logic. In this subject, students would begin to work on proper modes of reasoning. This subject, we can see, presupposed the rules of language; in that way, it depended on an adequate understanding of grammar. Once the basic rules of speech and communication were understood, students were taught to think about how best to *synthesize* and bring together various sentences and propositions. Students would learn rules of induction and deduction, rules of arguments and other modes of reasoning. In that way, they could be equipped not simply to evaluate grammatical rules, but to judge whether certain statements or collections of statements were plausible or even true.

The last of the three basic subjects of the *trivium* was *rhetoric*. In rhetoric, students would begin to apply their knowledge of grammar and logic to proper ways of *speaking* and communicating. In this subject, the focus was on oratory in such a way that an audience could be properly informed, motivated, or persuaded.[3]

These three subjects are no longer emphasized as basic to education. Yet they remain crucial for proper thinking. Perhaps much of what was taught in them can be picked up more casually through reading and thinking through particular concepts and ideas on our own. But a dismissive or neglectful attitude toward them will surely produce people, and a society, that are woefully deficient in real and vital speaking, communication, thinking, and persuading. Such, it seems, is the state of affairs in so many places and contexts currently.

We must also note that none of these three subjects is neutral with respect to its understanding. Like everything else, all three are informed by one's view of the world and one's covenant status before God.[4]

The Theology of Persuasion

One of the more frustrating aspects of a covenantal apologetic may perhaps already be felt by some who have read this far. In the sample dialogs set out thus far, there remain questions that *could have* come up, issues that *might have* been discussed, objections that *were not* addressed. This is not a flaw, but is endemic to the approach itself, and may be one of the reasons why some initially find this approach to be so daunting. But there is a very fruitful and biblical reason why gaps remain in any dialog set forth in this way. It has to do with the way in which we think about apologetics—a way that has its focus, as we have said, not so much in demonstrative *proofs* for God's existence, but in *persuasion*.

The discussion that ensues in this chapter may seem a bit more technical to some readers than in previous chapters. The discussion thus far has sought to communicate material addressed in various forms in other literature. Thus, other resources can be pursued with profit for elaborations of the subject matters discussed. In this chapter, however, the subject that we are going to explicate has received scant

---

[3] From the *trivium* students could move to the *quadrivium*—mathematics, geometry, music, and astronomy—and thus complete the seven "liberal arts."

[4] For an analysis of the relationship of our worldview to language and logic, see Vern Sheridan Poythress, *In the Beginning Was the Word: Language—a God-Centered Approach* (Wheaton, IL: Crossway, 2009); and Poythress, *Logic: A God-Centered Approach to the Foundation of Western Thought* (Wheaton, IL: Crossway, 2013).

attention, especially in the context of a covenantal approach to apologetics. Even so, it is so directly related to a covenantal apologetic that it is crucial for us to see it properly within that approach. In that connection, the explanations and elaborations given in this chapter will be brand-new to almost all readers. For that reason, I have determined to be a bit more thorough as I lay out the crucial place of persuasion in a covenantal defense of Christianity.

The reason why we must prefer persuasion in apologetics over strict, demonstrative proofs is deeply theological; it is a direct implication of tenet 2. Recall that "God's covenantal revelation is authoritative by virtue of what it is, and any covenantal, Christian apologetic will necessarily stand on and utilize that authority in order to defend Christianity." Given tenet 2 and what I have argued in the previous chapters, we can now begin to see that the word of God, as we have it in the canon of Holy Scripture, is our *most basic* and solid foundation for all that we want to say in apologetics. That Word is never in any way divorced from God's revelation in creation. But it is the central and most basic principle upon which anything else that we are going to say, including what we say about natural revelation, must be based.

This notion of a basic and foundational principle flies in the face of the "Cliffordian" maxim that we saw in chapter 3 (i.e., "it is wrong always, everywhere, and for anyone, to believe anything upon insufficient evidence"). Clifford (and those who either follow or preceded him in working from this maxim) thinks that everything we choose to know or believe, in order to be rational, must have behind it sufficient evidence. As we have seen, that view breaks down in a number of ways.

We should also recognize that Clifford's maxim cannot meet its own criterion for rationality. "What evidence is there," we could ask, "that everything must have sufficient evidence in order to be rationally held?" Indeed, what evidence *could there be* for a committed Cliffordian?

Suppose a disciple of Clifford's maxim were able to establish, say, three evidential propositions meant sufficiently to support that maxim. Would it not be the case that each of *those* evidential propositions would themselves be in need of sufficient evidence in order to be rationally held or believed? And what if there were evidential propositions sufficient to support the evidential propositions that sufficiently supported Clifford's maxim. Wouldn't *those*, too, be in need of sufficient evidence? And on it goes.

The dilemma is obvious. There simply cannot be sufficient evidential propositions *ad infinitum*. There has to be some "place"—some proposition, some concept, some idea, some foundation of authority—that is sufficient to carry the conceptual weight of what we claim to know, believe, and hold.

It is for this reason, among others, that the founding fathers of the Reformation placed the Scriptures as the proper foundation for *everything else* that we claim to know or believe. They came to that conclusion, in part, in response to the standard medieval view. During the Middle Ages, insufficient attention was given, in general, to the problem of sin as it relates to our reasoning process. There was not, we could say, a sufficient commitment to (something like) tenet 7.[5] Because the effects of sin were thought to be less extensive in their application to us (as compared with Reformation thought), in that sin was not seen as radically affecting our reasoning, there was an improper view of the faculty of reason, especially with respect to reason's ability to understand and discern God's revelation and his existence. Reason was regarded as fairly well intact, even after the fall, such that all men followed the same basic rules of thought.[6]

During the Reformation, there was a radical shift in emphasis, from the medieval focus on the power of reason as a foundation of knowledge, to a central and foundational focus on the power and necessity of Scripture. This focus was the result, in part, of the biblical teaching on sin's power. Depravity was seen not simply as a problem of the *will*, such that people do not *want* to choose properly (though that is true); it was recognized as a problem of the *intellect* as well, such that people sinfully reject that which they *know*. Because of sin's effect on the mind, there is no way that reason can provide a needed foundation for knowing and believing.

---

[5] "There is an absolute, covenantal antithesis between Christian theism and any other, opposing position. Thus, Christianity is true and anything opposing it is false."

[6] So Thomas Aquinas held that the light of natural reason participated in the light of God's own knowledge. See Thomas Aquinas, *Summa Theologiae: Latin Text, English Translation, Introduction, Notes, Appendices and Glossary*, 60 vols., ed. Thomas Gilby (London: Eyre & Spottiswoode; New York: McGraw-Hill, 1964), 1.12.11. There is some truth to this in that, as image of God, we are able to reason. But the problem of the effects of the fall on our minds was not adequately taken into account.

Thus, a central aspect to "re-forming" theology in the sixteenth and seventeenth centuries included a renewed focus on Scripture as our only foundation for knowing, for believing, and for reasoning properly.[7]

This Reformed focus ensured that Scripture, not a general notion of (all) men's reasoning ability, would serve as the ground on which all knowledge, including all theology, and all Christians must stand. Scripture is the *principle* upon which everything else that we say, believe, think, and argue must rest. And because it is the most basic and foundational *principle*, it is not possible to "go behind" that principle in order to demonstrate its status as foundational. Any "going behind" would necessarily show that there is something more foundational on which Scripture itself must rest.[8]

So the first theological foundation that informs the priority of persuasion is the *principial* status of Scripture. The importance of this can hardly be overstated. Scripture serves as our *most basic* foundation.

The second theological foundation is like unto the first.[9] Here, however, we move from God's special revelation in Scripture to his general, natural revelation in creation, and specifically *in us*. Because, as we have seen and discussed, all people *know the true God*, whenever we speak of this God to others, what we say—in apologetics, in preaching, in evangelism—automatically "connects" with what they already know. It is, therefore, the *sensus divinitatis* (sense of deity) that provides the connecting link between what we say in apologetics and what God is always and everywhere "saying" in and to his human creatures.

It is this all-important truth—the truth that all people, because made in God's image, *know God*—that provides the "point of contact" between what we as Christians believe and espouse and what anyone else might believe and espouse.

This is why, even though there are always (at least) two opposing views in every apologetic encounter, we can be assured that the

---

[7] In a discussion of the difference in prolegomena (doctrine of revelation) between medieval theology and the Reformers, Richard Muller notes: "*This view of the problem of knowledge [during the Reformation] is the single most important contribution of the early Reformed writers to the theological prolegomena of orthodox Protestantism.* Indeed, it is the doctrinal issue that most forcibly presses the Protestant scholastics toward the modification of the medieval models for theological prolegomena." Richard A. Muller, *Post-Reformation Reformed Dogmatics: The Rise and Development of Reformed Orthodoxy, ca. 1520 to ca. 1725*, vol. 1, *Prolegomena to Theology*, 2nd ed. (Grand Rapids: Baker Academic, 2003), 108, my emphasis.

[8] Recall our discussion of tenet 2 in chap. 1.

[9] For this theological point, and the one following, recall tenet 9.

Christian, covenantal view we are defending is "making contact" with those to whom we speak. It is making contact because everyone to whom we speak is in constant covenantal contact with the true God, who continues, night and day, to pour forth the revelation of his character to them and in them. Since we have already discussed the *sensus* and will have occasion to return to it again, I won't say anything else about it here. Its truth, nevertheless, is vital to any and every apologetic encounter.

The third theological truth that significantly impacts the way we think about persuasion is God's universal mercy over all that he has made.[10] Because this aspect of theology may be new to some, it might help to spell out its main contours.

Since man is totally depraved, it follows that there is nothing that man is able to do or think that is, in itself, good—nothing that we can say is fundamentally impervious to the effects of sin. All of man, in every aspect, is depraved, sinful, in rebellion against God. How, then, are we to account for those things that are done by the unregenerate that are, at least on the surface, not evil? How do we explain the fact that many unbelievers outshine believers with respect to some aspects of a virtuous life?

In answer to those questions, it is important to recognize that we have not simply invented a theological category that would bring some coherence to an otherwise unworkable notion of total depravity. That is, what we are *not* doing is interjecting theological "balance" to the notion of total depravity so that we can continue to hold such an idea but explain it away with other ideas.

Rather, during the time of the Reformation, as we have seen above, there was a renewed awareness of the clarity and sufficiency of Scripture so that where and when the Scriptures speak, affirmation was given to doctrines and concepts that had been obscured in much of the Middle Ages.

In an attempt to understand Scripture's affirmation of God's universal mercy, then, three basic aspects of that mercy, all interrelated, have been emphasized.

---

[10] God's universal mercy is usually referred to as "common grace." For a more thorough discussion of this mercy and its relationship to apologetics, see Cornelius Van Til, *Common Grace and the Gospel*, ed. K. Scott Oliphint (Phillipsburg, NJ: P&R, 2015).

1. The first aspect of God's universal mercy includes the fact that God's attitude toward his creatures made in his image is one of wrath, because of sin (Rom. 1:18), but is also one of mercy and kindness toward them. Note, for example:

The LORD is good to all,
  and his mercy is over all that he has made. (Ps. 145:9)

But I say to you, Love your enemies and pray for those who persecute you, so that you may be sons of your Father who is in heaven. For he makes his sun rise on the evil and on the good, and sends rain on the just and on the unjust. (Matt 5:44–45; cf. Luke 6:35–36)

From the biblical teaching that the Lord is good and merciful over all that he has made, Christ implores us to love our enemies. In so loving them, we demonstrate something of God's own disposition toward them. Notice also: "In past generations he allowed all the nations to walk in their own ways. Yet he did not leave himself without witness, for he did good by giving you rains from heaven and fruitful seasons, satisfying your hearts with food and gladness" (Acts 14:16–17). Again, the Lord "did good" by giving rain and fruitful seasons without discrimination. Every good gift that anyone has comes from God's merciful hand.

The apostle Paul even connects God's general revelation with his universal mercy toward all. Just after explaining the revelation of God's wrath in Romans 1, Paul asks, "Or do you presume on the riches of his kindness and forbearance and patience, not knowing that God's kindness is meant to lead you to repentance?" (Rom. 2:4). Included in God's kindness, in other words, is his constant and abiding natural revelation of himself and his character to every single individual. Clearly, then, there is a merciful disposition of God toward every person, even toward those who abide under his wrath.

John Calvin recognized the implications of God's goodness and mercy to all men. He knew that anything that a person (in Adam) is able to do that is deemed in any way "good" must itself stem from God's undeserved favor toward them. So, says Calvin:

Meanwhile, we ought not to forget those most excellent benefits of the divine Spirit, which he distributes to whomsoever he wills, for the common good of mankind. The understanding and knowledge of Bezalel and Oholiab, needed to construct the Tabernacle, had to be instilled in them by the Spirit of God [Ex. 31:2–11; 35:30–35]. It is no wonder, then, that the knowledge of all that is most excellent in human life is said to be communicated to us through the Spirit of God. Nor is there any reason to ask, What have the impious, who are utterly estranged from God, to do with his Spirit? We ought to understand the statement that the Spirit of God dwells only in believers [Rom. 8:9] as referring to the Spirit of sanctification through whom we are consecrated as temples to God [1 Cor. 3:16]. Nonetheless he fills, moves, and quickens all things by the power of the same Spirit, and does so according to the character that he bestowed upon each kind by the law of creation. But if the Lord has willed that we be helped in physics, dialectic, mathematics, and other like disciplines, by the work and ministry of the ungodly, let us use this assistance to suffer just punishment for our sloths. But lest anyone think a man truly blessed when he is credited with possessing great power to comprehend truth under the elements of this world [cf. Col. 2:8], we should at once add that all this capacity to understand, with the understanding that follows upon it, is an unstable and transitory thing in God's sight, when a solid foundation of truth does not underlie it.[11]

And then later Calvin says:

To begin with, I do not deny that all the notable endowments that manifest themselves among unbelievers are gifts of God. . . . For we see that he bestows many blessings of the present life upon those who cultivate virtue among men. Not because that outward image of virtue deserves the least benefit of him; but it pleases him so to prove how much he esteems true righteousness, when he does not allow even external and feigned righteousness to go without a temporal reward. Hence, there follows what we just now acknowledged: that all these virtues—or rather, images of virtues—are of God, since nothing is in any way praiseworthy that does not come from him.[12]

We can see, then, that when the unregenerate commit deeds and engage in acts that are honorable, we should not in the first place note in our minds and hearts how good they are. We cannot assume as

---

[11] John Calvin, *Institutes of the Christian Religion*, ed. John T. McNeill, trans. Ford Lewis Battles, 2 vols., The Library of Christian Classics (Philadelphia: Westminster Press, 1960), 2.2.16.
[12] Calvin, *Institutes*, 3.14.2.

much because we know that they are "dead in the trespasses and sins" (Eph. 2:1). Instead, if we are to think biblically about such matters, we immediately recognize in our minds and hearts how good *God* is. We realize that the committing of those honorable deeds and the doing of those honorable acts are in direct opposition to the very principles and motives on which the unregenerate operate. They could not even engage in those good deeds and do those honorable acts, or even see them as worthy, unless the mercy of God were operative to guide and to overrule their basic heart commitments.

2. The second aspect of God's universal mercy has to do with the restraint of sin in the lives of individuals and of society. Paul tells us:

> Therefore God gave them up in the lusts of their hearts to impurity, to the dishonoring of their bodies among themselves. . . .
>
> For this reason God gave them up to dishonorable passions. For their women exchanged natural relations for those that are contrary to nature. . . .
>
> And since they did not see fit to acknowledge God, God gave them up to a debased mind to do what ought not to be done. (Rom. 1:24, 26, 28)

Paul's thrice-repeated phrase that "God gave them up" assumes that God had been restraining or holding back the sinful tendencies of those on whom his wrath abides. To put it positively, the only reason those whom God gave up had not engaged in more and deeper sin is that God had been mercifully restraining them from operating according to their own depraved hearts.

Note also Calvin's point in this regard:

> But here it ought to occur to us that amid this corruption of nature there is some place for God's grace; not such grace as to cleanse it, but to restrain it inwardly. For if the Lord gave loose rein to the mind of each man to run riot in his lusts, there would doubtless be no one who would not show that, in fact, every evil thing for which Paul condemns all nature is most truly to be met in himself.[13]

This helps us to see that it cannot be the case that those who are in Adam are partly good and partly sinful, or that sin has had a less-than-total

---

[13] Calvin, *Institutes*, 2.3.3.

effect on them. Rather, as we have said, people who are totally depraved are also, generally speaking, not as bad as they could otherwise be. The reason that the unregenerate are not as bad as they would be is the universal, restraining mercy of God toward them.

3. The third aspect of God's universal mercy is a consequence of the first. It includes the fact that the unregenerate can perform "righteous" acts, even though still slaves to sin. This point need not be developed here. It is a vitally important theological truth, however. It means that there is much *religious* good that an unbeliever can participate in and accomplish without himself being regenerate.

We cannot give Hebrews 6:4–6 the attention it deserves here, but the truth of God's mercy is, in part, what the author to the Hebrews is describing:

> For it is impossible, in the case of those who have once been enlightened, who have tasted the heavenly gift, and have shared in the Holy Spirit, and have tasted the goodness of the word of God and the powers of the age to come, and then have fallen away, to restore them again to repentance, since they are crucifying once again the Son of God to their own harm and holding him up to contempt. (Heb. 6:4–6)

There are those, in other words, who can fully participate in the life and doctrine of the church, but who themselves have never bowed the knee to the lordship of Christ. But how can this be? Again, we cannot give this its due attention, but perhaps a couple of points from John Owen can help us see this.

In volume 4 of his *Collected Works*, Owen makes a good and proper biblical distinction between the gifts of the Holy Spirit, on the one hand, and the fruits of the Spirit, on the other. The former—the gifts of the Spirit—are such that anyone can participate in them; the fruits of the Spirit are reserved only for the regenerate. Gifts come from the outside; fruit grows from within. Says Owen:

> These gifts are not saving, sanctifying graces; those were not so in themselves which made the most glorious and astonishing appearance in the world, and which were most eminently useful in the foundation of the church and propagation of the gospel, such as were those that were extraordinary and miraculous. There is

something of the divine nature in the least grace, that is not in the most glorious gift.[14]

Further on Owen continues:

> With gifts, singly considered, it is otherwise. They are indeed works and effects, but not properly fruits of the Spirit, nor are anywhere so called [in Scripture]. They are effects of his operation upon men, not fruits of his working in them; and therefore, many receive these gifts who never receive the Sprit as to the principal end for which he is promised. They receive him not to sanctify and make them temples unto God; though metonymically [so to speak], with respect unto his outward effects they may be said to be made partakers of him. This renders them of a different nature and kind from saving graces; for whereas there is an agreement and coincidence between them in the respects before mentioned, and whereas the seat and subject of them,—that is, of gifts absolutely, and principally of graces also,—is the mind, the difference of their nature proceeds from the different manner of their communication from the Holy Spirit.[15]

So there is a common manifestation of God's universal mercy in that he may, at times and for his own sovereign purposes, give to those who are not a part of his church gifts of the Spirit, which are good and virtuous gifts, but which, in the end, do not in any way flow from a regenerate heart.[16]

There are a number of important apologetic aspects to this notion of God's universal mercy, particularly as we think about the proper way to assess the unregenerate lifestyle. We sometimes might think that it is "just natural," for example, that the unbeliever would love his family, or respect human life, or pursue a fairly orderly lifestyle. But when we think biblically about these things, we recognize that if left to the unregenerate heart completely, these "good" acts would immediately dissolve. The problem of sin, as Jesus reminds us, is that

---

[14] John Owen, *The Works of John Owen*, trans. W. H. Goold, vol. 4, *The Reason of Faith* (Edinburgh: Banner of Truth, 1977), 420.

[15] Owen, *Works*, vol. 4, *The Reason of Faith*, 420.

[16] This important point reminds us that there are significant apologetic implications of preaching as well. Since the wheat and the tares grow together, we can expect that there will often be those who are unregenerate, even though they themselves might manifest spiritual gifts, within our own congregations.

even though light has come into the world, "people loved the darkness rather than the light" (John 3:19). Sin, if allowed solely and without God's mercy to reign in the hearts of unbelief, will seek with the most fervent vigor what is dark, wicked, irrational, vile, sick, confused, and chaotic.

So the very fact that unbelievers do not, at all times and in all places, seek the darkness of their own hearts is owing not to a vestige of goodness in their hearts, but completely to God's merciful disposition toward those who are his enemies and thus are under his wrath.

What this means for us apologetically is that when we take note of something that is, even if superficially, good—something that is virtuous, that is honorable—we immediately recognize that such things come from God, and from him alone. And we may want to challenge the unbeliever at the very point with which we superficially agree. That is, if it is the case that the unbeliever is practicing these virtuous acts because of what *God* is doing, then it is also the case that the unbeliever cannot give proper account for the very things he holds to be of value.

So we may want to agree with him that they are indeed of value (at least to some extent), but then ask him how he can make sense of such things, given his own (unbelieving) commitments. We may want to tell him, for example, that his general love for his fellow man is a good thing, but then ask him how he proposes to make sense of such a thing. Thus the notion of God's universal mercy, given our understanding of total depravity, gives us a significant understanding of just where we might want to challenge unbelief. In that sense, it is an indispensable apologetic truth.

The "*Trivium*" of Persuasion

We began our discussion in this chapter with the *trivium*: those three central aspects that form the beginning of a liberal arts education. Following on that, we saw that there were three theological truths, a theological "*trivium*"—the *principial* nature of Scripture, the *sensus divinitatis* (i.e., knowledge of God), and God's universal mercy—that provide the foundation for a biblical view of persuasion in apologetics. With the educational *trivium* and theological *trivium* now in place, we are ready to discuss the *"trivium"* of persuasion, three aspects that help us understand something of the *structure* of persuasion itself.

It is appropriate, following on a discussion of God's universal mercy, that we look to Aristotle in order helpfully to frame our understanding of rhetoric and persuasion. According to Aristotle, "Rhetoric may be defined as the faculty of observing in any given case the available means of persuasion."[17] There is, then, a necessary link between rhetoric and persuasion. Before we proceed to the *trivium* of persuasion, however, a little groundwork is needed. We need to put our apologetic emphasis on persuasion in historical context.

Generally speaking, one of the reasons that the "evidential challenge" and the emphasis on proofs for God's existence has been prominent in apologetics has to do with the influence of the Enlightenment. There has been since the Enlightenment a hegemonic emphasis on reason. The reigning princes of this influence have been Descartes[18] (the rationalist philosopher), Hume (the empiricist philosopher), and, supremely, Kant (who tried to synthesize the rational and empirical). From Descartes to the present, the predominant mode of thinking, whether in philosophy or in theology, has been, for the most part, unduly dependent on these schools of thought.

With an emphasis on the rational, we can begin to see why the notion of demonstrative proofs held sway in (much of) theology and apologetics. The motives were good ones; there was an attempt to show Christianity (or theism, more generally) to be rational and not opposed to reason. But we have already seen how such an emphasis, when not properly scrutinized, can sacrifice basic and central truths of the Christian faith.

With an emphasis on the empirical, we can see why the notion of evidences for theism or Christianity held sway in (much of) theology and apologetics. Again, the motives were good; there was an attempt to show Christianity to be connected with real history and to be manifest in creation itself. But, again, we have already seen

---

[17] Aristotle, "Rhetorica," in *The Basic Works of Aristotle*, ed. Richard McKeon (New York: Random House, 1968), 1329.
[18] René Descartes (1596–1650) was the first prominent rationalist philosopher. He attempted to find one foundational "clear and distinct idea" upon which all knowledge could be based.

how such a view can compromise basic and central truths of the Christian faith.[19]

The Kantian influence, as we have seen, gave rise to the present praise of all things scientific at the expense of true, biblical faith. "Faith," in a Kantian context, can only have experience as its governing principle, *not knowledge*.

Given the theological *trivium* that I have laid out in the previous section, however, it should be clearer now why there is a biblical imperative to shift the emphasis, in a covenantal apologetic, from the notion of proofs or evidences *per se* to that of persuasion.[20] But in moving from a context in which demonstrative proofs and empirical evidences were foundational, to a context of persuasion, we are not thereby rending asunder what God has joined together. We are *not* saying, in other words, that the two sides (proofs/evidences, on the one side, and persuasion, on the other) are mutually opposed to each other or in any way contradictory. Nor are we saying that the two are mutually exclusive. As we will see, put in their proper place, *both* sides are mutually dependent. Persuasion, then, is the proper *mode* in which to consider the rational and the evidential.

What we are saying is that modern and contemporary discussions have placed an unwarranted and thus deleterious emphasis on only one side of the discussion—the side of proofs/evidences—not to mention the assumption of religious neutrality that pervades discussions of what is rational or evidential. This unwarranted emphasis, as we ought to expect by now, is due to an unwarranted *theological* emphasis. It is an emphasis on the faculty of reason, as in some way religiously neutral, that has been at least partially responsible for the lopsided view of a proper approach to apologetics.

Thus, the theological *trivium* discussed in the previous section (along with the ten tenets) must be firmly embedded in our thinking

---

[19] The details of this historical hegemony are beyond the scope of our discussion here. For a helpful analysis of this in light of a renewed emphasis on rhetoric, see Chaim Perelman and Lucie Olbrechts-Tyteca, *The New Rhetoric*, rev. ed. (Notre Dame, IN: University of Notre Dame Press, 1991). For a brief discussion of the antipathy of rationalism and empiricism to rhetoric, see David S. Cunningham, *Faithful Persuasion: Theology* (Notre Dame, IN: University of Notre Dame Press, 1992), 19–24.

[20] We should emphasize here again that a covenantal approach to apologetics is dependent on Reformed theology. The elements of the theological *trivium* above are themselves deeply and centrally Reformed. While other theologies might affirm aspects of those three truths, no other theology has seen the structural and sweeping implications of them for apologetics.

if we are going to see the necessary place of persuasion in a covenantal apologetic approach. Let's look at the structure of persuasion in its proper theological context.

Ethos

Now to the *trivium* of persuasion. Aristotle delimited three "kinds" or categories that were present in any and every persuasive discourse:

> Of the modes of persuasion furnished by the spoken word there are three kinds. The first kind depends on the personal character [*ethos*] of the speaker; the second kind on putting the audience into a certain frame of mind [*pathos*]; the third on proof, or apparent proof, provided by the words of the speech itself [*logos*].[21]

So, as Aristotle laid it out, persuasion consists of three central aspects—*ethos, pathos,* and *logos*. A bit of explanation is needed for each of these. In order to see them in their proper biblical and theological context, it will be useful to highlight Paul's ministry, with a special focus on his address at the Areopagus, as we elaborate on these three categories.

First, we need to focus on the *ethos* of persuasion, which means, generally, one's *character*. In Acts 17:18, Luke records that the Epicurean and Stoic philosophers referred to the apostle Paul as a "babbler." The Greek word could be literally translated as "seed-speaker." It is, as we can see, anything but complimentary. The philosophers were convinced that Paul was simply grabbing a hodgepodge of ideas (i.e., "seeds") from various places and trying to make some cohesive sense of them by randomly stringing them together. Like a hungry bird searching for food, Paul, they thought, was just grabbing seeds wherever he could find them and employing those disparate seeds to build a "new" philosophy (see Acts 17:21). Clearly, then, at least for some in Athens and at the Areopagus, Paul's character, his *ethos*, was in question.

It is instructive, however, to recognize that the philosophers' quickness to attack Paul's character was *not* based on any moral deficiency they saw in him. Rather, it was based solely on what Paul

---

[21] Aristotle, "Rhetorica," 1329.

was *saying* to them in the marketplace. He was dubbed a "babbler," says Luke, "because he was preaching Jesus and the resurrection" (Acts 17:18).

The criterion of *ethos*, of character, in the art of persuasion, therefore, cannot be measured solely by those to whom we speak. If our audience is the sole judge of our character, then we might be tempted to compromise our message in order to gain a hearing. The *ethos* of Jesus himself, we will remember, was called into serious question by some. He was called a "Samaritan" and was accused of being possessed by a demon (John 8:48, 52). The measuring rod by which we judge the *ethos* of persuasion, then, must be something other than what our audience, be it many people or one person, might think; it must be Scripture itself.

Another example of this from Paul's ministry, in light of our emphasis on persuasion, is most instructive here. For that, we need to look briefly at Paul's ministry in Corinth. Though the Corinthian church had responded to much of what Paul had written in his first epistle to them, there were still very serious issues with which Paul had to deal in Corinth. Specifically, false teachers had infiltrated the church and were making progress in undermining Paul's ministry. So Paul wrote his second letter to the Corinthians both to encourage them in their obedience and to warn them and to discourage them concerning their acceptance of these false teachers.

It is difficult to know precisely who were these "false apostles" (2 Cor. 11:13) to which Paul refers. One of the most plausible (though not definitive) explanations is that, whoever they were, they were heavily influenced by the Greek Sophists. Though there may have been other influences in the church at that time, the theory that the false teachers were influenced by Sophists seems (to me) to be one of the most plausible explanations.

Who were the Sophists? By the time of the writing of the New Testament, the Sophists were not seen, for the most part, to be people of integrity. Our word *sophistry* is taken from their movement, and it is typically defined as the use of fallacious arguments in order to deceive. In the beginning, however, the Sophists were seen to be philosophers of integrity whose main purpose was persuasion. They were, initially, people of superior skill or wisdom (*sophia* is the Greek word for wisdom).

We learn from Plato, however, that even in the fifth century BC there was a prejudice against the term *sophist*. By this time, the term by and large bore a contemptuous meaning. Plato refers to the Sophists as those who reason falsely for the sake of gain. One of the primary differences between Sophists and the other philosophers of the day was that they would charge exorbitant fees for their services. They were, in fact, the first in Greece to take fees for teaching wisdom (which seems to be the main reason for their ill repute).

Of interest to our current discussion, the Sophists largely concentrated on teaching rhetoric and persuasion. Their task was to persuade their listeners of whatever they wished them to believe. For Sophists, the search for or acquisition of truth was not a priority. Consequently they undertook to provide a stock of arguments on any subject or to prove any position. Some asserted that it was not necessary to have any knowledge of a subject in order to give satisfactory responses. To attain these ends, mere quibbling and the scoring of verbal points were employed. In this way, the Sophists tried to entangle, entrap, and confuse their opponents. They sought to dazzle their listeners by means of strange or flowery metaphors, by unusual figures of speech, by epigrams and paradoxes, and in general by being clever and smart rather than earnest and truthful.

Around the time of Paul's ministry, with the revival of Greek eloquence, the name Sophist had attained this pejorative distinction. Sophists had become professional orators who appeared in public with great pomp and delivered declamations either prepared beforehand or improvised on the spot.

The false apostles who were influencing the Corinthian church seem to have had these same characteristics. While they may not themselves have been Sophists in any official sense, they were no doubt influenced by them. Remember the indictment against the apostle Paul. Speaking of these false apostles, Paul writes, "For they say, 'His letters are weighty and strong, but his bodily presence is weak, and *his speech of no account*'" (2 Cor. 10:10). This was meant to be a serious charge. If Paul's speech was thought to be "of no account," then he was not someone who could be trusted or who was in any way persuasive. All that he said, including the gospel itself, was empty and without substance. If Paul was not persuasive, then his message itself was nothing.

This type of sophistry was obviously present in Corinth. Notice Paul's references to the notions of "speech," "wisdom," and "knowledge" in the Corinthian letters:

> I give thanks to my God always for you because of the grace of God that was given you in Christ Jesus, that in every way you were enriched in him *in all speech and all knowledge*—even as the testimony about Christ was confirmed among you—so that you are not lacking in any gift, as you wait for the revealing of our Lord Jesus Christ. (1 Cor. 1:4–7)

The Corinthians, says Paul, were enriched *in speech and knowledge* because of their union with Christ. Notice, though, that Paul's concern is not simply with such speech and knowledge in itself:

> And I, when I came to you, brothers, did not come proclaiming to you the testimony of God with lofty speech or wisdom. For I decided to know nothing among you except Jesus Christ and him crucified. And I was with you in weakness and in fear and much trembling, and *my speech and my message were not in plausible words of wisdom*, but in demonstration of the Spirit and of power. (1 Cor. 2:1–4)

It was not simply *speech* and *wisdom* that Paul was concerned to demonstrate, but speech, knowledge, and wisdom *in Christ*, and in *demonstration of the Spirit and of power* (see also 2 Cor. 6:3–7; 8:7).

Paul's summary statement of this false kind of sophistry is evident and made clear at the beginning of his instruction to this church: "Where is the one who is wise? Where is the scribe? Where is the debater of this age? Has not God made foolish the wisdom of the world?" (1 Cor. 1:20). This is an important—we could almost say monumental—point with respect to apologetics. While we want to be concerned with how we present the message (grammar), while we want to follow basic rules of thinking so that our speech and our message are coherent (logic), while we want to be concerned with persuasion and with our rhetorical technique (rhetoric) (Paul was concerned with these things as his letters show), we must never let those things be the basis upon which we have hope or upon which we rest as we present our message.

There will always be those who are better orators or who are perhaps more persuasive, whose skills of speech or writing we cannot match. Persuasion can never be seen as a neutral art or an end in itself. Our hope does not rest in those things; it does not rest in anything that we can make or produce. Our hope, as Paul reminds the Corinthians, rests in the foolishness of the cross, in the gospel and its power, not in us and our abilities.

In that light, Paul was not concerned simply to defend *himself*, but he was speaking in the sight of God, in Christ, for the encouragement, the building up, of the church of Jesus Christ: "Have you been thinking all along that we have been defending ourselves to you? It is in the sight of God that we have been speaking in Christ, and all for your upbuilding, beloved" (2 Cor. 12:19). When Paul had to "take off the gloves" and defend his own ministry, he did not do so on the basis of his attackers' own methods. He was not concerned *merely* with persuasive speech or wisdom, as defined by the false apostles. Instead, he determined to know nothing among the Corinthians except Jesus Christ and him crucified. "For we are not, like so many, peddlers of God's word, but as men of sincerity, as commissioned by God, in the sight of God we speak in Christ" (2 Cor. 2:17).

Paul did not come to battle the false teachers on their own ground; he would not "peddle" the gospel as the false apostles peddled their own teachings. He came with the weapons of Christ (2 Cor. 10:3–5). He came with true knowledge, true wisdom, with the speech and wisdom that could be found only in Christ. The *ethos*, therefore, that is a requisite aspect of persuasion, must be measured by the word of God itself.

This is, in part, what Peter means in that classic passage that we have already noted. In 1 Peter 3:15, as Peter commands the church to be ready to defend her faith, he is careful to note the *ethos* in which such a defense must be given. Defend your faith, Peter is saying, "with gentleness and respect."

This reminds us that our defense is not a defense that depends on us; it is not something that is successful only to the extent that our oratory is polished. Rather, it is a defense that recognizes that

Christ is Lord, that it is he who accomplishes the purposes that he desires in that defense. We need not, therefore, be hostile or abrasive or pugnacious in our defense. Christ reigns. We serve him. Our defense should reflect Christ's sovereignty and our willing service to him.

To be gentle and respectful does not, of course, obviate boldness. Paul knew that he might have to display such boldness to the Corinthians, even as he implored them with the meekness and gentleness of Christ (see 2 Cor. 3:12; 10:1–2). But boldness is not caustic or harsh; it stems from our confidence in Christ and his lordship. Boldness, we could say, is meek and gentle confidence in what we have to say.

What should also be obvious concerning the *ethos* of persuasion, and what we have not broached to this point, is that in our defense of Christianity, as in the entirety of our Christian lives, we are to be a *holy* people. We are to mirror the holiness of our Father in heaven. We cannot and should not expect that anyone or any audience will be anxious to listen to us, or be persuaded by us, if our own character is obviously and explicitly immoral or otherwise suspect. So obvious is this that Aristotle himself thought *ethos* to be central to the art of persuasion: "It is not true, as some writers assume in their treatises on rhetoric, that the personal goodness revealed by the speaker contributes nothing to his power of persuasion; on the contrary, his character may almost be called the most effective means of persuasion he possesses."[22]

It seems to me, anecdotally, that this may be one of the most neglected aspects of Christian living currently. Someone whose ministry is focused exclusively on college-aged people recently said to me that the burning need among that age group of Christians is holiness. It may just be that the cultural pressures are winning a subtle victory in this regard. If that is true, then it is serious indeed. Scripture is clear that without holiness no one will see the Lord (Heb. 12:14). In wanting to be "relevant" to those who are not in Christ, we may be displaying more of a life "in Adam" than we might think. This bodes ill for the art of persuasion in covenantal apologetics. If Christianity makes little difference in the way we *walk and talk* on a day-to-day basis, we should

---

[22] Aristotle, "Rhetorica," 1329.

not think that there will be any obvious reason for others to want to consider a life in Christ.[23]

Though Paul's character may have been in question in Athens, there can be no question that he was pursuing holiness in his gospel ministry there. It is doubtful he would have been asked to address the crowd on Mars Hill if his own character were in shambles. The charge of "babbler" was likely just the philosophers' way of trying to deflect what Paul was preaching.

The message, however, in the art of persuasion is clear: a defense of the Christian faith must first demonstrate Christ in our character. Without that, we have nothing of substance to say.

Pathos

In a highly charged political atmosphere, such as the ones often experienced in the United States, the notion of *partisanship* is most often discussed as a negative characteristic. According to David Cunningham, "The thinkers of the Enlightenment had hoped to undermine vested political interests by resorting to a discourse of liberalism or pluralism. They believed that, if every point of view were given a voice, no single ideological structure would be able to take absolute control."[24]

This Enlightenment attitude of "partisanship as pejorative" is based on a supposition of neutrality. It assumes that the very diversity of ideas is itself an end, rather than a means to an end. The problem that pluralism produces is that it destroys itself in the process. Contradictory and opposing ideas, by definition, cannot all be held and applied by one society. Some *partisan* notion will always dominate and, in so doing, will smother any notion of pluralism.

So partisanship is an essential aspect of persuasion. In the art of persuasion, as applied in a covenantal apologetic, we understand that there are, always and for all discussions, two opposing views present, each of which is held tenaciously by its adherents; the very fact of

---

[23] For further discussion on the nature and necessity of holiness, the best classic resource is J. C. Ryle, *Holiness: Its Nature, Hindrances, Difficulties, and Roots* (various editions). The best contemporary resource is Kevin DeYoung, *The Hole in Our Holiness: Filling the Gap between Gospel Passion and the Pursuit of Godliness* (Wheaton, IL: Crossway, 2012). See also K. Scott Oliphint and Rod S. Mays, *Things That Cannot Be Shaken* (Wheaton, IL: Crossway, 2008), esp. chap. 3.

[24] Cunningham, *Faithful Persuasion*, 77.

partisanship creates the persuasive context. One view, the Christian faith, is true. It adheres to the truth as it is found in God's revelation, and supremely in Christ, and is consistent with the way the world actually *is*. The other view, any view opposing Christianity, is by definition false.[25] It adheres to a false understanding of the world, but it nevertheless seeks to apply that view to the actual world. Such application will end in frustration; it cannot be consistently thought or practiced.

Whenever we speak of the *pathos* of persuasion, though the word itself has reference, roughly, to one's emotional state, we are thinking much more broadly than just how those to whom we speak might *feel*.[26] When we think of *pathos*, we are interested in a proper and personal understanding of those to whom we speak. In persuasion, it is the task of the speaker properly to construe his audience, with a view toward communication that is "adequate to the occasion."

In his book *Faithful Persuasion*,[27] Cunningham argues that the "objective" ways (of which he notes four) of construing the audience are all flawed. One view of apologetics, the Thomistic view discussed in the previous chapter, though it has been a predominant view historically, nevertheless fell prey to an externalist or objective view of the audience, in that it too easily "objectified" its opposing audience. Because of that externalist, objectified view of the audience, the apologetic approach did not—indeed presumably *needed not*—vary from person to person. No matter the audience, the apologetic subject matter to be discussed was always going to be causality or contingency or gradation of being or design (or some combination of these).

As we saw in the last chapter, it is not that these subjects are themselves off limits or in some way inferior or illegitimate. But the problem for purposes of persuasion is that they come without consideration of the *actual* situation, including the actual *problem*, with which those to whom we speak are themselves wrestling. "In the modern period," says Cunningham,

---

[25] Recall tenet 7.
[26] Our English words *empathy*, *sympathy*, and *antipathy*, for example, are formed in part from the Greek word *pathos*.
[27] Cunningham, *Faithful Persuasion*, 72. There are problems in Cunningham's overall analysis, problems that stem from an implicit denial or dismissal of our theological *trivium* above. Those problems, important as they are with respect to Cunningham's overall argument, will not occupy us here.

Christian theologians [and apologists!] have very rarely elaborated on their notion of the audience. This reticence can be attributed to a number of factors. First, given the rise of rationalism and the simultaneous demise of rhetoric in the modern period, the specificity and uniqueness of the audience has gradually been replaced by the assumption that the arguments are universal and self-evident. Second, the modern emphasis on pluralism and diversity rebels against the imposition of a single point of view.[28]

In such an objective approach to apologetics, persuasion has little relevance. No wonder, then, that the focus in this kind of apologetic has been on proofs. Proofs can be memorized and touted without respect to the audience. As Cunningham notes, "This view of human communication effectively neutralizes the diverse assumptions, opinions, and ideological commitments with which human beings approach the rhetorical task."[29]

As we consider the *pathos*, therefore, it is necessary for us to take account of the actual audience that we are addressing. Our objective "is to persuade the audience to *identify* with a particular position. The rhetor seeks to move, even to *impel*, the audience toward a particular point of view."[30]

In our persuasive construal of the people to whom we speak, that is, the *pathos*, two central aspects are always in play and must be considered by the covenantal apologist. These two we can denominate as (1) the aspect of *suppression* and (2) the aspect of the *sensus*.[31] In order to see how these two aspects operate in a real, concrete situation, with a real, concrete audience, we can return again to the Areopagus.

In the midst of his address on Mars Hill, Paul quotes two Greek poets. Why would Paul, in a defense of Christianity, choose to use statements by pagans? Here Paul employs what we have dubbed the *suppression* aspect of *pathos*. Paul, in the interest of persuasion, has properly construed his audience; he knows something of their culture and beliefs. So he seeks to identify with his hearers by using statements that they themselves know and many of them believe. In using

---

[28] Cunningham, *Faithful Persuasion*, 52.
[29] Cunningham, *Faithful Persuasion*, 68.
[30] Cunningham, *Faithful Persuasion*, 68.
[31] It will be obvious by this point that these two aspects are an application of Paul's discussion in Rom. 1:18ff.

such statements, he automatically draws them into his discussion. He is interpreting for them statements that they have already accepted.

The first quote Paul uses is from Epimenides of Crete (whom Paul quotes again in Titus 1:12). Epimenides notes of Zeus that it is "in him [that] we live and move and have our being." The other poet quoted is Aratus, who notes that we are all God's offspring (Acts 17:28). It is vital, for a proper understanding of apologetics, and of persuasion, to understand how Paul uses these Greek poets. He enlists them in order to build a bridge between his own presentation of the gospel and what his audience holds to be true. It seems obvious that Paul is persuasively connecting what he himself is arguing for with what his audience already knows. He is using quotations familiar to them in order to advance and clarify his own points about the gospel.

It is also important to notice that Paul could have simply told the Athenians that they were all wrong, but he does not take that approach, even though that is perfectly true. Paul could have stood up and, rightly and truthfully, denounced his audience's loyalty to Zeus and called them all idolaters.

Suppression of the truth always manifests itself in terms of idolatry. Given that idolatry has moved him to this occasion, that is what we might expect from Paul. Not only so, but given the paucity of interest in persuasion today, most current apologetic methods would simply "tell the truth" without concern for connecting with the audience. If the only concern were to tell the truth, then the Areopagus address would begin, "Men of Athens, I see by your rampant idolatry that you are all suppressing the truth in unrighteousness and worshiping something created rather than the Creator. Repent!" But Paul is wiser than that. He is interested in telling them the truth persuasively. So to that end, he quotes these two poets, using statements familiar to his entire audience. And he does so in order to bring them into his own (Christian) context. This is a perfect example of the proper application of *pathos*.

We must recognize, however, that Paul imports a substantially different *meaning* to these adopted quotations. This is vital to understanding the persuasive element of *pathos*. It is sometimes thought that in quoting these Greek poets Paul is agreeing that they have gotten at least part of their description of God right. All that Paul is doing, it might be thought, is adding the gospel to the Greeks' (semi)proper notion of God. But this is not what Paul is doing at all. Remember that Paul knows the source of his audience's beliefs. He knows that these beliefs are suppressed, "twisted truths" that come from sinful reactions to God's natural revelation of himself. As suppressed and twisted truths, they are, in the hands of the Greeks, condemnable. They are in error. The Greeks would be without excuse if they stood before God with these notions (Rom. 1:20). When they die, they will not be able to say to God, "See, we got it half right!" In that sense, the things that they believe simply are not true at all; they are false propositions, and Paul knows that.

So when Epimenides says that "in him we live and move and have our being," he does not say that in reference to the true God at all. He is writing about a god of his own creation, a false god. When Aratus says that we are "his" offspring, he is not referring to the true God; *he is referring to Zeus.* And in case we miss the point, it simply is not true that we live and move and have our being in Zeus; we are not the offspring of Zeus. These suppressed and twisted truths have become foolish exchanges of the truth of God for a lie (Rom. 1:25).

But when taken and transplanted into their rightful context, to the context of Christianity, these are glorious truths. So Paul surgically removes these poetic propositions from the diseased body that can only kill and destroy their meaning, and transplants them into the healthy body of Christian truth, where alone they are able to thrive.

The Greeks have used these ideas to suppress the true knowledge of God. Paul takes them and puts them back into their proper context, in which alone they communicate the truth about the true Creator and Lord. In that sense Paul is saying, "Your ideas and concepts can be true only if they refer to the true God." This is masterful *pathos,* and it is persuasion at its finest.

As a matter of fact, one of the peculiar aspects of persuasion in a covenantal approach to apologetics, we could say, is *parasitos* (though if we add *parasitos* to *ethos,* *pathos,* and *logos,* that would turn our *trivium* into a *quadrivium*). A parasite is one who lives at another's expense. The only way those who are in Adam can live in God's world, as God's creatures made in his image, is by taking notions, ideas, concepts, and truths from Christianity and attempting to import them into their own belief structure.

Given that their own unbelieving position is false, it cannot, by definition, comport with the way the world actually is. So instead of living entirely in an illusory world, they take things from the real world—the world that Christianity alone describes—in order to try to make sense of their own thinking and living. This is, indeed, parasitic behavior. But it is necessary if one is to live and think at all in God's world, all the while believing that God does not exist or that his existence is not relevant to one's life and thought. There is a *parasitos*, a parasitic element, in all aspects of unbelieving thought and life. Remembering this will help us to see further connections in our apologetics discussions below.

Once returned to their proper context, however, these parasitic ideas—these suppressed, twisted, and exchanged truths, turned into lies, of the Greek philosophers and the Athenians—take their rightful place as absolute truths about the Christian God.[32] That is Paul's point in quoting these poets, a point of persuasion in his defense of Christianity. The *suppression* aspect of the *pathos* of persuasion includes a "reading" or construal of the audience such that we take and use their own ideas and beliefs in our defense of the Christian position.

But there is also the *sensus* aspect working powerfully in Paul's persuasive presentation. This aspect of *pathos* is completely absent from all notions of persuasion in discussions of apologetics today. For that reason, such notions become nothing more than one person's opinion against another's. In discussions of *pathos*, as we have seen, the predominant idea is that we must properly construe our audience. As we have seen, that has merit and should be a part of our persuasive dialog. But the more important, central, and crucial point to remember and apply in our persuasive discussion is that *God has already "construed" our audience* for us, to the extent that he has told us, in his Word, just what unbelief is like.

Cunningham, for example, seems to have no place for a *principial* view of Scripture or of God's revelation in creation. So for him, the best

---

[32] Recall tenet 8.

the "rhetor" can do in his talk about God is utilize notions of analogy and metaphor. He says:

> If theology takes seriously the notion that human beings cannot achieve complete knowledge of God through their own endeavors, then the discipline should also recognize that the language of empirical description will be incapable of providing a complete vocabulary for talking about God. Metaphor is thus central to Christian theology because it helps bridge the gap between the familiarity of empirical language and the relative strangeness of talk about God.[33]

This kind of thinking, however, effectively strips the *pathos* of persuasion of its power, leaving it lifeless and without radical effect.

The good news for a covenantal apologetic, the news that truly bridges the gap between what we are communicating and what our audience claims to believe, is that, with any and every audience, any and every person, God has already and always been there, revealing himself both within and without them in such a way that they already, really and truly, *know him.*

It would be enlightening, if we could, to stand back and ask objectively how we might have gone about speaking to the crowd at Mars Hill on that day. What would we have wanted to say to a group of people, many of whom were only interested in hearing something new, and some of whom were committed to a centuries-old philosophy? Some, undoubtedly, were just average, everyday Athenian relativists, and some were highly educated and committed academics. How might we have addressed such a crowd?

Perhaps we can envision the apostle Paul on his way from Athens to Mars Hill, thinking carefully about how he might begin to address persuasively such an audience. And what does Paul decide to say?

He first acknowledges the "common ground" that he and the Athenians have.[34] They are, together, "very religious" people. So he begins by bringing them into his own general orbit. From that point, however, Paul makes it very clear that his "religion" is worlds apart from theirs. It would be a useful and edifying study to work through Paul's

---

[33] Cunningham, *Faithful Persuasion*, 85–86.
[34] This is "common ground" only in the sense that Paul speaks of in Rom. 1:23, 25. It is "common" that all people worship *someone* or *something.*

initial comments in his Areopagus address in this regard. At this point, however, we will simply highlight the salient features that relate to the *sensus* aspect of the *pathos* of persuasion.[35]

Notice that Paul's discussion, in the main, is a discussion of *the character of God*. He takes, as an entrée to his address, the Athenians' inscription "To the unknown god." But then he immediately announces that he will make this supposed unknown god known to them. The altar with its inscription to an unknown god is Paul's cue. He knows that altar is not there as a result of ignorance on the part of the Athenians. Rather, it is a result of their suppression of the truth. The city is full of idols, in other words, *because people who know God have refused to honor him as God, or to give thanks* (Rom. 1:21). So Paul first establishes that the God of whom he speaks is the Creator of all things. He will, as we have seen, reiterate that point with a quotation from Aratus—"we are indeed his offspring." But the first thing Paul wants his audience to know is that they are God's creatures.

This, of course, is replete with covenant connotations. Being God's creatures means, at least, that we are *obliged* to him. He has given us life; we, therefore, *ought* to give him our lives in return. This would not have escaped Paul's listeners, even if they would have no substantial understanding of the notion of covenant itself.

Paul has to immediately make clear to them that, unlike the gods of the Greeks, this God who created them and all things is not a God who needs us, or anything else, in order to be who he is. This seems to indicate that there is some kind of "covenant" notion present in Paul's audience. The Greek view of covenant, however, was one that placed obligations on *both* parties. It was a covenantal *quid pro quo*—if I do *x* for this god, then he (it) will do *y* for me. The gods of the Greeks were essentially dependent on humans in some ways. Paul makes it clear that the true God is in need of nothing.

This point is one that the philosophers might have grasped immediately. If it is the case, as Paul says, that God has created and is sovereign over *everything*, then it must be the case that *everything* is dependent on him, and that he is dependent on nothing. In other words,

---

[35] For more on the relationship of the *sensus* to Reformed theology historically, see Muller, *Post-Reformation Reformed Dogmatics*, 3:192ff.

"in the beginning, God . . ." assumes that before there was anything created, *God was* (cf. John 1:1). So it could not be that he needed anything, since he existed when there was nothing else.

Paul then goes on to establish that God gives life, breath, and all things to every person, and that all people are descendants of one man. Given God's absolute sovereignty over every person, from the beginning Paul tells his listeners that the reason they are in Athens and not in Egypt is that God has appointed the boundaries and habitations of every person who has ever lived on the face of the earth.

As we said, further study of this passage would reap substantial spiritual dividends. The point we are concerned to make here, however, is that the *pathos* of Paul's audience, as with the *pathos* of any and every person to whom we speak, is that they already know God. When Paul begins, therefore, to speak to them about God as Creator and sovereign Lord, as independent, as the One who gives every person everything that he has—life, breath, all things, the boundaries of his dwelling place, etc.—Paul knows that, deep down, because they are image of God, they *know* what he's saying is the truth. In other words, to understand the *pathos* of any audience, the *fact* of their being image of God and thus of truly knowing him must always be taken into account. In Paul's case at the Areopagus, it is the first thing he wants them to know.

It is not the case, then, as Cunningham argues, that because God is altogether incomprehensible, language about him is going to be confusing. God is always and everywhere making his character known. He is successful in every case. Those to whom God reveals himself clearly see and understand what God is revealing. It is that clear understanding that renders them without excuse. If God's revelation were not clear—if it were obscure or ambiguous—then Paul's argument would be in error. People *would* have an excuse if God's truth given through natural revelation did not get through. But it does get through; it gets through to every person. Whenever we think of defending the Christian faith, we must recognize that whoever our audience is, God has already and always been speaking to them.

There is one more important point to make about the *sensus* aspect of the *pathos* of persuasion. It is a point that is overlooked in discussions of this kind. It is also a point that could occupy us for some time, given its monumental importance for discussions and questions about how and what human beings can know. I cannot develop those important discussions here, however. All I will do at this point is introduce the details relevant to persuasion in a covenantal apologetic.

I said above that the notion of persuasion is not antithetical to the rational or evidential; it simply puts the rational and evidential in their proper context. In Descartes's philosophical method, he sought to doubt everything that it was possible to doubt in order to arrive at some indubitable truth (he likely took this basic method from Augustine). As Descartes began to doubt everything, he recognized that there is one thing that he could not doubt: that he was doubting. And if he was doubting, then he was thinking. The supposed indubitable that Descartes adopted was his now famous dictum *Cogito ergo sum*, "I think, therefore I am."

There are a number of substantial criticisms of Descartes's method and dictum, some of which Descartes himself was fully aware of. One of the most common criticisms, however, is that Descartes's goal was set far too high. Because of his rationalism, he thought it possible to stand on a statement or proposition (such as "I think, therefore I am") and to begin to know everything else on the basis of that one indubitable truth. The problem with Descartes's dictum, however, is not that his goal was too lofty. Neither is it that Descartes was searching for a truth that would have all the properties of mathematical certainty, a "clear and distinct idea," as he put it. The problem was that Descartes thought he was able to generate and locate such a truth in and of himself.

When we begin to reckon with what Paul tells us in Romans 1:18ff., however, we see that what Descartes wanted and thought he could acquire on his own is actually what God gives us in his natural revelation. That is, part of what it means to be "image of God" is that we inevitably and eternally, as God's creatures, know him. To use Descartes's language, because of what *God* has done (not because of anything in us), we all, as his human creatures, have a "clear and distinct idea" of God himself. Even more, we all have "clear and distinct" knowledge of his character.

This, then, helps us to see that which is certain—the knowledge of God in all people—as one of the primary aspects of the *pathos* of persuasion. In other words, the *sensus* of the *pathos* of persuasion is a clear and distinct knowledge of God. This knowledge will manifest itself in various ways. It will be twisted, decontextualized (from its proper source), and perverted in some ways, but it will stem from the knowledge of God that all of us have and that cannot be utterly annihilated in us.[36]

The significant difference between what Descartes wanted in his dictum, on the one hand, and the *sensus*, on the other, is that because of sin, the *sensus* is not indubitable. As a matter of fact, again because of the sinfulness that pervades us in Adam, the *sensus* is the one thing that we will diligently work night and day to doubt, even to deny. But this doubting and denial is just an expression of the suppression of the truth that is attached, like a cancerous tumor, on our Adamic status. In Adam we will, even if it kills us, do all that we can to avoid what is patently and clearly made obvious to us by God himself.

This is where the rational and evidential meet with persuasion. We appeal, in persuasion, to that which is utterly rational because certainly known, and to that which is exhaustively evidential because given in all that God has made, when we persuasively appeal to the *sensus* that God has given us all.[37]

This is one of the reasons, as we saw in the sample dialog given in the previous chapter, that the "theistic proofs" can at times and in certain contexts be useful. They are useful to the extent that they appeal to the *sensus*; and that appeal, in the course of the "proof," might need to be made explicit in the argument. It is certainly *true*, in other words, that God is the first cause, the necessary being on which all contingency depends, the designer of all that is, and so forth. But these truths can only *be true* if framed in terms of the *real* world, the world that God has condescended to make and control. Thus, the "proofs" are actually means of persuasion, rhetorical discourses, and can be useful, given the right audience.[38]

---

[36] Recall tenets 8 and 9.

[37] It is interesting to note that Alvin Plantinga, in a discussion about William Paley and arguments from design, suggests that we might better think of such arguments not as arguments *per se*, but rather as design *discourses*. Plantinga does not include a notion of the *sensus* in this discussion, but it seems to me he is on to something, if we better construe the typical "proofs" as persuasive discussions. So construed, they are better dubbed discourses. See Plantinga, *Where the Conflict Really Lies: Science, Religion, and Naturalism* (New York: Oxford University Press, 2011), 244ff.

[38] In his analysis of the Reformed view of theistic proofs, Richard Muller notes: "The Thomistic 'five ways' take on a character not at all familiar to their famous author: *they are now rhetorically, not demon-*

The content and application of the *sensus* bodes well for the art of persuasion. We never come into a context in which our audience is a *tabula rasa* (blank slate). Instead, every person, every audience, is a slate that is exhaustively marked from top to bottom with the revelation of God's character.

We can see, then, why Paul began his Areopagus address with the character of this God whom each person in his audience knew. And we can see that when Paul appealed to the *suppression* aspect of this audience by quoting the two Greek poets, he had already made clear to whom he was referring in those poems. Both statements—"in *him* we live and move and have our being," and "we are indeed *his* offspring"—given Paul's presentation of God's character, referred to the true and triune God. Paul was telling his listeners what they knew all along, and he used those quotations to make his point abundantly clear. Having wooed them into the orbit of his discourse by using their own poets, Paul then turned their worldview upside down by "reminding" them of who the true God is.

Logos

We can be brief in our explanation of the *logos* (translated as "word"), in part because all that we have said throughout this book about the principles of a covenantal apologetic (including the ten tenets) deals in some way with its *message*. The *logos* of persuasion focuses our attention on the actual arguments, including the content of those arguments, that we aim to present to a given audience.

In our *trivium* of theology, above, the first point that we set out was the foundational and basic (i.e., *principial*) status of God's revelation in Holy Scripture. We will recall that it is just *because* of this status that persuasion can take its proper place in our covenantal defense of Christianity. If our apologetic did not include the *principial* status of Scripture, but instead saw the Bible as something the status of which needed to be rationally or evidentially *proved*, then the central place of persuasion would necessarily recede into the background.

Since, however, a covenantal apologetic affirms Scripture as foundational, it will be obvious to us that it is Scripture's *content* that must

---

stratively, framed, and they are presented together with and as having the same status as the standard rhetorical arguments like *e consensu gentium*." Muller, *Post-Reformation Reformed Dogmatics*, 3:193.

be highlighted as the primary and preeminent *logos* of persuasion. The content of our discourse and all of its arguments must have its genesis in Scripture. What we wish to communicate, in other words, as the *logos* of persuasion, is the *logos*, or Word, of God himself, and ultimately God's Word made flesh, who is the Lord Jesus Christ.

There is a fascinating connection with respect to the *logos* of persuasion that we need to highlight as we look one last time (in this chapter) at Paul's address on Mars Hill. Remember that in Acts 17:31, Paul tells the Athenians that God has "fixed a day on which he will judge the world in righteousness by a man whom he has appointed; and of this he has given *assurance* to all by raising him from the dead." The word translated "assurance," we will recall from chapter 3, could also be rendered "proof" (as it is in the NASB). But there is another fascinating aspect to Paul's use of the Greek word *pistis* in this passage. One of the words in classical Greek for a persuasive, rhetorical proof is this very same word that Paul uses in verse 31. As a matter of fact, *pistis* is the word that Aristotle uses for rhetorical proof.[39] It is also the word that is more often in Scripture, depending on context, translated "faith."

Understood in this way—and this is undoubtedly how the Athenians would have understood it—we can begin to see Paul's persuasive *logos* in his Mars Hill address. When Paul tells the Athenians that God has given *pistis* to all that judgment will come by his raising Christ from the dead, Paul is, in effect, saying that God's *rhetorical proof*, God's persuasive *word*, that all men will be judged is the resurrection of Christ.

The power of what Paul is saying here to this Athenian audience can hardly be overestimated. Remember that it was this fact of the resurrection that motivated the philosophers and Athenians in the first place to bring Paul to the Areopagus in order to present his case. It was the resurrection that seemed to be the "new" thing Paul was presenting (17:18–21). That "new" thing was both an agitation to the philosophers and an item of curiosity to the Athenians generally (17:21). So in the midst of a masterfully persuasive argument utilizing both the *suppression* and the *sensus* aspects of persuasion, the apostle concludes with a masterstroke of persuasive rhetoric.

---

[39] Cunningham, *Faithful Persuasion*, 39.

The very thing that piqued both interest and scorn was the capstone of Paul's entire persuasive argument. It was the *telos* (end goal) both of Paul's presentation and, as he makes clear, of all history. It was the rhetorical proof (*pistis*) of the resurrection of Jesus Christ that ensured that history would someday be complete and that Christ, who was dead but is now alive, would come back to judge the living and the dead.

Paul could have easily used other words for proof; there were others available to him. The use of *pistis*, however, was meant to move his hearers not simply to an abstract, cognitive conclusion, but, given its close connection with the Greek word for faith, and given its connotation of a whole-souled change of mind and heart (remember that *pistis* is most often translated as *faith*), Paul was making it clear that his listeners were responsible to *commit* themselves to his message. He was not interested in a syllogistic conclusion; he was intent that the Athenians would come to faith in Christ.

Thus, the word (*logos*) that we present always aligns itself with the word of God, and our goal in a covenantal apologetic is that we present *the Logos* himself, the very incarnate Word of God, who is the Lord Jesus Christ (John 1:1–9, 14).

Conclusion

Two important points with respect to a covenantal approach to apologetics will conclude our discussion of persuasion.

First, Luke tells us the outcome of Paul's address on Mars Hill: "Now when they heard of the resurrection of the dead, some mocked. But others said, 'We will hear you again about this.' So Paul went out from their midst. But some men joined him and believed, among whom also were Dionysius the Areopagite and a woman named Damaris and others with them" (Acts 17:32–34).

Some commentators have surmised, given this response to his address, that Paul was so discouraged as he went from Athens to Corinth that he decided to rid himself of discussions and presentations like that on Mars Hill and instead "decided to know nothing . . . except Jesus Christ and him crucified" (1 Cor. 2:2). But this idea is completely foreign to Paul and his ministry; it misses the point both of his address to the Athenians and of his ministry among the Corinthians (who were still "infants in Christ" and thus were not ready for the solid food of Christian truth—1 Cor. 3:1ff.). Paul understood, as we must, that the ultimate persuader is God the Holy Spirit. It was not the persuasive cunning or caliber of his argument that would change minds and hearts in Athens or in Corinth; it was the sovereign testimony of the Holy Spirit, working by and with the Word, that would do that.

So, as Luke reports it to us, the responses to Paul's Areopagus address ran the gamut. There were some who continued to mock Paul—some, no doubt, who continued to think him to be nothing more than a "babbler." There were others who wanted to hear more. They were not yet convinced, but something(s) Paul had said resonated with them, and they were curious to hear him expand on what he had said. And then there were some who joined him and believed. There can be no doubt, given this last response, that it was clear from Paul's presentation that the proper response was *faith*. In other words, the *pistis* (rhetorical proof) of the resurrection of Christ was meant to evoke a response of *pistis* (faith) from Paul's audience.

Was Paul's speech, then, successful that day on Mars Hill? His success cannot be measured by the responses given. Even if every Athenian there had believed in Christ, that would be no sign of *Paul's* success. It is the sovereign Spirit alone who can create that kind of success. But Paul *was* successful in that he communicated the truth of God. In our defense of Christianity, we are successful to the extent that what we say comports with what God has said in his Word. Our goal in a covenantal apologetic cannot be the conversion of those to whom we speak. That is a goal that we cannot accomplish. It is our prayer, but should not be our goal. Rather, our goal is to communicate, as persuasively as we are able, the truth of God himself, as that truth finds its focus in the Word who became flesh and dwelt among us.

This point helps us to understand that our apologetic discussions and dialogs are not about "winning" the argument. We are not called to be intellectually superior or rhetorically better than those to whom we speak. We are not in an intellectual contest when we do apologetics. We are in a spiritual battle in which only the Spirit of Christ can conquer the true enemy.

The second concluding point that we need to remember was mentioned at the beginning of this chapter. Because arguments of persuasion have to take into account the *pathos* of persuasion, there will not be just one way, or just one set of truths, or one answer given, in every apologetic encounter. What we say, how we say it, and what words and responses we choose to give will depend to a large extent on those to whom we speak. Paul would not have used quotations from Aratus in his defense of Christianity in the synagogue. To do so would have misunderstood the *pathos* of his audience there.

So in a covenantal approach to apologetics, the question, "What do you say when someone says *x*?" will likely have many possible answers, since that question is abstract as it stands. A proper response requires a fuller *pathos*. What cannot change is the *ethos* and the *logos* of what we say. In any situation—apologetic or otherwise—we are meant to be holy as God himself is holy. And in any situation—apologetic or otherwise—we are meant, when the opportunities arise, to communicate that which is in and consistent with the word of God. The *pathos*, however, calls forth from us the application of wisdom. We have to be able to take what we know and to apply it in the given situation we are in at that moment.

In the coming chapters, I will provide examples of what that wisdom might look like. I will spell out a *possible* way that certain challenges might be addressed in a covenantal approach to apologetics. But these can only be examples; they should not, for the most part, function as templates, except insofar as the examples illustrate various aspects of the ten tenets. Hopefully, however, examples can stimulate other possible avenues of persuasion and further solidify our ability, by the grace of God, to give an answer to objections, attacks, or questions that might come our way.

Heaven above is softer blue,
Earth around is sweeter green;
Something lives in every hue
Christless eyes have never seen.[40]

---

[40] George W. Robinson, "Love with Everlasting Love," 1890.

5

We Destroy Arguments:
The Achilles' Heel

If God does exist as man's Creator, it is as we have seen, impossible that evil should be inherent in the temporal universe. If God exists, man himself must have brought in sin by an act of wilful transgression. Hence, existence, as it now is, is not normal but abnormal. Accordingly, to maintain that existence, as it now is, is normal, is tantamount to a denial of man's responsibility for sin, and this in turn makes God responsible for sin, and this simply means that there is no absolute God.[1]

The Good Fight

We destroy arguments (2 Cor. 10:5). That is one of the things that characterizes the ministry of the apostle Paul. We know that there is, and will always be, hostility to the Christian faith. We also know that anything that opposes Christianity is, by that very act, false. We know this not because we are smarter or more rational or more consistent than others. We know it because of what God has said and because of what God's grace has done in our lives.

Paul knew that the intruders in the Corinthian church were building up their own cause by tearing down his ministry. He knew that an attack on his ministry was an attack on the truth of the gospel message itself. So he wrote the last four chapters in 2 Corinthians to respond to those attacks. The first six verses of chapter 10 form the general introduction to what Paul says in the rest of the letter. So he wants

---

[1]Cornelius Van Til, *The Defense of the Faith*, 4th ed., ed. K. Scott Oliphint (Phillipsburg, NJ: P&R, 2008), 85.

his readers to know the summation of his response: he will demolish arguments.

While it is true that Paul is describing in verses 4 and 5 his apostolic ministry, that does not mean that what he does and says is only descriptive. As an apostle of Christ, he is showing us how we should respond to attacks on our faith. If Paul was ready to demolish arguments, we must be ready as well. In other words, Paul meant for his statement to be applied by his readers also. One reason we know this is that Paul uses expressions in verses 4 and 5 taken from at least two different biblical passages. His notion of demolishing strongholds, in verse 4, is akin to the Septuagint (the Greek translation of the Old Testament) version of Proverbs 21:22. There we are told, "A wise man scales the city of the mighty and brings down the stronghold in which they trust." Paul no doubt has this in mind as he thinks of the pseudo-sophistry of his attackers.

He also knows that some in the Corinthian church would have made this connection. By using this terminology and by referring them to the book of Proverbs, he is telling his readers that true wisdom consists of demolishing strongholds in which the mighty trust. It is not true wisdom simply to erect an argument, whether true or false, as Paul's opponents had done. Rather, the wisdom that is from above must, at the right time, tear down the fortresses that are falsely erected. Christians who seek to be wise must also "pull down the strongholds" when the need arises.

The terminology Paul uses is also close to terminology used of the Sophists in Paul's time. In this way, he is also getting the attention of his challengers. He is telling those "deceitful workmen" that their facades are going to fall. They may be intent on developing and selling arguments meant to refute and destroy Paul's ministry, and thus the church in Corinth itself, but Paul is putting the church on notice that he himself will demolish the arguments advanced against him.

This is the "good fight of the faith" (1 Tim. 6:12). It is the responsibility of every Christian to defend and commend the gospel. That defense is a process of demolition, a demolition of the arguments presented against Christianity. Paul's word for "arguments" in 2 Corinthians 10:5 (*logismous*) is directed specifically against his opponents' appeal to authority. They were attempting to establish themselves as authorities in the church solely because of their own expertise, their own intellectual power. So their arguments were only as strong as their own ideas.

Paul is reminding us that the arguments presented by these intruders were only as authoritative as the intruders themselves. And their authority, in the end, was merely in their own minds. It was in their own ideas and reasonings—quite literally a figment of their imaginations. So Paul is saying that he is going to go after and demolish the false authority on which these false apostles rested. (More on these false apostles in chapter 6.)

This will be the case whenever we engage in apologetics. Apologetics, in many ways, is simply a battle over authorities. It involves making plain just where we stand, or better, where we rest, with regard to what we claim. It also involves encouraging our opponents to make plain where they rest their own case. The authority issue is always primary.

The idea that Paul presents in the next clause tells us a good bit about the kinds of arguments he was opposing. The clause could be translated "every high thing raised up against the knowledge of God." While Paul is alluding to the sinful pride of his attackers, he is also pointing out that the sophistry that had taken some of the Corinthians captive came under the pretense of sophistication and erudition. The arguments may have sounded lofty and substantial, and they may have been intimidating because of their vocabulary, but they were really, in the end, just one more rebellious opinion. They had as much authority behind them as did the false teachers themselves.

Paul is pointing out, as well, that these arguments are not just verbal debates. They are arguments that, if believed, will have eternal, and eternally damaging, consequences. Though they carry no authority, their sophistry can lead people to reject the gospel itself. The very danger of the arguments is that they are so subtly subversive of the gospel. They are, in fact, arguments raised up against the very knowledge of God itself.

The Western intellectual tradition is full of these kinds of arguments. This may be one of the reasons why many Christians have chosen to stay well away from that tradition. It can be intimidating and make us feel intellectually inferior.

Two related points might be useful to remember in this regard. First, we recognize that any argument raised up against the knowledge of God can be destructive to any and all who adopt them. Second, we remember that Christianity does have answers to these arguments. Even if we are unfamiliar with the precise terminology and technicalities of the arguments themselves, once we grasp the question those arguments are designed to answer, our understanding of Scripture can begin to supply the true and needed answer. So, in this chapter I hope to show how one particularly predominant argument might be demolished.

As we noted in the beginning, it is sometimes said that the apologetic approach advocated in this book has great difficulty with actual application. "Once the principles of your approach are laid out," someone might say, "there is nothing left to do but preach the truth. A real argument is foreign to your approach." Maybe there is some justification for this complaint. It may be that there has been a focus on the truths that make up the approach itself without much application to objections against Christianity. I propose, then, to present another example of an argument raised against Christianity and a response that is consistent with what I have thus far set forth and that demonstrates the force of an *argument* for Christianity.

Broadly speaking, apologetics includes anything we say or do that fortifies and demonstrates the truth of Christianity. Any time Christian truth is spoken or lived out, it is inevitably done in the context of some kind of opposition, whether from the sin that remains in us, or from the world, or from the devil—or any combination of these. There is always something(s) opposing the truth. Such is the war that we as Christians are in.

More specifically, however, it is sometimes helpful to think of apologetics as including two distinct tasks—a positive one and a negative one. Positively, the task of apologetics is to commend the Christian faith to those who are affected by, even enslaved to, unbelief. This is perhaps most obviously done when we have a discussion with someone about the gospel in which objections to it are raised.

Whenever we do that, we are commending the Christian faith in the face of opposition. This is what we called the "Christian context" in chapter 2.

Negatively, the task of apologetics is to refute challenges to the truth of the Christian position. Here the focus is on countering arguments that say Christianity is inconsistent or irrational. To use Paul's terminology, the negative approach destroys the arguments, tears them down, and weakens, lessens, or in some way undermines whatever force they may seem to have. Often included in this negative aspect of apologetics is what we called the Quicksand Quotient in chapter 2. We seek to show that the position advocated against Christianity sinks of its own weight.

These two tasks, the positive and the negative, should not be separated; they can sometimes be incorporated and applied simultaneously, and it should be our goal to accomplish both, if possible. One can commend the Christian faith even while defending it against attacks. One can destroy an argument even while building another one. As we will see later, this is the best way to think about Christian apologetics, all things considered; we want both to defend and to commend.

But these tasks can also be distinct. It is possible to defend the Christian faith, thus answering or responding to a particular attack on Christianity, without immediately offering it as the truth of the matter. One reason to do this might be to "clear the field" of an obstacle or obstacles to Christian belief, in order to offer its truths afterward. There is a place for this kind of defense; it is a good thing to clear the field. So we should not dismiss the negative aspect of apologetics as useless. It is true that a cleared field, to continue the metaphor, needs something beneficial planted in place of the weeds that have been uprooted or they will inevitably return. But clearing the field is itself an important task in its own right.

In the remainder of this chapter, we will look at an example that highlights this dual distinction.

Negative Apologetics

Whenever our focus is to neutralize or otherwise weaken an objection to Christianity, we are engaged in (what we have called) negative apologetics. The initial goal of a negative apologetic is to ward off objections and complaints that come against Christianity.

There are a host of these and it would be impossible to address every objection. In negative apologetics, responding to attacks that come against Christianity has more to do with understanding the particular complaint in view than with (as in positive apologetics) commending Christianity as true. *Both tasks are essential aspects of apologetics and should go together*. But there may be occasions when the best response, at least initially, might be to address the complaint head-on with the hope that it would clear the way for commending Christianity. An illustration of how this could be done might be helpful here.

The existence of sin and evil in the world is as good a place as any to begin thinking about negative apologetics. It may even be that most of the objections against Christianity reduce down to the sin/evil problem in some way, shape, or form. In any case, it is one of the most obvious problems that Christianity has to face. Given the real incompatibility between who God is and the existence of evil, some have dubbed this problem the "Achilles' heel" of Christianity; it is the one problem that brings the whole thing tumbling down. In its most generic form, it is typically called "the problem of evil."

It seems that the problem of evil is the most implacable challenge that Christianity must face. It comes in various forms. The late atheist-turned-nonatheist Antony Flew told the parable of the "Invisible Gardener." The parable included two travelers in a jungle who came across a perfectly manicured garden. One traveler insisted that the garden entailed the existence of a gardener, but the other was not convinced. Whenever the first traveler was faced with new objections to his belief in a gardener, he would add qualifications that would support his belief, rather than give up on the belief itself.

The parable was meant to show that the God of Christianity has "died the death of a thousand qualifications." That is, what Flew was trying to argue was that whenever an objection arose with respect to theism or Christianity, the response of the Christian or theist was to add yet another qualifier to God's existence, such that the objection wouldn't "stick." Rather than give up on a belief in God, Christians just add qualification on qualification. Because of those qualifications, according to Flew, Christianity is not "falsifiable" and thus is itself a meaningless position to hold.

Of interest in Flew's discussion, however, was his rationale for the parable. He was so taken with the reality of the death of innocent children that he set out the parable to try to show how ludicrous a belief in God is in the face of such horrific evils. His parable was designed to show that the best Christians are able to do in the face of a multitude of objections like this is continually to qualify their understanding of God in order to try to get him "off the hook" when such predicaments are posed. Thus, it was the problem of evil that motivated Flew's conclusion that Christianity is meaningless.

The problem of evil itself goes back a few millennia and has been articulated by many thinkers throughout the ages. Perhaps David Hume sums up the problem as well as any: "Epicurus' old questions are yet unanswered. Is [God] willing to prevent evil, but not able? Then he is impotent. Is he able, but not willing? Then he is malevolent. Is he both able and willing? Whence then is evil?"[2] Hume, in quoting Epicurus, is highlighting the same problem that bothered Flew. How can it be, they ask, that a good, omnipotent, and omniscient God can exist when there is so much evil in the world? Surely if he is good, and if he knew what would happen, and if he is able to stop evil, there would be no evil in the world. But there is obviously much evil in the world. It must be, then, that this kind of God does not or could not exist.

This way of formulating the problem of evil, as it is discussed in Hume and others, has its focus on an intellectual difficulty. Its focus is on the obvious incompatibility between God's existence and the existence of evil. But we should not think that this intellectual focus is *only* intellectual. As we mentioned above, the motivation for Flew's parable was the fact that children suffer. So the intellectual problem has very real and practical applications and implications.

One of the reasons that the problem of evil is so powerful as an objection to Christianity is that it points to two actual truths. (1) There is an incompatibility between God's character and the evil that exists, and (2) the evil that exists is real and touches everyone in deep and abiding ways. These two truths all Christians would affirm.

---

[2] David Hume, *Dialogues Concerning Natural Religion*, 2nd ed. (London: 1779), 186.

Because of its multifaceted character, there is more than one way to respond to the problem of sin and evil. There is a pastoral response, which would seek to show how the Lord himself provides comfort for those who suffer, and how he overcomes his enemies. This is, perhaps, the most central and important response to the problem. But the problem as stated by Hume has a strong intellectual component as well. There is something amiss, in this construal, when we try to hold the two truths of "God exists" and "evil exists" together in our minds. Surely these two truths defy our standard ways of thinking; we seem to lack the intellectual tools needed to bring them together in a satisfactory way. Thus, this aspect of the problem of evil has sometimes been called the "logical problem of evil."

We should note, however, that to say that this problem has a strong intellectual component and that it is a "logical" problem is not to say that it is abstract, removed from daily life, or otherwise irrelevant. To say that it has a strong intellectual component, we should see, is also to affirm that it is a practical problem. We dare not succumb to an all-too-typical bifurcation of the theoretical and the practical. While such things can be virtually unrelated, there is no room in Christianity for such a dichotomy. If we have trouble thinking about some truth, then surely we will have difficulty applying it to our daily living and our worship. So our response to the logical problem of evil, if considered properly, will have direct practical consequences. It will affect how we think about God and our relationship with and to him.

A good example of negative apologetics can be seen in a response to this so-called logical problem of evil. As we saw above, the logical problem of evil is typically framed in such a way as to highlight the intellectual incompatibility between the existence of a good, omniscient, omnipotent God, on the one hand, and the existence of evil, on the other. Since the problem has often been framed in logical terms, it may be useful to attempt to give an apologetic response to it.

We should first mention that there are deep and knotty discussions surrounding a response. One of the best overall defenses of this problem has been set forth by Alvin Plantinga.[3] We will adapt and adopt

---

[3] Alvin Plantinga, *God, Freedom, and Evil* (New York: Harper & Row, 1974). Plantinga is arguably the most influential Christian philosopher in the English-speaking world today. Much of what he develops can

some of the principles of his response to the logical problem of evil below. In doing so, however, we will not adopt the view of free will on which Plantinga's response depends; that view is outside the parameters of Reformed theology (because it is outside of Scripture) and therefore is not an option for a covenantal approach to this problem.

Without going into detail, a couple of points will help here. First, just to reiterate what we hope to do in this section, we should state clearly in response to the logical problem of evil that what we will offer is a *defense*. We are not yet interested in offering a theodicy.[4] That is, we are not interested, at this point, in responding in a way that would seek to show how there can be both this kind of God and evil. We are not interested in actively commending the truth of God's existence and his ways, given the existence of evil and sin, in this response. To do that would be to begin to advocate for the position we are defending.[5]

Rather, our concern is to stave off the attack, to show that it is in some way illegitimate, and therefore to take away its force. This is, we should note, a completely acceptable mode of argument, though it is a strictly defensive mode. It is useful, even at times necessary, to meet attacks head-on and to push them back so that their force is either weakened or altogether annihilated.

Perhaps it will help to think of it this way. Suppose you are an occupant of Edinburgh Castle in the early fifteenth century. Under Henry IV, England attempts to take the castle, but fails, owing to the strong defense of your army. You have successfully defended the castle. The attack has not succeeded. What is your position now with respect to the castle? You haven't gained any new ground or territory; you haven't gained anything, so to speak. You have not advanced your position in any positive way. What you have done is stave off an attack that would attempt to take the castle from you and place it under foreign control. In this sense, you have kept the castle strong.

---

be helpfully adapted and utilized in a covenantal approach to apologetics. The points made below about a defense all come from his work.

[4] One reason I borrow heavily from Plantinga's approach here is that it is such a fine example of what a defense *is*. For another analysis of Plantinga, see K. Scott Oliphint, "The Old-New Reformed Epistemology," in *Revelation and Reason*, ed. K. Scott. Oliphint and Lane G. Tipton (Phillipsburg, NJ: P&R, 2007), 207–219.

[5] I will attempt to show how to commend the Christian faith in the context of this objection in the next section. All I mean to do here is to show how the negative and positive aspects of apologetics can be distinct. We should not, however, think thereby that they can or should be separated.

So it is with a negative apologetic defense. In your defense of the castle, you are not arguing for your rightful place in the castle. You could do that (and should do that, if possible), but the need of the hour is to respond to the attack, to hold your ground. So you seek only to keep the attacks at bay, so that the walls and gates remain strong and resistant to the enemy. You are defending your position without commending your position. This is what a negative apologetic defense, strictly speaking, is meant to do.

How, then, could we defend our position against the attack above? Remember, the attack centers on the logical problem of holding both that God exists as (at least) good, omniscient, and omnipotent and that evil (or sin) exists as well. A negative response may require some perseverance on the part of the apologist (and the reader!). But it is oftentimes necessary in order to diffuse the initial supposed strength of the attack itself.

The first thing to note is that the logical problem of evil is not, in fact, a logical contradiction. That is, there is no violation of the canons of formal logic when it is asserted that both God and evil exist. It is not, after all, an assertion that (1) God and evil exist and (2) God and evil do not exist. (That would be a contradiction.) So the logical problem is not one of logical contradiction.

Perhaps the logical problem of evil is best understood as a problem, let's say, of incompatibility. This kind of problem is not as clear as a problem of contradiction would be; it is a bit more difficult to define precisely. The problem may be that there are properties inherent in the existence of God, on the one hand, and of evil, on the other, that we are unable to explain or to bring together in our own minds. They seem mutually to exclude each other. We have either no information or too little information to make their coexistence intelligible.

How can we make sense of the fact that God is good, is all-knowing, and is all-powerful, and yet that evil is a daily, painful reality? Given the obvious existence of evil, so the argument goes, it must be that the "not so obvious" existence of God must be given up.

So the respective propositions—i.e., (1) God exists and (2) There is evil—are thought to be incompatible. This, we should recognize, is exactly right; it *is* a problem, and Christians should acknowledge that. How can it be that a God who is indeed good and who knows all things and who is all-powerful would allow for the presence, even the overwhelming presence, of evil and sin in the world?

An "easy" (albeit unorthodox) way out of this dilemma would be to deny one of the three attributes above ascribed to God so that the incompatibility disappears. For example, if God were not good, then even though he is all-knowing and all-powerful, the existence of evil would be understandable since it would be consistent with his character. He would be, as Hume notes above, malevolent. Or if God were not all-knowing, we could explain the existence of evil and sin as something that even God did not know would happen; we could assert that it caught him by surprise. In the same way, if God were not all-powerful, then evil and sin could be explained as that which God was unable to stop; he simply did not have the requisite power to ensure that evil would not come into the world.[6]

But this way of explaining things is a high price to pay for Christians. It goes against the biblical teaching of who God is, and, as might be expected, it goes against the Christian tradition's teaching about God's character. Christianity has historically affirmed that included in God's character is his sovereign power over all things created. To reduce or otherwise negate one of these attributes is not, in other words, a biblical option for the Christian.

So we have two statements—(1) An omnipotent, omniscient, and good God exists, and (2) There is evil—which themselves are not easily brought together. How could such statements be more easily merged together?

Plantinga notes that what is needed is a third statement, (3), that is consistent with (1) and that entails (2). In other words, another statement that does not conflict, but is consistent, with the fact of God's existence, but which also includes the fact of evil's existence, would help us see how the incompatibility might be overcome.

Not only so, but as Plantinga evaluates the objection, he rightly contends that the incompatibility between God's existence and the

---

[6]This latter option, i.e., altering our understanding of God's omnipotence, is the sum and substance of many answers given to this problem. In Plantinga's response, the possibility that God, given the creation of man, could not in any meaningful way control what man would do alleviates the incompatibility between his existence and evil. Once he chose to create man, he simply could not be sovereign over what man might do.

existence of evil, in order to be a substantial objection, must, for anyone lodging the complaint, itself be a necessary incompatibility. For
the argument/attack to have its force, it would need to be *necessarily* the
case that the existence of God and of evil are incompatible. This is the
case because if the existence of God and of evil were only *possibly* (and
not necessarily) incompatible, then the existence of God and of evil
would possibly be compatible, and the problem would lose its punch.
So those complaining about the lack of compatibility between God and
evil must show that lack of compatibility as necessarily the case. They
must, in other words, hold that it is *impossible* (not just improbable)
that God and evil coexist.

But that claim is, as a matter of fact, a bold one. On what basis
could one assert such an impossibility? Plantinga works through some
very technical arguments in order to show that it is possible that the
existence of God and of evil are compatible.[7] Without looking at the
details of a response to this argument, the point to observe here is that
the attack can be fended off by introducing another truth or situation
that could allow for the compatibility of the existence of God and of
evil.

So what we need is a statement that includes God's existence
and entails the existence of evil—a statement that we have labeled
(3). One prime candidate for (3) is this: "Adam responsibly and
freely[8] chose to disobey God, to eat the forbidden fruit, after which
time he and all of creation fell." This statement, we should note, is
consistent with (1)—it is consistent with the existence of a good,
omniscient, and omnipotent God. And it is consistent with (2)—
it entails the existence of sin and evil since the fall of Adam and all
of creation brought evil into the world. So is it *possible*, we could
ask, that the fact that Adam responsibly and freely chose to eat the
forbidden fruit brings together God's existence and the existence
of evil such that they are now seen to be compatible? That is, in

---

[7] I should say here that I have to take exception to Plantinga's analysis of the problem of evil, as it requires Molinism. I do agree that the one objecting to the intelligibility of the coexistence of God and evil
needs to see such an incompatibility as *necessary* or the argument is merely one of degrees of possibil-
ity/probability. This does not destroy the objection, but it does significantly weaken its assumed force.
[8] I use the word "freely" here defined according to the Westminster Confession of Faith 9.2: "Man, in
his state of innocency, had freedom, and power to will and to do that which was good and well pleas-
ing to God; but yet, mutably, so that he might fall from it." "Freely" here does not include Molinism.

affirming (3)—"Adam responsibly and freely chose to disobey God, to eat the forbidden fruit, after which time he and all of creation fell"—do we avoid denying (1)?

Given (3), God's goodness, omniscience, and omnipotence all can be affirmed, and we also have an explanation for (2), the entrance of evil and sin into the world. Thus, while we still maintain that God and evil are contrary entities, we can see how both exist by virtue of Adam's responsible and free choice.[9]

One objection to proposition (3) might be that it introduces a claim that presupposes the truth of biblical revelation. Any understanding or knowledge of the predicament of Adam and Eve assumes what is taught in Scripture. Because of that, an objector might say, it is illegitimate to appeal to something that the objector himself does not believe. Perhaps he thinks the argument can only be answered in the context of an agreed-upon source or authority. It is at this point that we need to be careful to focus on those things that lay behind the objection itself. If we do, this objection will have little force, and for at least two reasons.

First, because the incompatibility between (1) and (2) is only a *possible* incompatibility, all that is needed is that (3) itself be *possible*. That is, one does not, initially, have to contend for the *truth* of (3) (though it is true; but remember we are offering a defense here, not, at this point, a commendation of the Christian faith), but only that (3) itself be possible and plausible. What might make the appeal to Adam and his action plausible and not simply possible?

Perhaps that it is a central tenet of Christianity, that it has been believed by countless Christians (and Jews) for millennia. Though the objector may not believe it himself, that is no argument against its truth or plausibility, and certainly not against its possibility. Remember, the objector is asking us to make sense of the existence of God and of evil. Because the objector does not believe in the existence of God, he will also not likely believe the answer provided, but that is no argument against its plausibility or against its truth.

---

[9] There is obviously more that needs to be said here, especially with respect to the contingency of Adam's choice, but it would take us too far afield and would necessitate technicalities that might obscure our basic point. To see how this might be worked out, see K. Scott Oliphint, *The Majesty of Mystery: Celebrating the Glory of an Incomprehensible God* (Bellingham, WA: Lexham Press, 2016), chap. 7.

Second (and this is a monumentally important point that is never brought out in these discussions), consider that the problem of sin and evil itself, as posed by the objector, is a problem *that includes within it the existence of God*. That is, although an atheist does not believe in God's existence, the problem that he poses to Christianity at this point is *not a problem that attaches to atheism*, at least not directly, but rather is one that attaches to Christianity; it is a problem that obtains in such cases when a good, omniscient, and omnipotent God is affirmed.[10]

There are at least two ways to interpret this problem as presented. Maybe the atheist is saying, "I can't believe in this kind of God, given the ubiquitous problem of evil; if I could see compatibility, that would remove at least one objection." On this scenario, the atheist sees incompatibility as an obstacle to belief. But maybe the atheist objector is saying, "You can't believe in both God and evil, given the incompatibility between the two." In this case, the objector is accusing the Christian of believing (some kind of) irrationality or falsehood. So the objection could be an attempt to remove a problem with Christianity (as the atheist sees it), or it could be an attempt to show one instance in which Christianity is itself not true or rational.

Here is the cornerstone of the response. However the objector wants to frame the problem, the response will generally be the same. Since the problem posed operates with the working assumption *that God exists, and that he has certain characteristics* (i.e., goodness, omniscience, and omnipotence), it is consistent with the problem, as posed, to *appeal to the place wherein we learn of these characteristics* and where "the problem of evil" is itself discussed.

Given that the objection itself operates with the working assumption that there is a God who has these characteristics, the all-important focus and central question to ask is this: On what basis does the objector posit a God who is good, omniscient, and omnipotent? Certainly he does not believe in such a God. Rather, he knows that it is we Christians who believe in that God, and believe him to have (at least) these characteristics. Not only so, but since the objector presents the problem as one intrinsic to Christianity, there is no fallacy or logical

---

[10] One might want to insist that this problem is a problem of theism generally, which it may be. However, this does not require, nor is it possible, that one's response be one of generic theism. It is perfectly acceptable to appeal to Christian theism in this case, since the problem is contained in its truths.

breach if one answers the objection from the same source in which the alleged problem itself, including the characteristics of God, is found.[11]

So the fact that the objector may not believe (3) is not relevant to the response that we give, nor is it relevant to whether or not there is an answer to the problem. He does not believe in the existence of God either, but he posits such in order to lay out the problem. So what the objector himself believes is not directly relevant to our answer, even as it was not directly relevant to his objection.

This is an important point and should not be glossed over lightly. It is sometimes thought or assumed by both parties in a debate of this kind that the context, including the response, we posit must be one that each party in the debate will gladly accept. But there are too many other factors present that do, or could, block one or both parties from accepting a particular response. What is needed, in this case, is not a statement that the objector will accept, since the very problem that he poses—the attack that he wages—is one that includes a statement Christians accept, but the objector *does not accept*, namely (1). So the acceptability of a certain state of affairs (i.e., the existence of God) is itself not a part of the objector's own beliefs. It can hardly be untoward, therefore, to respond to the objection in a way that is consistent with the challenge itself, even though it is not consistent with the objector's position; his very objection is inconsistent with his own position!

Think of it this way: the objector comes to us and says, "You Christians believe two propositions which themselves are incompatible. It is your responsibility to show me how these propositions can be compatible." Now suppose the objector also demands that you show the compatibility of these truths on the basis of the objector's own atheistic position. That, of course, cannot be done. The only way to show the compatibility of the two propositions is by appealing to the source and substance of those propositions themselves. And the first statement, "God exists," is absent from the atheist's position. No response, therefore, can take that position as the proper context for an answer.

---

[11] It should be said here that to respond to the atheist objector by noting that he himself has no ground for asserting something *as* evil or wicked (since no absolute standard exists in atheism) is *not* to speak to the specific objection or problem posed. There certainly is a problem with respect to atheism and the ground or standard by which one could determine evil, but the problem here has to do with the compatibility of the existence of God and evil. It is, therefore, a *Christian* problem, not an atheistic one, and should be seen as such, so that a *Christian* answer can more naturally be given.

Thus, we have an objection that stipulates the incompatibility of two truths, both of which are integral to Christianity. In that way, the objection presupposes two truths of Christianity, which truths themselves could only be known by way of God's own revelation. It is no stretch, therefore, to introduce (3), which itself is another truth of Christianity, in order to show how (1) and (2) can be seen to be compatible.

As a matter of fact, it is the only legitimate way to respond. If the objector cries foul, if he deems the response illegitimate, he has introduced or attempted to interject something else into the discussion that he has not made explicit. He has changed the rules. If that is the case, then more needs to be discussed, and perhaps it is time to begin commending the Christian faith, rather than just letting the defense rest. We will discuss the commendation of Christianity, in light of this objection, in the next section.

The point I want to highlight here is that to the extent that our response is successful, the so-called logical problem of evil is severely weakened. The attack has come; the response is meant to beat back the attack so that it lacks force. No attempt has been made, in the explanation that we have given above, to move the discussion to the grounds of what we believe, or positively to introduce the objector to the realities of the Christian gospel.

Such things can and, as opportunity is given, *should* be introduced (more on this below). But we should not conclude that unless such things are introduced, no real defense has been given. Though primarily negative, this approach has a proper place and can be useful in apologetic dialog and discussion.

Positive Apologetics

In the previous section we have attempted to weaken the force of the logical problem of evil, which has been offered as an atheistic objection, that is, one that seeks to conclude for the nonexistence of God. We have construed the objection as one of incompatibility, rather than of contradiction. This construal is uncontroversial.

We have also attempted to offer two aspects to our initial response. The first aspect focuses on the force of the objection itself. This aspect recognizes that an objection of this sort, in order to have the impact it is presumed to have, must see the coexistence of God and of evil as impossible. There must, therefore, be a *necessary* incompatibility between God's existence and the existence of evil. If the incompatibility is merely *probable* rather than necessary, then the two are *possibly* compatible and the argument loses whatever strength it was presumed to have.

An illustration here may help. It is true that in a round of Texas Hold'em, the card dealer *probably* will not deal four aces to me. But it is also true that he *might* give me four aces. So any argument against my having four aces cannot exclude the possibility that I could have four aces in my hand. Though improbable, it is not impossible.

So also for the coexistence of God and of evil. Any argument that concludes for the improbability of the coexistence of these two is no strong argument against it. Improbable things happen all the time. If all the argument produces is an improbability, it is no real objection to Christianity; improbability of this kind oftentimes has more to do with opinion and predisposition than with logical force (more on this in chapter 6).

The second aspect of our response took into account that the objection itself draws its content from a conception of God consistent with Christianity. In so doing, the objector has, *by way of his own objection*, opened himself up to a response that would take seriously just how it is that we know such things about God. That is, the objection assumes that God is good, omniscient, and omnipotent.[12] And we know who God is only by virtue of his revelation to us. Once the topic of revelation is introduced, as it is at least implicitly *by the objection*, it is legitimate to pursue a response that would utilize the teaching of that revelation.

In other words, the objector is asking us to "make sense" of our belief that God exists, that he has the aforementioned characteristics, and that evil exists. The way to "make sense" of that is the way that the objection surfaces in the first place and is the same way that we know God to be good, omniscient, and omnipotent—by way of revelation.

---

[12] Just to reiterate, it is not the case that the objector believes this about God. Rather, it is the case that the objection requires this understanding of God. Thus, the objection assumes a certain knowledge of God and just how that knowledge is obtained is directly relevant to the objection itself.

In the course of our response above, however, it may have been obvious that there was another aspect of the objection that has not yet been addressed. There is, one might have recognized, another objection to our above-proffered solution to the logical problem of evil that the objector may want to set forth and that is implicit in what we have offered as an answer thus far.

The further objection to our response could look something like this: "You have stated that Adam responsibly ate the forbidden fruit and, thus, we have the entrance of sin and evil in the world. But you have not yet explained in any way how Adam could be responsible for his disobedient choice, given God's own character." In other words, the incompatibility that is suspected in the original objection could easily reduce down to an incompatibility between specific characteristics of God and the reality of evil, to which this same God is opposed.

This is a legitimate inference from the original objection posed. It may indeed be that the general objection in the problem of evil is now more specifically directed against the Christian in order to require him to make sense of Adam's *responsible* choice in the context of God's omniscience and omnipotence. Let's call this the Incompatible Properties objection (IP), in that it focuses the incompatibility on specific characteristics or properties that each—God and man (or creation)—has.

In Plantinga's response to the problem of evil, noted above, this IP objection becomes the crux of the issue. The problem, in other words, is not simply a general incompatibility between God's existence and the existence of evil or sin. Rather, the problem implies a more specific incompatibility that is assumed when it is affirmed that God has the characteristics mentioned above, on the one hand, and that Adam brought about a state of affairs that was and is in opposition to this God.

How could it be, to put the matter more specifically, that God's omnipotence and omniscience could not "protect" or prevent Adam from bringing the created world into ruin? Surely, as omniscient, God would have *known* what Adam would do in any possible circumstance, so could he have determined not to bring about those circumstances. Or, given his omnipotence, he could have *stopped* Adam from eating the forbidden fruit so that evil and sin would not have brought creation into bondage.[13]

Plantinga's response to this more specific problem was to construe God's particular characteristics—specifically his omnipotence—in such a way that the creation of Adam imposed limits on God's essential power. That is, once God determined to create Adam, it is possible, Plantinga would say, that God's omnipotence was itself limited by the fact of Adam's moral and ethical responsibility before God.

This particular understanding of the relationship between God and man is not a new one and is one that brings together the incompatibility between God's power and man's ability by attributing to man the power to live and act independently of God's control. Thus, though God is powerful, he restricts his power in order for man to be able to choose freely. But difficulties remain with this particular response.

The problem, to be clear, is not that God's omnipotence is thought to be limited *simpliciter*. Like all attributes of God, his characteristics must be understood and defined according to his own revelation of himself. So, for example, God's having all power does not mean that he has the power or ability to lie. This "inability" is not a lack in God; it is rather contained in the very character of who God is. So "all-powerful" is not defined in terms of "can do anything"; that definition remains abstract and assumes a notion of possibility that is foreign to biblical Christianity. "All-powerful" rather means that God can do anything that is consistent with his own character. He can do, as the children's catechism states, "all his holy will."

So the problem with Plantinga's response is not that he restricts the "omni" in *omnipotence*. Everyone in Christian theology must qualify the "omni" of *omnipotence*. The problem, rather, has its focus in just how the omnipotence is thought to be restricted. It is thought to be restricted, as Plantinga makes clear, by virtue of Adam's (libertarian) free will, a will that itself could bring about a state of affairs that God's

---

[13] The IP objection, it seems to me, is the crux of the problem. Without going into detail, it seems also that the Molinist or Plantingan response to the IP objection still leaves huge questions unanswered. Though Plantinga's response is meant to be a defense *only*, it does border on a theodicy in that it distances God's control from the act of sin or evil itself. For example, in Plantinga's construal, it is possible that God could not strongly actualize a state of affairs that was only morally good. But if that is the case, surely he *knew* what Adam would do, even if that knowledge was so-called middle knowledge. If he did know, why then go ahead and create?

own power *could not* bring about. In other words, Adam's will was such that it acted independent of God's control. Or God is not sovereign over Adam's choices; those choices must be independent of God. Any will acting in conjunction with God's control, so the argument goes, could not be free and therefore could not be responsible. Moreover, any will acting in conjunction with God's will would put the responsibility for its acts squarely on God. Thus, God would be the author of sin.

But this response which construes God's sovereignty as limited is not open to one who embraces a covenantal apologetic. It is not open to anyone who holds that the theology reaffirmed during the Reformation is itself most consistent with biblical truth.[14] Anyone holding to Reformed theology will need to find another way to respond to this objection.

It just so happens that there is another way, and it is a way that moves more explicitly and intentionally toward the reality of the gospel as the only real solution to the problem of evil and sin. It seems to me fair to say that no other approach or response to this problem so naturally moves to the good news of the gospel. And that seems to be a fatal flaw with any other approach to this problem.

Perhaps this particular objection can best be illustrated by way of a fictional dialog between the atheist objector (AO) and a covenantal apologist (CA). Any fictional dialog of this sort will invariably be "cleaner" than a real dialog, but it should at least provide some general parameters within which a suitable response to this IP objection could be given. The atheist objector begins:

> AO: If I understand where we are at this point, you have attempted to argue that my objection must include the *necessary* incompatibility of the coexistence of God and evil. You have also introduced a proposition (concerning Adam) that has its source in biblical revelation, and you have justified that by insisting that the objection itself has its source (at least in part) from biblical revelation. I am prepared to concede these points. [Remember, I said this dialog would be "cleaner" than most in real life.]

---

[14] In theological terms, Plantinga opts for a kind of Molinism, in which God's acts are determined by his middle knowledge, which itself takes account of man's libertarian choices. This is akin to the position of historic Arminianism. Reformed theology has opposed this notion, and for good reason. For more on these distinctions, see Oliphint, *The Majesty of Mystery*, chap. 7.

What you have not explained, to my satisfaction, is the crux of my objection. The objection is not simply that God and evil cannot coexist, but rather that this kind of God, with all the attributes enumerated, cannot coexist with evil. It is specifically God's omniscience and omnipotence that rule out his compatibility with evil (since no theist will concede that God is not good). Given the overwhelming evidence for evil's existence in this world, it is irrational to conclude that this kind of God exists as well.

CA: In order to respond to your objection, it might be useful to frame it in its more general context. The objection, taken generally, argues that there is an incompatibility between who God is, on the one hand, and some property, or properties, of creation, on the other hand. In other words, the objection entails certain assumptions with respect to God and creation, assumptions that are involved in the conclusion that, given this property, or these properties, in creation, God cannot exist.[15] You are specifically concerned with the incompatibility of the properties of God, on the one hand, and man (in this case, Adam), on the other.

A couple of clarifying points before we address the objection directly. First, just how do we go about understanding "compatibility" here? This question could take us too far afield, so perhaps we can agree on a fairly general definition: "Two statements e and h are compatible if and only if neither of them logically implies the negation of the other."[16]

Now the objection that you offer indicates that the existence of God as omniscient and omnipotent is not compatible with the existence of evil. In terms of our definition, we could say, the existence of evil logically implies the negation of the existence of this kind of God. And let's just say, again for the sake of brevity, that logical implication, as used here, simply means that the truth of the existence of evil ensures that a God of this kind cannot exist. In other words, the implication relation is such that the reality of evil's existence rules out the reality of (this kind of) God's existence. So far, so good.

At this point, however, we need to clarify a few more general points in order to move to the more specific ones. Generally, we are considering exactly *how* God and the world are, or can be, related.

---

[15] These kinds of incompatibility arguments, as we noted in chapter 1, are the sum and substance of Michael Martin and Ricki Monnier, eds., *The Impossibility of God* (Amherst, NY: Prometheus, 2003).
[16] Mario Augusto Bunge, *Critical Approaches to Science and Philosophy* (Piscataway, NJ: Transaction, 1998), 57.

You will understand, of course, that I approach this consideration from the standpoint of Christianity. Though you may mean the objection to cover all forms of theism, you must understand that responses to the objection depend on a particular understanding of who God is. My response depends on an understanding of the God of Christianity.

In any understanding of the God of Christianity, it is affirmed that God exists necessarily. That is, it is not possible for him not to exist. He is not self-caused, but rather is acausal. His existence just is who he is; he needs no causation in order to exist. As a matter of fact, he needs nothing in order to exist and to be who he essentially and necessarily is.

Not only is God necessarily who he is, but everything else that exists, does so only by virtue of his free decision to create and sustain it. He did not have to create, but he freely determined to do so.

Once God creates, he establishes a relationship with his creation, and a special relationship with those made in his image. Those made in his image, unlike the rest of creation, are responsible to "mirror" his character; they are to be human replicas of who he is.

Instead of mirroring God's character, as we have said, Adam violated God's character by eating of the forbidden fruit and thus plunging himself and all of creation into ruin—a ruin that man himself cannot fix. If there was going to be a remedy to this problem, God alone would have to provide it.

By this point, the objector may be getting impatient. He may suspect that we are on the verge of launching into a recitation of redemptive history. He may also suspect that we are moving away from his objection. So the covenantal apologist continues:

CA: Just how God provided the solution will be addressed in a few minutes. What we have to highlight at this point is that God's solution to the problem that Adam brought about was that he himself would come down, in the person of the Son of God, to remedy the problem of sin.

AO: Oh, I see. When I present to you a problem of incompatibility, your immediate reaction is to start to preach to me about such absurdities as God dying on a cross. Surely this response is a massive red herring. How does this address the compatibility problem between God and evil?

CA: I do want to talk to you about such "absurdities," but it is exactly the compatibility problem that I am trying to introduce here.

As you may know, Christianity is so-called because it has its focus not in some generic god, but in the triune God—Father, Son, and Holy Spirit. I acknowledge that you do not believe such things, but as I said, that is not relevant to our particular discussion, or your specific objection.

You are not asking me to make sense of the coexistence of God and evil given what *you* believe. Since you do not believe in God, such a request would indeed be absurd. But you are asking me to make sense of it *given* the existence of God. I am simply stating what Christianity has believed since its inception.

Since we are discussing God's relationship to creation, generally, you should be aware that the central, quintessential, and primary example of God's relationship to creation is found in the person of Jesus Christ, the Son of God. Christianity has held that it was in the condescension of the Son of God, in taking on a human nature, that the relationship of God to creation reached its climax.

AO: I thought we were going to discuss compatibility. Is it really necessary to get into the fine points of your religion in order to discuss such things?

CA: As a matter of fact, we are not discussing the fine points of Christianity, but its very *essence*. If you are honestly asking for a response to the problem of the compatibility of God's existence and the existence of evil, then I must give you an honest answer, one that will get at the heart of our disagreement.

Now to the problem of compatibility.[17] In one of our historic creeds, the Chalcedonian Creed (AD 451) (which has its genesis in the text of biblical revelation, which we can delve into later if you wish)[18] the description of the incarnation of the Son of God was that he was "acknowledged in two natures, inconfusedly, unchangeably, indivisibly, and inseparably."

The creed goes on to affirm, concerning this "hypostatic" (or personal) union, that with regard to these two natures, "the distinction of natures [is] by no means taken away by the union, but rather the property of each nature [is] preserved, and concurring in one Person

---

[17] By now, a pattern should begin to be evident in my response. This pattern takes tenet 1 seriously and offers a response that is distinctively Christian. This pattern should also make clear that it is the substance of the Christian faith that offers responses to many of the objections out there, since only in Christianity has God condescended, and preeminently so in Christ.

[18] For a look at some of the passages relevant to this discussion, see Oliphint, *The Majesty of Mystery*, chap. 4.

and one Subsistence, not parted or divided into two persons, but one and the same Son, and only begotten, God the Word, the Lord Jesus Christ."

Let me emphasize here that this understanding of "God in the flesh"—of the Son of God taking on a human nature—is affirmed by both Catholic and Protestant churches. There is nothing that I have said so far that veers from the basic historic norm of Christian theology.

If you look carefully at what Christians have believed for almost two thousand years, you will recognize that the way in which God relates himself to creation in the incarnation is by the union of two distinct and otherwise separate natures in one person.

These natures, we might say, are *incompatible*. God, as infinite, is united with a finite human nature, for example. When the Son of God took on a human nature, he did not cease to be who he was and is—he did not give up his infinity, eternity, immutability, aseity, etc.— but rather he took on something he did not previously have: a human nature, with all that it entails. In so doing, as the creed reminds us, he remained one and the same person—the Son of God—but now also with a human nature.

In other words, given the Christian understanding of the Trinity, the Son of God is himself fully and completely God, as is the Father and the Spirit. Because each of these three persons is fully and completely God, each person has (and is) all the essential properties of the one God. Each, therefore, as the one God, is "in and of himself infinite in being, glory, blessedness, and perfection; all sufficient, eternal, unchangeable, incomprehensible, everywhere present, almighty, knowing all things."[19]

Now notice that the Chalcedonian Creed affirms that when the Son of God took on a human nature, there was no confusion of natures, there was no change in the natures, no division of them, and no separation.

That is, the natures *did not blend* together to make a third nature, each property essential to each of the two natures *did not change; nor* were the two natures *divided* or *separated*. The *union* of natures, in one person, in the incarnation did not negate the *distinction* of natures, but the properties of each nature are preserved in the union. All of this is affirmed even as these two natures are said to be "concurring in one Person and one Subsistence, not parted or divided into two persons,

---

[19] Westminster Larger Catechism, answer 7.

but one and the same Son, and only begotten, God the Word, the Lord Jesus Christ."

Can you see where I am going with this? What Christians have confirmed and believed for millennia is that *there is compatibility* between the essential characteristics of God and the essential characteristics of (in this case) man, such that the two can be united in one person without the properties of either of the two natures changing. What some would take to be essentially *incompatible* characteristics are actually *united* in one person.

AO: This is where I have to cry foul. I was willing to put up with your discussion of Adam, even of Christianity. But now you are offering a model of compatibility to me that, even by the reckoning of Christianity, is *sui generis*. How can you establish a notion of compatibility from something that is a one-time miraculous event according to your own religion?

CA: You are right to recognize the unique character of the incarnation. I do not want to undermine that in any way. But here is the point to notice before we move on. In the person of Jesus Christ, according to Scripture, and as given in our historic creeds, we have a unifying of the divine and the human. So, at minimum, we have to recognize that there is no intrinsic or essential incompatibility between properties that God has necessarily and the essential properties of creation, even of human beings.

God was able to bring them both together—to unify them—without violating any of the respective properties. Any notion of compatibility will have to allow that if this is true, then there is no incompatibility between God's character and the character of human beings. God can unite them both into one without merging or changing either.

What, then, does this compatibility look like? In part, it looks like the life of Christ, as we have it in Scripture. Consider, for example, Christ in the garden of Gethsemane (Matt. 26:36ff.; Mark 14:32ff.). Here is the Son of God, the Word himself, the One who was in the beginning with God and who is God (John 1:1). He is about to take on the agony of suffering for sin. And what does he do? He prays to his Father. And what does he pray? That this suffering might be taken away from him, that there be another way to remedy the sin problem.

Does this mean that the suffering of the cross was *merely and only* a contingency, that it was ultimately possible that it would not take place? Scripture is clear (Christ himself is clear) that the cross was

necessary for Christ (cf. Matt 26:54). How, then, can it even be meaningful for this same Christ—who knew what Scripture demanded,
who knew what his task of obedience to the Father entailed, who
knew before the foundation of the world what he must do, who even
planned the cross itself—to go to his Father and plead for another way?

It is meaningful in the same way that it is meaningful that Christ
himself has two distinct natures, which are unified (made compatible) in one person. The relationship of God and creation generally is
unique such that it is up to God to determine exactly *how* the two will
be related and brought together.

That is, the necessity that is God's alone is not negated or undermined when God determines to reveal his character through and by
various characteristics (such as wrath, grace, etc.) in order to relate
himself to creation. Or, to be more specific, just because God speaks to
Moses on Mount Horeb does not in any way negate that he is eternal
and therefore transcends temporal categories. He can remain eternal
even while he speaks to Moses. He can remain omnipresent and infinite even while he is located on Mount Horeb.

To put the matter more generally, God can and does remain who
he is essentially even while he freely relates himself to all of creation. He condescends to reveal himself to us without "violating" his
character.

AO: But wait a minute! You are trying to explain compatibility by
pointing to something that is ultimately inexplicable! You are asking
me to believe that aspects of God's character and of creation are compatible just because God made them compatible, even though I have
no categories of thought that allow me to see *how* these things can
be! Surely you don't expect a reasonable person to check his brain at
the door and just bow to the unreasonable as an explanation, do you?

CA: That is a very good question; it deserves a response. As you
might expect, my understanding of the world and of reality is quite
different from yours. That is one reason we are having this discussion.

Whenever questions of what is reasonable or unreasonable
arise—just like questions of what is compatible or incompatible—
they can only be answered according to larger questions of what the
world is like and how we might know what it is like. According to
Christianity, that which is reasonable is that which is consistent with
Christian truth. So, for example, Christians understand the world as it
is now to be *abnormal*, rather than normal, because of the entrance of
sin. That can be the case only if the "norm" for what the world should

be is given some place other than experience. Surely, given experience only, the world is "normally" a mixed up, and sometimes awful and horrible, place. But it was not created that way. The "measuring rod" for determining what the world is like is what God has said in Scripture. This is basic to Christianity.

AO: So now I suppose you are going to tell me that the "measuring rod" for determining what is rational or irrational is what God has said in Scripture. If that is what you think, it seems you have now thrown out any and every standard of thinking, including our typical laws of thought. This is nothing but utter irrationality. Now contradictions can be "normal," which means, of course, that they are not "normal," which is a contradiction. And on it goes.

CA: You've got it partly right. The "measuring rod" for determining what is rational is the revelation of God, including the word of God in Scripture. But this in no way destroys or eliminates our standard ways of thinking, any more than Scripture being the "measuring rod" for what exists destroys the existence of my laptop computer.

As the "measuring rod," Scripture sets the parameters within which we live and think. It does not destroy or essentially alter the world; it guides our understanding of it. I should say at this point that the only alternative to this scenario is that we assume we ourselves are able, in and of ourselves, either individually or as a group, to determine these things. Surely the history of thought has shown this to be highly suspect, at best.

Now, just as the ecumenical creeds have adequately expressed the biblical truth of the incarnation, so also have they expressed the biblical truth of the Trinity. For example, in the Athanasian Creed, the church has confessed the following: "This is what the catholic faith teaches: we worship one God in the Trinity and the Trinity in unity. Neither confounding the Persons, nor dividing the substance. For there is one person of the Father, another of the Son, another of the Holy Spirit. But the Father and the Son and the Holy Spirit have one divinity, equal glory, and coeternal majesty. What the Father is, the Son is, and the Holy Spirit is."

In other words, the church has historically confessed that God is one in essence and three in persons. Moreover, the church has also recognized that it is impossible fully to comprehend this. How can it be, one might ask, that each of the three persons can be fully and completely God—not partly God—and there not be three Gods? The answer given in Scripture and supported in Christian history is that Scripture will allow neither a diminishing of the three persons nor an addition to the one God. Both the threeness and the oneness are true.

Is this an irrational truth? It certainly is beyond our ability to understand it. We lack the intellectual tools to bring these truths together in what you might think is an "ordinary" way. But that simply points us to a standard beyond our own brains; it points us to God's character and his Word as our standard, even though his character is above our intellectual capacity to comprehend fully.

This should be no surprise, even to one who does not believe in God. If God exists, surely he would not be God if his creatures could fully comprehend his character (nor, if we could do such a thing, would we be creatures, for that matter).

This brings us back to the matter at hand. What you are seeking in your objection is an answer to the problem of evil, a problem that, as we have seen, has its focus on the incompatibility of certain properties of God and of evil. With respect to compatibility generally, however, we have already noted that there is no incompatibility between God being who he essentially is and his having a real, dynamic relationship with creation, including man. This he does quintessentially in the person of Christ.

And in the person of Christ, as we saw earlier, this unifying of the divine and human natures entails no essential property change in either nature. The divine remains fully divine, and the human remains fully human. There is no divinizing of the human, nor humanizing of the divine. Both natures remain what they are, but they are also unified, brought together, functioning in harmony, in the person of Christ. Christ was not schizophrenic. There is no indication that he struggled to hold his two natures in harmony. He simply operated, as the God-man, according to each nature in a way appropriate for each.

Now we need to discuss all of this within the context of your particular objection. In some answers to this objection, it is argued that God's omnipotence is not such that it can affect our choices. As a matter of fact, so it is said, the opposite is the case. We choose, and those choices form the initial basis and foundation for God's actions and reactions to us and our choices.

But this response has no warrant in Scripture. As some who hold this view admit, it is based on a particular understanding of free will, which itself has its source in certain experiences and common beliefs.[20] However, since the world is "abnormal," we need a more suitable guide as to which intuitions and common beliefs are legitimate and which are not. Common beliefs and experiences have to be seen through the lens of Scripture in order properly to be understood.

The reason why this notion of free will is brought into the discussion, however, is understandable. It has its roots in a number of related concepts and ideas with respect to God's character. God's foreknowledge and sovereignty are often thought to negate any notion of freedom, or contingency, including our responsibility in matters we choose.

Surely, some would say, if God is in any meaningful way in control of all things, or if he knew in eternity exactly what I would choose, can that choice be meaningfully free? What God knows in eternity *will* take place; it follows, some would say, that God's control must include his responsibility in what is controlled. So free choice and responsibility seem to be negated by the necessity of what God knows, or the direct action of God's sovereign control.

So let's frame the discussion in terms of the compatibility of necessity and contingency.

AO: Wait a minute. I have patiently listened to you work through your theological tenets, but now it looks like you are moving away from the IP objection. The IP objection sees a conflict, for example, between God's omniscience and, as you have presented it, Adam's responsible choice. How does that relate to the general categories of necessity and contingency and their compatibility or lack thereof?

CA: That is a very good question, and I hope to get to it soon. If you can bear with me just a little bit longer, I think you will see the connection.

Suppose, as the Christian tradition holds, God is *a se*. That is, he is, in and of himself, self-complete, lacking in nothing, and altogether absolutely independent. For God to be God, he must not be dependent on anything outside himself to be who he essentially is.

---

[20] To cite two examples: "Molinism is most properly viewed as the philosophical development of prephilosophical beliefs which are widely shared both within the Christian community and beyond it. . . . Far more common, at least in my experience, is the reaction that Molinism is but an elaboration of a view which they have held implicitly all along." Thomas P. Flint, *Divine Providence: The Molinist Account*, Cornell Studies in the Philosophy of Religion (Ithaca, NY: Cornell University Press, 1998), 76. And: "Free will theists of all types point to experience to support their belief in libertarian free will. That we act freely at least some of the time is a matter of intuition. Determinism is counterintuitive." Bruce A. Ware, ed., *Perspectives on the Doctrine of God: Four Views* (Nashville, TN: B&H Academic, 2008), 157. In fairness, Olson does argue that free will is taught in Scripture, but his examples point to texts that say God relents and repents. See Oliphint, *The Majesty of Mystery*, chap. 7.

If that is the case, it is also the case that when God freely creates the universe, he knows everything about that which he creates. There is nothing hidden from him; there is nothing that would or could take him by surprise. All that he creates, he exhaustively knows. As One who transcends time, he exhaustively knows the past, present, and future of everything that is.

Now, as Father, Son, and Holy Spirit, once this God creates, he also condescends to relate to his creation. To put it simply, he eternally "begins" to relate to creation once he creates, a relation that he did not have prior to his creating activity; God is now related and self-bound by something that did not previously exist. Not only so, but as he issues commands to his creation, he does so by virtue of his sovereign authority over what he has made. As Scripture says, he works *all things* according to the counsel of his own will (Eph. 1:11). There is nothing—*absolutely nothing*—outside of his meticulous and sovereign control.

Is it the case, then, that God's working "all things" is incompatible with the contingency and responsibility of our choices? Certainly not according to what Scripture tells us. According to Scripture, God knows and plans the end from the beginning (Isa. 46:10), but this in no way relieves his human creatures from the responsibility of their choices. In fact, when God declares his omniscience and omnipotence, it is that very declaration that should motivate us to listen to him (Isa. 46:12) and to heed his Word.

Or, to go back to our discussion of Jesus Christ as the second person of the Trinity, the God-man: did Jesus conclude that because he knew and planned the end from the beginning, the contingency and responsibility of prayer were thereby taken away? On the contrary, in the garden, he prayed in such agony that "his sweat became like great drops of blood" (Luke 22:44). He petitioned his Father "with loud cries and tears, to him who was able to save him from death" (Heb. 5:7).

Was the Father really *able* to save him from death? Didn't his eternal decree, his omniscience, and omnipotence negate his *ability* to save his Son? No, it didn't; not according to Scripture. He remained able to do it, but he was not willing. Indeed, it was the will of his Father to crush him (Isa. 53:10). And he was willing to do that because he knew that there was only one way to destroy and eradicate the horrendous sin and evil that we had foisted upon his good creation. In order to solve the problem of evil, the One who was himself God had to take on that evil and bring it with him to the grave (2 Cor. 5:21). The only way to conquer the evil that we brought into the world was for God himself to destroy it by dying.

AO: So let me get this straight. Are you trying to tell me that the perceived incompatibility between the existence of (a wholly good, omniscient, and omnipotent) God and evil is simply a *perception* problem?

CA: In one sense, yes. It is *not* a perception problem in that clearly God and evil are not compatible. But it *is* a perception problem in that the problem itself forces us to see the world, and God's participation in it, according to how God describes it, rather than how we might construe it ourselves.

You see, as long as you insist on viewing the world according to your own principles, you will never understand the world that you think you know. The only way properly to see yourself, the world, or anything else is through the spectacles of Scripture. Because Christians view the world through those spectacles, the issue of compatibility—whether of God's triunity, or of the incarnation, or of his decree and our responsibility, or many other things—has to be seen in light of the incomprehensible mystery that just is God himself.

AO: So what you are telling me is that the incompatibility that I perceive is due to my refusal to accept God at his Word. Can't you see that this response is only true if Christianity is true, and it in no way offers me, an atheist, a satisfactory answer?

CA: I do see that. But you need to remember two things. First, you asked me how I can affirm compatibility between the existence of God and evil. I have told you how I can do that. You have not asked me, nor could you, how *on an atheistic basis* I can affirm the two. On an atheistic basis, there is no such problem because you think there is no God. I know God exists, and so my answer has to have access to exactly how I know that.

Second, you are right that on an atheistic basis this answer is not satisfactory. But there are no satisfactory answers to any of these questions on an atheistic basis. Atheism is an illusion, an attempt to suppress what is patently obvious. How, then, could an illusion provide a real, concrete answer to the problems and questions that surface in the real world? That, you see, is the true incompatibility. An illusory belief will never be made compatible with the real world; it cannot make sense of it. The two simply cannot be made to go together.

AO: Well, much as I disagree, you have given me much to ponder. I hope we can renew our discussion at a later point.

As one can readily see, conversations such as this one could go in a number of directions, and the way this one went was only one possibility. However, what can also be seen in this conversation is that the principles of Christianity are powerfully and persuasively able to address the problem without in any way compromising the truths of a covenantal approach to a Christian defense. Specifically, that the problem of evil can so readily and easily move the conversation in the direction of the *gospel* is unique to this approach.

We will not be content merely to point out generic aspects of God and of our choices in order to show a *possible* compatibility. Rather, having (negatively) dismantled the (presumed) strength of the objection, we can then (positively) challenge the very root of the problem itself, which is the objector's presumed autonomy, and his notion of compatibility that is built upon that presumption. Our aim is to highlight his need to remove his self-made and rebellious spectacles and, positively, to put on the spectacles of Scripture by entrusting himself to him who knew no sin, but who became sin for us, that in him we might become the righteousness of God (2 Cor. 5:21).

'Tis mystery all: th'Immortal dies:
Who can explore His strange design?
In vain the firstborn seraph tries
To sound the depths of love divine.
'Tis mercy all! Let earth adore,
Let angel minds inquire no more.
'Tis mercy all! Let earth adore;
Let angel minds inquire no more.[21]

---

[21] Charles Wesley, "And Can It Be," 1738.

6

Walk in Wisdom
toward Outsiders

But the theory of evolution, which presently serves as explanation, is equally antithetical to Scripture. Just as the natural sciences attempt to infer the animate from the inanimate, the organic from the inorganic, human beings from the animal world, the conscious from the unconscious, the higher from the lower, so also the science of religion of modern times seeks to explain religion in terms of an earlier areligious state of affairs and pure religion from the primitive forms of fetishism, animism, ancestor worship, etc. Earlier in this volume we have already sufficiently explained and refuted this theory of the origin of religion.[1]

The Wisdom of Persuasion

In chapter 4 we discussed the mode of persuasion as the preferred, biblical tactic in a covenantal apologetic, a tactic that wisely discerns the *pathos* of our audience.

The theological reasons for preferring that mode relate to the ten tenets, but have their particular focus in the theological *trivium*: (1) the *principial* status of Scripture, (2) the knowledge of God that all people possess (i.e., the *sensus divinitatis*), and (3) God's universal mercy toward all people, even those who are and remain in Adam. With these tenets and the *trivium* as the background, persuasion is the most biblical way to think about and proceed in a covenantal

[1] Herman Bavinck, *Reformed Dogmatics*, vol. 1, *Prolegomena*, ed. John Bolt, trans. John Vriend (Grand Rapids: Baker Academic, 2003), 316.

defense of Christianity. But persuasion, in and of itself, can be danger-ous; it can be dangerous if it is ever divorced from its proper biblical and theological roots.

The apostle Paul wrote his letter to the church at Colossae so that the people there might hold fast and firm to their conviction of the centrality of Christ (cf. Col. 1:23; 2:3, 6; 4:12), and so that they might be quick to avoid any kind of false philosophy (2:8). It is clear that one of Paul's primary reasons for writing to this church was itself *apolo-getic*. Paul, who had not yet visited this church (2:1), was concerned for the false teaching that was making inroads into it. In his apostolic encouragement to them, therefore, he lifts up the supremacy of Christ (cf. 1:15–20) and warns them not to be "taken captive" by philosophy and empty deceit (2:8).

This entire epistle could be studied with great profit, especially when considered, in the main, a defense of Christianity against false teaching and false philosophy. In the interest of time and space, how-ever, we will focus on a couple of key points in Paul's address to the Colossians, points that will help us focus on the apologetic task at hand in this chapter.

First, in Colossians 2:1–4, Paul reiterates again the supremacy of Christ (as he has done in 1:15–20). He wants the Colossian Christians to know the reason he struggles so for them (and for the church in nearby Laodicea). In this struggle, Paul has as his goal that "their hearts may be encouraged, being knit together in love, to reach all the riches of full assurance of understanding and the knowledge of God's mystery, which is Christ, *in whom are hidden all the treasures of wisdom and knowledge*" (2:1–3).

The depth of what Paul is saying here is almost inexhaustible. But notice that he wants his readers to have as their central focus "the knowledge of God's mystery, which is Christ." His desire for them, in the face of the false teaching and philosophy that had apparently permeated this church, is that they recognize the supremacy, reality, and centrality of who Christ is and what he has done. Paul then ex-plicitly tells the Colossians why he wants to encourage them in this way: "I say this in order that no one may delude you with plausible arguments" (2:4).

Whatever false philosophy was having its way with some in the church there, it apparently had its own persuasive force. Paul's word here, translated "plausible arguments" (*pithanologia*), is used only here in the New Testament and is a word used by Plato to indicate *persuasive*, as over against logically demonstrative, arguments. In other words, as we have already seen with Paul's relationship to the Corinthian church, this church in Colossae apparently was being duped by the persuasive speech of false teachers. Paul's solution for them is as profound as it is simple, and it is a solution that is true in any and every situation for the Christian. We are to be taken captive *only* to a philosophy that is "according to Christ."

I remember when our children would reach a certain age, they would sometimes allude to the fact that since we as their parents were so far removed (in time) from their own experiences, we simply could not have any idea what they were actually experiencing. Twenty to thirty years removed constituted, for them, a total ignorance of their own struggles.

It seems to me that we sometimes think that way about Scripture. Sure, we might imagine that Paul had to battle problems; he had to defend the Christian faith. But our experiences, now some two thousand years later, are so far removed from Paul's that his admonitions in Scripture could not directly apply to *us*. After all, Paul could not have understood the struggles that *we* go through.

But this attitude betrays a misunderstanding. While *specific* details and circumstances between our struggles and Paul's will be different, the fact remains that the *categories* of sin that Paul was combating are exactly the same as those we are meant to fight today. Paul wouldn't have envisioned the Internet, but that in no way diminishes the need for him to warn the churches over and over again about the deadly dangers of sexual immorality.

So also in this passage in Colossians. Paul could not have known the details of, say, neo-Kantian philosophy or Sartrean existentialism. But that in no way detracts from Paul's admonition in Colossians. The false philosophy in Colossae had its own details. It seems to have involved both Greek and Jewish components. Nonetheless, it was a philosophy that was "according to human tradition, according to the elemental spirits of the world, and not according to Christ" (2:8).

You do not have to be "in the moment" to understand how spiritually deadly any given "moment" can be, whether the "moment" is false teaching in Paul's day or false teaching today. For all its myriad permutations, sin remains fundamentally the same across the ages. It remains rebellion against the triune God. And its only solution is to turn to Christ, taking every thought captive to his obedience. In him *alone*, says Paul, are hidden *all the treasures of wisdom and knowledge*. That was true then; it is true now.

Whatever the nature of the "philosophy" that was plaguing the pilgrims in Colossae, the solution was to be taken captive to the philosophy that is according to Christ and to renounce any philosophy that is according to human tradition.

With this background, we can see why Paul concludes his letter as he does, and this conclusion has to be stamped across any covenantal (persuasive) attempt to defend the Christian faith: "Walk in wisdom toward outsiders, making the best use of the time. Let your speech always be gracious, seasoned with salt, so that you may know how you ought to answer each person" (4:5–6). Since Christ is the One in whom are hidden all the treasures of knowledge and wisdom, our responsibility as Christians is to "walk" in that wisdom when we are dealing with those who are "outside" of Christ. We could, with profit, spend the rest of the chapter on this verse, but we can only highlight three points here.

First, "wisdom" in Scripture is the application of biblical truth to a particular situation. To put it in terms of our *trivium* of persuasion, wisdom is the accurate (*ethos*) assessment of the *pathos* in order persuasively to offer the *logos*. What Paul is saying here is that our responsibility toward outsiders is to be wise in what we say to them; to say to them those truths that will most accurately and appropriately address the actual problems and needs with which we are confronted.

This wisdom, we should reiterate, is the opposite of trusting in our own abilities and oratory. As Proverbs, that great book of wisdom, reminds us,

> Whoever trusts in his own mind is a fool,
>> but he who walks in wisdom will be delivered. (Prov. 28:26)

The false teachers in Colossae were encouraging Christians to trust in their own minds, in human tradition. But whoever trusts his own mind is a fool; our trust, and thus our wisdom, is rooted in Christ alone.

Second, in "walking" wisely, says Paul, we are "making the best use of the time." It is difficult to know precisely what Paul means by this; the words he uses can be understood (and translated) in different ways. Apparently, he has in mind the proper *use* of wisdom as we speak with those who are outside of Christ. If we conduct ourselves wisely when we are engaged with those who do not believe, then we will inevitably get to the heart of the problem, a problem which has its focus in the rebellion that characterizes the "outsiders."

Part of what it means to be "wise," in other words, is to "redeem the time," to use the time we have with "outsiders" in a way that both addresses their issues and focuses the solution on Christ. It is not wise or appropriate, therefore, simply to approach every situation with some kind of premade apologetic "template" that is set in stone and to attempt to make that template fit every *pathos*.

To put this in the context of our previous emphasis on persuasion, would we be making the most of the time if we determined, in any and all apologetic situations, to discuss the fact that God is the first cause? Or the ultimate designer? Or the only necessary being? It wouldn't seem that such responses are, in every case, a proper use of our "outsider" occasions. Instead, when wisdom dictates our discussions, we understand the *pathos* in order to communicate more persuasively the *logos* (assuming, of course, that the *ethos* of holiness is operating as well).

Notice, thirdly, that Paul moves to the character of our *logos* (this is the word Paul actually uses here, translated "speech"). Our *logos* is to be both gracious and seasoned with salt. What Paul means, according to one commentator, is this:

> Paul is calling on Christians to speak with their unbelieving neighbors and friends with gracious, warm, and winsome words—all with the purpose of being able to "answer" unbelievers. . . . An appropriate Christian response will, of course, communicate the content of the gospel, but it will also be done in a manner that will make the gospel

attractive. Peter makes a similar point: "Always be prepared to give an answer to everyone who asks you to give the reason for the hope that you have. But do this with gentleness and respect" (1 Pet. 3:15b).[2]

In other words, merging together what God has said through Paul and Peter in these two passages, we are, in our apologetic encounters, to respond with wisdom in such a way that our speech is gracious and persuasive (winsome) as we treat those to whom we speak with gentleness and respect.

This is a tall order; it is perhaps the tallest orders of all the orders that can be given in apologetics. Only the Spirit of Christ can produce such things. In and of ourselves, we are not able to respond with wisdom, grace, gentleness, and respect to those who challenge us. But God will not command what he does not provide, so we trust him to instill in us those qualities necessary for a biblical, covenantal defense of the faith that he has graciously given to us. Again, according to the wisdom of Proverbs,

> With patience a ruler may be persuaded,
>   and a soft tongue will break a bone. (Prov. 25:15)

To respond in wisdom, then, means to respond with a view toward the *pathos*, understanding the *ethos* and *logos* to be firmly set in place.

The Spirit of Persuasion

Before we move to a sample dialog, one more biblical and theological point is necessary to remember. It is useful to think about the task of defending the faith as a task of "premeditated evangelism." It is *evangelism* in that our goal is a defense of, and thus a communication of, the *Christian* faith. That point should be clear by now. It is also *premeditated* in that our defense includes our own thinking and analysis of the implications of our Christian faith to situations, problems, attacks, and objections that might come our way.

But since no one can be argued into heaven, could it be that to spend our time thinking through or working on arguments—actually

---

[2]Douglas J. Moo, *The Letters to the Colossians and to Philemon*, The Pillar New Testament Commentary (Grand Rapids: Eerdmans, 2008), 331.

meditating on possible Christian responses—is a fruitless endeavor?[3] Could it be that Jesus himself discouraged us from spending thought-time on what we should say in the face of objections and challenges to our faith?

> But before all this they will lay their hands on you and persecute you, delivering you up to the synagogues and prisons, and you will be brought before kings and governors for my name's sake. This will be your opportunity to bear witness. Settle it therefore in your minds not to meditate beforehand how to answer, for I will give you a mouth and wisdom, which none of your adversaries will be able to withstand or contradict. (Luke 21:12–15)

This passage (and related passages in Matthew and Mark) seems to discourage any preparation for or concern about defending our faith. The Greek word Luke uses for the phrase "how to answer" is from the verb *apologeomai*, from which we get our word *apologetics*. It looks as though Christ is telling us not to think about, or thoughtfully prepare for, the apologetic task. Is Jesus commanding his disciples *not* to be ready to defend their faith? Is he telling them that they need not prepare for challenges to the faith that will come their way? Because this passage is easily misunderstood, we will highlight three aspects of the ministry of the Holy Spirit in the context of the apologetic task.

First, it is important to see what Christ is *not* saying in this passage. He is not saying that the disciples, or we, should neglect to prepare ourselves at all for a confrontation with those who oppose him. The integrity of Scripture will not allow for such an interpretation. If Christ were saying that, then Peter would be explicitly contradicting him when Peter commands us to prepare ourselves to give an answer. Surely Peter in his epistle would not contradict what he heard his Master, Jesus Christ, tell him. Since it is the same Spirit that inspired these and all texts of Scripture, the option of "contradictory texts" is not open to any Christian.

To be sure, we are not to take a laissez-faire attitude to the confrontations that might come to us, but neither are we to be anxious or

---

[3]The material in this section is a modified and edited version of "Apologetics and the Holy Spirit," in K. Scott Oliphint, *The Battle Belongs to the Lord* (Phillipsburg, NJ: P&R, 2003), 179–94. See that chapter for a more complete explanation.

to fear in the way that the world fears when objections come. Instead, as we have already discussed (1 Pet. 3:15), we are to set Christ apart as Lord. Just as Christ commands his disciples not to worry, but to trust, so Peter commands us not to fear, but to sanctify the lordship of Christ in our hearts.

The second aspect of the Spirit's ministry is what we might call his work of *synergy* (working with). The Spirit works with Christ's Word, the Bible. This is the work that the Spirit does as he speaks in and through the Word itself. This is one of those truths that could easily revolutionize our practice of apologetics, of preaching, and of evangelism. The best expression of this work of the Spirit comes from chapter 1 of the Westminster Confession of Faith, section 10:

> The supreme judge by which all controversies of religion are to be determined, and all decrees of councils, opinions of ancient writers, doctrines of men, and private spirits, are to be examined, and in whose sentence we are to rest, can be no other but the Holy Spirit speaking in the Scripture.

This last phrase, "the Holy Spirit speaking in the Scripture," is worth remembering; we have alluded to it already. It emphasizes for us this truth: we should never think that God the Holy Spirit works independently of the truth of God's Word or that the Word goes out *without* the Spirit.

For example, it is often said among well-meaning Christians that "the Lord told them" what they must do or say, or how they must act. We need to understand that with the finished work of Christ came the finished work of Christ's Word (see Heb. 1:1–4). God the Holy Spirit does not speak audibly to people, even to *his* people, apart from the word of Christ in the Bible. Hebrews does remind us that, in days gone by, God spoke through his appointed representatives—that is, "by the prophets." But he has ceased speaking in that way.

In these last days, Hebrews says, he has spoken to us in his Son. The completion of the Son's work marks the completion of the Son's Word as well. But that does not mean that his Word is dead. Part of the Spirit's ministry in glorifying Christ (John 16:14) is to speak by and with Christ's own Word, the Bible.

By the same token, we should avoid thinking of God's Word as simply a text without a living and active testimony; God's Word *is* living and active; it is sharper than any two-edged sword in that it cuts deeply (Heb. 4:12). We should see the words of Scripture as alive; they are the words of a living God who is speaking to us *now* through them. Viewed in that way, our study of Scripture could never be a simple matter of gathering facts.

The Bible is God's completed "conversation" with us about who he is and what he has done in and through his Son. As the hymn writer puts it, "What more can he say than to you he has said?"[4] He has said all he needs to say in his Word. With the Spirit speaking in that Word, it is never a dead letter, but is life itself. "The highest proof of Scripture," according to John Calvin, "derives in general from the fact that God in person speaks in it."[5]

The third aspect of the Spirit's ministry is his work of testimony. I remember talking to a young man about the gospel one day. As I talked, he affirmed all that I said. He believed that Christ had come, had died on the cross for sins, and had risen again. He believed that he had sinned and that he could not get to heaven on his own. Toward the end of this discussion, he turned to me and said, "Yes, I believe all this, but so what?"

It is not enough simply to believe that Christ came, died on the cross for sins, and so forth. We must believe *into* Christ; we must trust him. To believe that Christ came and all the rest is to believe that certain statements are true. It's like believing that my wife will not poison me at supper tonight. But to believe *into* my wife would be to eat the dinner that she prepared. To believe into people means to put our very lives into their hands, to act in a way that betrays a fundamental trust. It means to follow their instructions, to trust that what they say and are doing is needful and not harmful to us.

The only way to move from "believing that" to "believing into" is by the testimony of the Holy Spirit. The Spirit's speaking in Scripture is

---

[4] From "How Firm a Foundation," John Rippon, *Selection of Hymns*, 1787; the full stanza is:
How firm a foundation, ye saints of the Lord,
Is laid for your faith in His excellent Word!
What more can He say than to you He hath said,
You, who unto Jesus for refuge have fled?
[5] John Calvin, *Institutes of the Christian Religion*, ed. John T. McNeill, trans. Ford Lewis Battles, 2 vols., The Library of Christian Classics (Philadelphia: Westminster Press, 1960), 1.7.4.

crucial. It is a necessary corollary to the inspired ("God-breathed"—2 Tim. 3:16) word of God as it brings together the authority of God's Word with the Holy Spirit's activity in the world. But the Spirit's speaking by and with the Word will not, in and of itself, change a sinful heart. Sinful hearts need supernatural work. That work is the testimony of the Holy Spirit *in us*.

The testimony of the Holy Spirit answers the "so what?" question. It assures me that *I* am in desperate need of a Savior, that the death of Christ on the cross was for *my* sins, that the most important thing in my life is to glorify and please God, that I am his child and he will never leave me or forsake me, and so on.

Without the testimony of the Spirit, I may agree to the great truths of the gospel; I may believe that they are true, but I will not—I cannot—believe in them. I will not put my life into the everlasting arms of Christ unless his Spirit testifies to and in me, changing my heart, so that my love for Christ overshadows everything else. The "so what?" question will be answered only if and when the Spirit testifies in me to the truth of the word of God.

The testimony of the Spirit gives us an assurance, a *certainty*, that can only come from above. It gives us an assurance that God is for us and that, therefore, no one can ultimately stand against us (Rom. 8:31). It tells us that we are children of God (see Rom. 8:15–16). Again, according to John Calvin:

> If we desire to provide in the best way for our consciences—that they may not be perpetually beset by the instability of doubt or vacillation, and that they may not also boggle at the smallest quibbles—we ought to seek our conviction in a higher place than human reasons, judgments, or conjectures, that is, in the secret testimony of the Spirit.[6]

So, back to our original question, how should we understand Jesus's words in Luke 21? We should notice three things about this passage.

First, the kind of situation that Jesus describes is apologetic in nature; it envisions a *defense*. "There will come a time," Jesus tells his disciples in effect, "when you will have opportunity to bear witness

---

[6] Calvin, *Institutes*, 1.7.4.

of me. You will be brought before the authorities because of your Christian faith."

This situation is likely foreign to most of us. The ruling authorities, at least in most of the West, have not made Christianity illegal (yet). But it was not foreign to the first- and second-century Christians. One of the first apologists of the second century, Justin Martyr, was called on to defend his faith, and the faith of his brothers and sisters in Christ, in the presence of the emperor. He knew what it meant to be brought before the governing authorities because of faith in Christ. And he knew that he might lose his life as he sought to commend the faith to the emperor.[7]

While we may not, in our lifetime, be called before the rulers, the same principles hold. Whenever we are challenged or our faith is questioned, we are in an apologetic situation. It is time, at that point, to defend and commend the faith.

Second, Jesus's command "not to meditate beforehand" (Luke 21:14) may at first seem to run counter to other passages we have seen. Why would Peter command us always to "be ready" in the context of Jesus's telling Peter and his other disciples "not to meditate beforehand" about the coming challenges? How does this comport with apologetics as *premeditated* evangelism?

We should notice, first of all, that the parallel passages in both Matthew and Mark use a different verb than Luke does. They use the verb not to "be anxious" (Matt. 10:19) or not to "be anxious beforehand" (Mark 13:11). Because these three Gospels are written in part to give us different perspectives on the same events, Matthew and Mark can help us understand Jesus's concern for his disciples. Jesus is telling them that they are not to be anxious or to worry about the various rules, laws, and customs that might cause a conflict with their Christian testimonies. He is telling them that they won't need to be legal experts or be familiar with every jot and tittle of Roman customs in order to defend their Christian faith. They are not to fear or be anxious because of what the government authorities will charge.

Jesus is teaching them something that every Christian must learn. He is telling them, as Paul later reminded the Philippians, that they

---

[7] For a more extended discussion of Justin's *Apology*, see William Edgar and K. Scott Oliphint, eds., *Christian Apologetics Past and Present: A Primary Source Reader*, vol. 1, *To 1500* (Wheaton, IL: Crossway, 2009), 35–64.

were to be anxious for nothing (Phil. 4:6). Anxiety is a heart confessing that Christ is not Lord. To be worrisome is to think that we are ultimately in control, that we can alter our own circumstances, ultimately, by our own power.

The disciples are not to think this way. Jesus knows the kind of suffering that they will be called on to endure. He knows that the Christian road will be rocky and ultimately deadly for them. He knows that they will suffer martyrdom for their faith (see, for example, Matt. 20:23; Mark 10:39). To be worried about how their Christian faith will fare in a hostile world would take their minds off of the task at hand. It would distract them from the defense of and preaching of the gospel. Worse still, it would betray a heart that is not resting in Christ and his authority (Matt. 28:18–20).

But Luke's account of Jesus's warning does not say "do not worry"; it says "do not meditate beforehand." Why the different wording? Given Matthew's and Mark's account, what Jesus is saying (in Luke's account) is that the disciples are not to set their minds on how they might respond when the challenges come from the governing authorities. Matthew Henry's explanation of Luke 21:14 is worth noting here. He rightly understands Jesus to be saying something like this:

> Instead of setting your hearts on work to contrive an answer to informations, indictments, articles, accusations, and interrogatories, that will be exhibited against you in the ecclesiastical and civil courts, on the contrary, settle it in your hearts, impress it upon them, take pains with them to persuade them not to meditate before what you shall answer; do not depend upon your own wit and ingenuity, your own prudence and policy, and do not distrust or despair of the immediate and extraordinary aids of the divine grace. Think not to bring yourselves off in the cause of Christ as you would in a cause of your own, by your own parts and application, with the common assistance of divine Providence, but promise yourselves, for I promise you, the special assistance of divine grace: I will give you a mouth and wisdom.[8]

It is this last statement that helps us see Christ's focus in this warning. If Jesus were *only* telling them not to meditate beforehand

---

[8]See Matthew Henry, *Matthew Henry's Commentary on the Whole Bible: Complete and Unabridged in One Volume* (Peabody, MA: Hendrickson, 1996), Luke 21:15–19.

on what they would say, it might be possible to read it as a universal prohibition—a warning against meditating beforehand on anything and everything. Instead, the import of what Jesus is telling his disciples is that, in the face of opposition, they must trust him—his authority, his Spirit, his grace—and not themselves.

Third, in all three accounts—Matthew, Mark, and Luke—the negative is followed by a positive. Jesus tells them not to worry, not to meditate beforehand, and then he tells them how to respond positively instead. The positive helps explain the negative prohibition. In Luke, the positive statement is "for I will give you a mouth and wisdom, which none of your adversaries will be able to withstand or contradict." In Matthew (Mark is basically the same), we read, "for what you are to say will be given to you in that hour. For it is not you who speak, but the Spirit of your Father speaking through you" (Matt. 10:19–20; cf. Mark 13:11–12).

These positive statements help us see what is meant in the negative statements. In all three cases, what Jesus wants to emphasize is what *he*, through the Holy Spirit, will give. This is where the Spirit's ministry, which we discussed above, is so crucial. The focus of Jesus's concern for his disciples is that they learn to rely on what the Spirit of Christ gives them when they are challenged. And what is it that the Holy Spirit gives? According to Jesus, he will give them "all the truth" (John 16:13).

When they are challenged, therefore, the disciples of Jesus Christ are to speak with mouths led by the Spirit of Christ and the wisdom that he alone gives at the time of the challenges they will face. What is required in situations like this is that Christ's disciples know the truth, that they understand the wisdom that comes from above, that they use the very "speech" (*logos*) or truth of God, as given in his Word.

To put it into our context, Jesus's instruction, as a matter of fact, is the opposite of what it is sometimes thought to be. Rather than telling us not to prepare for the challenges to come, he is saying that we must be ready with the wisdom that is given from above. We must be ready, in other words, with the truth of Scripture when our faith is challenged. Our hearts must be biblically prepared for such challenges (*ethos*) as we set our minds on his sovereign lordship in the midst of it all.

Our preparation, then, is not in focusing on every challenge that might come to us, as if we had the time and competence to learn enough about all of them to answer them adequately. Rather, it is to focus on that which is given by God, "breathed out" by him, and therefore is always and everywhere and for every person "profitable for teaching, for reproof, for correction, and for training in righteousness" (2 Tim. 3:16).

As we have said, it is true that no one can be argued into the kingdom. But it is also true, in the Lord's wise plan, that no one will come to faith in Christ without hearing about that faith (Rom. 10:17). As we defend the Christian faith and commend it to others, the Spirit promises to use us and to give us wisdom and knowledge. What a privilege we have in Christ to be agents of the Spirit himself as he glorifies the Son.

What I propose to do in the remainder of this chapter, and much of the next, is to take some specific examples of attacks against Christianity and to show how one *could* go about addressing those attacks.

I need to reiterate what I have been at pains to make clear. The fictional discussions below are simply *one way*—perhaps not even the best way, certainly not the only way—to respond to some specific attacks. Our hope is to respond in wisdom, with graceful and persuasive speech. But it will be obvious, as we have already seen, that such discussions could move in many directions that ours does not, and that responses also could vary from person to person, situation to situation, and point to point. What I do hope to show is that there is *a way* in a covenantal apologetic to address these specific challenges. Thus, at minimum, these discussions should provide some concrete examples of just how the principles we have been looking at throughout our study can actually be applied to real objections and attacks that might come our way.

The remainder of this chapter examines a current, common objection and attack on Christian faith. In the final chapter, we hope to be able to see how one might respond to unbelieving *religion* in the context of a covenantal defense of Christianity.

Dennett, Dawkins, and Doubt

With these two biblical applications in mind—the necessity of wisdom as the biblical avenue for persuasion, and the Holy Spirit's work, by and with the Word, as the ultimate persuader—we will attempt to set out an apologetic, a covenantal defense, to a fairly common attack or two on the Christian faith.

Perhaps most threatening to some in our current day is the predominance, even near-reverence, given to scientific knowledge and "dogma." This is a distinctly modern phenomenon, in that science itself, as we know, was birthed in the cradle of Christianity.[9] But it is a phenomenon that is front and center in our culture and in academia today, so it is likely one with which many Christians have struggled.

In most apologetic discussions about science, the topic of evolution is the primary challenge. That topic is so big that one book, even a small series of books, cannot do it justice. We cannot do it justice here; nor can we do justice to the overall "science versus Christianity" discussion in such a short space. What I propose to do, then, is very modest and simple, but is, I hope, helpful (even if minimally) as a *beginning point* in thinking about this particular challenge. This beginning point will not make use of the *evolutionary* debates and facts that swirl in the almost infinite regions of scientific discussion. Exploring this more fully would, of course, be a worthwhile project for those called and capable of doing such things.

Since our interest here is in a basic biblical apologetic response, we will focus on the biblical and theological data that can be useful in these kinds of discussions. We will hope to see, then, that one who is biblically literate and who engages in a little "premeditation" can, without being an expert in science, offer a *persuasive* (covenantal) defense of Christianity. All that is needed, then, for a discussion like this is the Bible and a little prayerful premeditation.

Let's first consider what we know of any scientific theory that proposes to eliminate God. We will assume that the more general principles already discussed in this book are firmly in place. For example,

---

[9] There are numerous works to consult in this regard. For a more complete analysis of the relationship of Christianity to science, see Vern Sheridan Poythress, *Redeeming Science: A God-Centered Approach* (Wheaton, IL: Crossway, 2006).

we know that any scientific theory that proposes to be atheistic is false and cannot give proper account of itself; the seeds of self-destruction are resident in any such theory.[10] We also know that we cannot simply place ourselves on some supposedly neutral "evidential" ground in order to discuss scientific objections and challenges to Christianity. What is "rational" and what is "evidential" depend, first of all, as we have seen, on where one presumes to stand to make such objections and challenges.

But what can we say, more specifically, with respect to evolutionary theories that propose to deal with the origin of man? The first thing we recognize is that no human being was there when the world and man were created. This may seem too obvious to point out, but it has significant implications for any evolutionary theory of origins. The second thing we can affirm is that no "missing link" between animals and human beings has been found, nor could it be.[11] This, of course, is what it means, in part at least, that God created man (male and female) in a special way, and not through some macroevolutionary means.[12]

Given these truths, what might we say to those who want to contend for an atheistic evolutionary theory of origins? Let's take two primary exponents of such a theory and see what we might initially be able to say in response.[13]

In his influential book *The Blind Watchmaker*, Richard Dawkins takes Paley's analogy (i.e., "watch implies watchmaker," as found in Paley's work *Natural Theology*) and argues, against Paley, that whatever it is that produces design in our universe cannot be a grand designer, but is, in fact, a blind force, a "blind watchmaker." That is, the design apparent in our world has no intrinsic purpose; it only functions ac-

---

[10] Recall tenets 7 and 9.

[11] As Van Til notes: "We are certain, as certain as our conviction of the truth of the entire Christian position, that certain 'facts' will never be discovered. One of these, for example, is 'the missing link.' The term 'missing link' we take in its current meaning of a gradual transition from the non-rational to the rational. As such, it is an anti-Christian conception, inasmuch as it implies that the non-rational is more ultimate than the rational." Cornelius Van Til, *A Survey of Christian Epistemology* (Nutley, NJ: Presbyterian and Reformed, 1969), 7.

[12] I recognize that this topic is a matter of debate in many Christian circles at present, and it is worthy of response. At this point, however, we are dealing with the more general problem of Christianity versus atheistic evolution. For a most helpful discussion of the necessity of the special creation of Adam, as well as his historicity, see J. P. Versteeg, *Adam in the New Testament: Mere Teaching Model or First Historical Man?*, 2nd ed., trans. Richard B. Gaffin Jr. (Phillipsburg, NJ: P&R, 2012).

[13] Just to reiterate, the responses I will give will be initial, and there is no doubt that rejoinders have and can come to these responses. My goal here, however, is to provide a *persuasive* response that would challenge the self-deception of the theories concerned.

cording to the latent properties of nature itself. It does not and cannot point to some ultimate designer.

Daniel Dennett in like fashion argues in *Darwin's Dangerous Idea* that the "dangerous idea" we glean from Darwin is that the complexity of design in the world is itself dependent on

> blind chance—coin flips, if you like—and on nothing else. No matter how impressive the products . . . , the underlying process always consists of nothing but a set of individually mindless steps succeeding each other without the help of any intelligent supervision; they are "automatic" by definition: the workings of an automaton.[14]

Not only so, but Dennett takes Darwin's dangerous idea and makes his own argument personal: "To put it bluntly but fairly, anyone today who *doubts* that the variety of life on this planet was produced by a process of evolution is simply ignorant—inexcusably ignorant, in a world where three out of four people have learned to read and write."[15]

Dawkins, as well, is not content to keep his scientific opinions within the cool confines of his laboratory; he slips them on his hands and jumps into the boxing ring: "It is absolutely safe to say that if you meet someone who claims not to believe in evolution, that person is ignorant, stupid or insane (or wicked, but I'd rather not consider that)."[16]

Without needing to immerse ourselves in a detailed *scientific* discussion of these proponents of blindness and danger, we can begin by highlighting that in the process of their discussion, both Dawkins and Dennett argue for the *plausibility* of their evolutionary thesis. This will be a significant point in our response, but we'll tend to that in a minute.

There is another aspect of Dennett's argument that is worth addressing, especially given its polemic and confrontational tone. In order to address it, we will need to quote him at some length. So, in

---

[14] Daniel Clement Dennett, *Darwin's Dangerous Idea: Evolution and the Meanings of Life* (New York: Simon & Schuster, 1995), 59. We should note here that Dennett attributes complexity and design to what he calls an "algorithm." The details of that, however, are not necessary for us to elaborate at this point.

[15] Dennett, *Darwin's Dangerous Idea*, 46, my emphasis. The notion of "doubt" will play a key apologetic role in our defense below.

[16] Richard Dawkins, review of *Blueprints: Solving the Mystery of Evolution*, by Maitland A. Edey and Donald C. Johanson (Boston: Little, Brown, 1989), *New York Times*, April 9, 1989, quoted in Plantinga, *Where the Conflict Really Lies: Science, Religion, and Naturalism* (New York: Oxford University Press, 2011), 33.

order to respond to him, let's suppose that you are a Christian (who is not a scientist) and are somehow confronted—in a book, in the classroom, by a relative—with these atheistic evolutionary ideas about origins. How might your response initially proceed? Let's move into our now-familiar dialog mode, this time between Daniel Dennett (DD) and a covenantal apologist (CA), and see one (*possible*) way to respond.[17]

A quick word of caution before we begin. Some of the criticisms I will offer in the dialog below will require some thought. Because we're just jumping into this, you may not have had sufficient opportunity for "premeditation." So after I offer a critique, I will give a bit of explanation in order to explain where and how premeditation was useful in these discussions.

Our goal in the critique is to highlight the "big issues" that motivate Dennett and Dawkins and not to get bogged down in the scientific and philosophic detail. We'll move selectively through the relevant section:

> DD: "The philosopher Ronald de Sousa once memorably described philosophical theology as 'intellectual tennis without a net,' and I readily allow that I have indeed been assuming without comment or question up to now that the net of rational judgment was up. But we can lower it if you really want to. It's your serve. Whatever you serve, suppose I return service rudely as follows: 'What you say implies that God is a ham sandwich wrapped in tinfoil. That's not much of a God to worship!' If you then volley back, demanding to know how I can logically justify my claim that your serve has such a preposterous implication, I will reply: 'Oh, do you want the net up for my returns, but not for your serves? Either the net stays up, or it stays down. If the net is down, there are no rules and anybody can say anything. . . . I have been giving you the benefit of the assumption that you would not waste your own time or mine by playing with the net down.'
>
> "Now if you want to *reason* about faith, and offer a reasoned (and reason-responsive) defensive of faith as an extra category of belief worthy of special consideration, I'm eager to play. I certainly grant the existence of the phenomenon of faith; what I want to see is a reasoned ground for taking faith seriously *as a way of getting to the truth,*

---

[17]There is so much material to respond to in just Dennett's book that I can only hint at a response to *some* of what is said. The goal here is to eschew the technicalities and to try to get at the presuppositions that motivate the overall method.

and not, say, just as a way people comfort themselves and each other. . . . But you must not expect me to go along with your defense of faith as a path to truth if at any point you appeal to the very dispensation you are supposedly trying to justify. Before you appeal to faith when reason has you backed into a corner, think about whether you really want to abandon reason when reason is on your side. . . . We're seriously trying to get at the truth here, and if you think that this common but unspoken understanding about faith is anything better than socially useful obfuscation to avoid mutual embarrassment and loss of face, you have either seen much more deeply into this issue than any philosopher ever has (for none has ever come up with a good defense of this) or you are kidding yourself. (The ball is now in your court.)"[18]

CA: Thank you for your clarity. Let me say first that there is much of substance on which you and I can agree. Specifically, I too am seriously trying to get at the truth in this discussion. And I want to do that in a way that is eminently rational.

But you and I have an initial problem that must be addressed, and it is manifest in your illustration. In speaking of the "net" of rational judgment, you think that there are only two options. Either the net is up or the net is down. When the net is up, rational judgment is in play; when it is down, anything goes, including your postulation that God is a ham sandwich wrapped in tinfoil. To put the net down, you think, is to open the game up to such absurdities.

The problem, however, which you have not recognized is the problem of the *net itself*. The net that you propose to use for our verbal volley is not one that I myself am able to use in your game. I cannot use it, *not* because I am opposed to rational judgment, but because what you think is rational judgment is, in fact, a judgment that precludes my position. You have argued elsewhere that my religious commitment is a natural phenomenon.[19] So whatever the net of rational judgment is, it must include the fact that my commitment is simply more of your own naturalism.

For you, if I might continue the net analogy, though now as a fishing net (and quote one of your forebears, Sir Arthur Eddington), "What my net can't catch isn't fish." In other words, whatever does not fit with your notion of rationality is automatically excluded.

You are anxious to have the net up, as long as the net contains only those principles that you claim to be rational. But if that is the

---

[18] Dennett, *Darwin's Dangerous Idea*, 154–55.
[19] Daniel C. Dennett, *Breaking the Spell: Religion as a Natural Phenomenon* (New York: Penguin, 2007).

case, then surely the game is fixed from the beginning, isn't it? What *I* think is rational, because of my authority for thinking such things, is going to be substantially different from what *you* think is rational. So the options are not, as you imply in your net illustration, "either rational judgment or absurdity." Rather, we have to determine just how we think about rationality *itself*.

And this speaks to one of the criteria that you lay down for a *reasonable* faith. You say, "But you must not expect me to go along with your defense of faith as a path to truth if at any point you appeal to the very dispensation you are supposedly trying to justify."

Now, perhaps you can see that this is exactly what you have done in requiring that your net be used in our discussion. If I might apply your own criterion against you, you yourself have appealed to the very dispensation you are supposedly trying to justify. You have appealed to a net that defines the "rational" naturalistically, and then you have urged me to make sense of my faith within it. No tennis player worth his salt would venture onto a court with such a net; if the opponent's net excludes his contender at the outset, the game is over before it begins.

The other, related, problem is that, as I'm sure you recognize, there is no way to justify what is rational by an appeal to something that is completely "outside of," and makes no use of, the rational itself. That is, rationality can be justified only by using and invoking the rational. So also for the empirical. In order for you to put up your net of rational judgment, you not only exclude your opponent's position at the outset, but you yourself "appeal to the very dispensation you are trying to justify." This appeal, you have argued, is illegitimate.

I agree, however, that "we're seriously trying to get at the truth here." So as we debate the composition of our respective nets, let me try to meet your request to "see . . . a reasoned ground for taking faith seriously as a *way of getting to the truth*." You will concede, I hope, then, that the question at hand is not who is the more rational according to my criteria of rationality? but, rather, which view explains the empirical data before us?

You readily admit that the book on Darwin's dangerous idea is not a book of science, but is rather a book about science. So you want to defer to the authority of the scientists for some of what you set forth. You say, "When I quote them, rhetoric and all, I am doing what they are doing: engaging in persuasion." You then note rightly that "there is no such thing as a sound Argument from Authority, but authorities can be persuasive, sometimes rightly and sometimes wrongly."[20]

I too am going to make use of an "Argument from Authority." Whether the argument is regarded as sound depends on what we think is true, but what I propose is both sound and persuasive. It has been deemed utterly persuasive for over two thousand years. Not only so, but its content, as you surely know, is what motivated the scientific enterprise in the first place. Whether you deem it "right" or "wrong" is a matter that is not up to me. But to dismiss it out of hand is to ignore a predominant view of what is rational in a vast quantity of the Western intellectual tradition, the entire Christian tradition, the bulk of the scientific tradition, and much of the tradition of philosophy.

First, I will readily grant that there are striking similarities between species, and that the more advanced the species, the greater (some of) the similarities. But the Christian tradition has always recognized such things.

One of the reasons for these similarities is that when God created, he created the animals from the same basic *stuff*, the dust, that he used to create man. In creating Adam, notice, "the Lord God formed the man of dust from the ground" (compare Gen. 2:7 with Eccles. 3:20). This is intended to show us, at least, that we, like the beasts, are children of dust (Gen. 3:19). Adam (and, indirectly, Eve also, since Eve came from Adam) came from the same "stuff" as the beasts (Gen. 2:19). Thus we are linked with the animals and with creation in one sense, because we are taken from creation; we are quite literally *a part* of it.

DD: Hold it! I thought we were talking about *science* and about *philosophy*. What right do you have to interject your own religious fables into this discussion? Especially since doing so brings "the net" down, so that anything goes. Do I have to remind you that I have already addressed this with my "God is a ham sandwich" retort?

CA: Perhaps I wasn't clear. I am doing two things here that you have already conceded doing yourself. First, I am presenting an "Argument from Authority." Unless you've had your naturalistic head in the ground, you will recognize that the authority from which I argue is the authority of Holy Scripture. Whether you accept it as an authority or not is not relevant here. You argue from authorities that you accept, so you must allow me to do the same. Surely, you won't expect me as a Christian to concede to your atheistic authorities, will you? Second, and taking from the first point, I am discussing with you which "net"

---

can provide what is needed for the game to even begin. You grant that there has to be a net; but I cannot use your net.

Perhaps you will not want to use mine either, but at least you can entertain my argument, rather than trying unduly to disregard it, as you did earlier by postulating your net as the only one available in the game. The argument, therefore, is not analogous to tennis with a net; it is more akin to the rules of the game that allow for it to be played at all. The net has no meaning apart from those rules.

If I may continue. Since we human beings are made from the same basic stuff as the animals, there is bound to be much continuity between us. But the question that your algorithms have not addressed, and cannot (and here I can only speculate as to why you would not address this problem), is the evidentially and rationally obvious *discontinuities* that exist between the rest of creation and human beings.

For example, you don't even address the most obvious and specific question as to how that which is mindless can produce the mind of a human being. Surely you would agree that our minds can transcend the "natural." They readily move beyond the "natural," for example, in the very activity that we are performing here—the activity of discussion and debate—a discussion and debate in which you and I assume that what we say and propose has *meaning*, that it resonates with the actual state of affairs in the world.[21] We disagree as to the *root* or *cause* of those states of affairs, but I doubt you would want to disagree that we are thus engaged right now.

The reason, you see, that your (or any other) evolutionary theory of origins does not address these central questions is that, by definition, it is not *able* to do so. Any study of the "natural" *only*, with the supposition that only the "natural" is rational, will by definition have to exclude anything that does not comport with the definition of the "natural." Your Kantian paradigm—in which there are the data of science, which one can *know*, and then the (at least logical) possibility of *faith*, which cannot partake of rational knowledge, is owing, I'm sure you recognize, not to science, but to a philosophical prejudice that itself is not scientifically or evidentially justified.

So, back to my "Argument from Authority." When God created human beings, he breathed into them the breath of life. He did not create them in the same way that he created anything else, including

---

[21] If Dennett wants to argue that even the meaning of our discussion is purely naturalistic, then he is stuck in the dilemma we noted in Harris's view of determinism. See Sam Harris, *Free Will* (New York: Free Press, 2012).

the animals. Instead, God conferred with himself and determined that human beings would, in a multitude of ways, "image" what he is like. Those "image" characteristics are readily and evidentially observable, even by science. Not only so, but they are the very characteristics that most obviously set us apart from the rest of creation. Yet you neglect even to mention them. Does that look like a fair "net" to put up in the game?

DD: Okay. I hear what you're saying. But you must not have read my book very carefully. In fact, you missed my first chapter. Did you not read my statement that belief in an "anthropomorphic" God, a God who "lovingly fashioned each and every one of us (all creatures great and small)" is a "myth of childhood, not anything a sane, un-deluded adult could literally believe in"? As I said, a belief in an "anthropomorphic Handicrafter God" is a "pathetic hodgepodge of pious pseudo-science."[22]

CA: Yes. I did read that, with much interest and amusement. What interested me most was how, *scientifically*, you were able to make such stark and dismissive claims. I wondered as I read that, "Just how is this diatribe against God itself a scientific pronouncement?" Of course, as I'm sure you know, what is said there is anything but science; it comes from an unjustified and presumed prejudice against Christianity, not from science.

DD: No, no. I am not prejudiced against Christianity. As I said in my book, I am only looking for a reasonable defense of it. So far, all you've given me are fables from your Bible.

CA: What I have explained to you thus far are facts from "my Bible." But they are facts, nevertheless, whether you or I believe them or not.

The reason I say that you are prejudiced against, rather than *scientifically* opposed to, Christianity is that you choose in various places to ridicule an "anthropomorphic" God. Perhaps it is you who needs to read a bit more about this. The first page of the Bible would be a good place to begin.

The reason Christianity is called "Christianity" is that it is just this God, the One who created all things, including you and me in his image, who himself has come down, in the person of his Son, as the Lord Jesus Christ. The history of Christianity has confirmed the Bible's teaching that he is both God and man. Without Christ as the God-man, there is no *Christ*ianity. What is it, may I ask, that motivates

---

[22] Dennett, *Darwin's Dangerous Idea*, 18.

you to think that the likes of so many millions over the last two thousand years are insane and deluded? You have no scientific reason to believe such a thing. You could not have such a reason, since your algorithms can say nothing about that.

The fact is, Dr. Dennett, you and I are *born* deluded and (given the proper definition) insane. We refuse to see the obvious. Not only so, but we work as hard as we can to reject it. So *Darwin's Dangerous Idea* is simply a very thoughtful and rigorous example of that delusion. Your own "Argument from Authority," which you readily admit to using, is not able to justify your more incendiary statements about God. Those statements have nothing to do with scientific authority. They simply display in bright red colors your own, may I say, irrational prejudice.

The only way to make sense of the actual and thoroughly evidential *discontinuities* between animals and human beings is to affirm that we are "image" of the God who himself is a knowing, loving, relational God, a God who has come down in his Son. Surely one can recognize, given the basic construal of cause and effect, that what is in the effect is *best understood* as coming from its cause.[23] But you propose to ignore "what is in the effect," that is, the human mind, so that your algorithms won't be called into question. There is no explanation of the human mind except the mind of the One who made it. There is no scientific evidence that the rational has come from the nonrational. None whatsoever. It seems delusion might justifiably be ascribed to such notions.

The problem of delusion, insanity, and self-deception is only remedied when we accept the anthropomorphic God, in his fully anthropomorphic character, as the Lord Jesus Christ, the Son of God. Apart from that, your algorithms will simply float in the void, unable to account for the very things that are most obvious to any philosopher or scientist.

My "Authority," then, is God himself, speaking anthropomorphically in his Word, and ultimately in his Son. Given that authority, your algorithms can take their proper place. Without that authority, you are left with your own deluded, irrational, and nonscientific diatribes, which themselves can have no scientific foundation.

Maybe this is the best way to put it. The children's song that you begin the book with—"Tell Me Why"—is not simply, as you say, a "sentimental declaration." That it is a children's song does not mean it

---

[23] As Copi notes, "Every use of the word 'cause,' whether in everyday life or in science, involves or presupposes the doctrine that cause and effect are *uniformly* connected. We admit that a particular circumstance caused a particular effect only if we agree that any other circumstance of that type will . . . cause another effect of the same kind as the first. In other words, similar causes produce similar effects." Irving M. Copi, *An Introduction to Logic*, 7th ed. (New York: Macmillan, 1986): 403.

eschews profundity. When the song affirms that "God made the stars to shine, the ivy twine, the sky so blue," it is affirming what science, *as science*, will never be in a position to affirm or deny. If you do not affirm this, it is not because you are so scientific or so rational. It is because you continue to avoid and ignore the obvious. The clear evidence of this is that in your book of almost six hundred densely written pages, you never even mention the most obvious and evidential discontinuity between man and animals.

This dialog, it will be apparent, could go in many different directions and continue for a very long time. The point of it, however, is to illustrate where one *might* want to begin if and when there is an occasion to ferret out the mindset of an evolutionary naturalist. Notice as well that the heart of the issue is not in the dense and technical material that Dennett offers. Rather, it is in the *way* he chooses to avoid or dismiss the foundational questions that inform everything else he says. So, I have tried in the discussion to focus on the all-important questions—the questions that relate to his initial assumptions—but to do that in a way that anyone who has and knows the Bible could do it. One need not be as astute as Dennett in science or philosophy to challenge the root assumptions of his argument.

One more, shorter, example will have to suffice at this point.[24] As stated above, both Dawkins and Dennett aver that anyone who *doubts* evolution, or who does not believe it, is (let's just list the defects they mention) "inexcusably ignorant," "stupid," "insane," or "wicked" (though Dawkins is charitable enough to say he does not want to consider the latter). But then, for both of them, the case made for an unguided evolutionary process is a case based on its *plausibility* and *not on its certainty*. Now, Dawkins and Dennett would both likely believe that certainty is unattainable in science, and perhaps in any other field.[25] The best we can do, they would likely say, is argue for plausibility.[26] But since you are now a

---

[24] Again, to reiterate, I am not proposing that these are the *only* issues to address, maybe even not the main issues to address. What I am doing is trying a means of wise persuasion that takes what the other person says seriously, while also showing its status as bankrupt. This is akin to the *ad hominem* approach introduced earlier.

[25] This brings up a point that we cannot discuss here, but that is monumentally important, especially in this day and time. Christianity alone can provide certainty. That certainty should inform part of our apologetic approach.

[26] We will not detail the arguments here. Dawkins is perhaps more explicit about this than is Dennett. See, for example, Richard Dawkins, *The Blind Watchmaker: Why the Evidence of Evolution Reveals a Universe without Design* (New York: Norton, 1996), 78–79.

wise and biblically literate apologist, you will immediately want to know just what this plausibility *is*. What is it that makes something plausible?

Let's use a standard philosophical definition of plausibility:

> A claim is plausible if it subjectively seems worthy of belief even if we have not necessarily studied its objective ground. Plausibility is thus acceptable credibility, and its *degree of credibility can depend in part on the authority that advocates it*. A plausible claim can turn out to be false, and an implausible claim can turn out to be true. *People can disagree on what they find plausible.* Plausibility is distinct from probability, which is related to alternatives. A belief is probable if its degree of likelihood is greater than that of its alternatives. On most accounts, probability is more objective than plausibility.[27]

At this point, a way forward should be obvious. If plausibility is what "subjectively seems worthy of belief," and its "degree of credibility can depend in part on the authority that advocates it," then we can see why one may want to accept evolutionary theory as plausible. Something will "subjectively seem worthy of belief" if the authority we accept advocates it. But now we're back to the problem and question of authority. Plausibility, like beauty, is in the eye of the beholder, and it depends on what authority we accept.

What this does, at least, is call into serious question the character flaws that Dawkins and Dennett ascribe to those who refuse to go along with them. It shows that irrationality accrues to those who think that anyone who does not see the plausibility they see is deluded or insane (but, thankfully, not wicked). The very notion of plausibility that they themselves admit as basic to their arguments allows for real disagreement, since one man's subjective impression may not comport with another's. The fact that Dennett finds his arguments plausible is a nice piece of biography, but it is no threat to Christian truth, and it surely does not justify his attempt to call into question the character of anyone who disagrees with him.

But perhaps what Dawkins and Dennett want to argue is more than plausibility. Perhaps what they're saying is that given the evi-

---

[27] From Nicholas Bunnin and Jiyuan Yu, eds., *The Blackwell Dictionary of Western Philosophy* (Malden, MA: Wiley-Blackwell Publishing, 2009), 533, my emphases.

dences or algorithms that they lay out, it is *highly probable* that evolutionary theory is correct. And as our definition above notes, "a belief is probable if its degree of likelihood is greater than that of its alternatives." Thus, "probability is more objective than plausibility." This is not the place to peruse various aspects of probability theory. But a little "premeditation" sees that what *is* obvious about probability is that it too depends on a "degree of likelihood" that is greater than the proffered alternatives.[28]

There are two points to make about this. First, any notion of probability that depends on a "degree of likelihood" in cases such as these depends itself for its calculus on the *background knowledge* of the calculator. As Copi notes, "[An event] can be assigned a probability *only on the basis of the evidence available to the person making the assignment.*"[29] But we have already seen that "the evidence available to the person making the (probable) assignment" will automatically exclude the fact that God's character is patently obvious in every bit of evidence used.[30] There is a determined bias and rejection of the Christian position at the outset of any notion of probability that Dawkins or Dennett would use.

Embedded in (this kind of) probability, therefore, is the knowledge (or assumptions) that one brings to the probability equation.[31] The probability of evolution, in this case, given (the background assumption of) naturalism is thought to be greater than the probability of evolution given (the background assumption of) theism. But that kind of calculus is a sleight of hand; it prejudices the equation at the outset. The *real* point of contention is with the background assumptions, not with the probability calculus *itself*. So what is *probable*, even if more objective than what is plausible, depends, from the start, on *what one determines to count as evidence, and what one determines to exclude.*

The other point worth considering might be what the probability calculus itself determines. Here we can step on the evolutionist's ground for a moment. If it is the case, as it must be, that the best one

---

[28] If our dialog above had continued, the covenantal apologist surely would have asked whether, with respect to the notion of cause and effect, it is more probable that the rational came from the nonrational, or that the rational came from the rational.

[29] Copi, *An Introduction to Logic*, 513, my emphasis. Copi goes on to give an example of how and why probability is relative to the one assigning the evidence.

[30] Recall tenet 10.

[31] For any interested in how this probability calculus might proceed, see Plantinga, *Where the Conflict Really Lies*, 50ff.

can offer is that evolution is *probable*, given naturalism, then is it not also the case that evolution (not to mention naturalism) is also *to some degree* improbable? That is, unless the probability of evolution can be shown to be 1, meaning it is *certain* (which it could not do), there are by definition *degrees* in which evolution is *im*probable. If *that* is the case, then the calculus that the evolutionist uses itself leaves room for doubt. It may be very little room in the mind of the evolutionary naturalist, but it is room nevertheless.

And if, on the arguments of the evolutionist himself, there is room to doubt, we might ask how could it be that one who doubts evolution is therefore "ignorant, stupid or insane"? Doesn't the notion of probability *require* that doubt be included in it?

In fact, using their own words, why could we not say that those who advocate such a probability, because they leave room for doubt, are themselves advocating for ignorance, stupidity, or insanity (but not wickedness)? Here, then, is a question that might be worth pursuing with Dennett: If, as you say, "anyone today who doubts that the variety of life on this planet was produced by a process of evolution is inexcusably ignorant," then how can evolution be simply plausible or probable, since both plausibility and probability leave room for doubt?[32]

The rejoinder to this kind of question, of course, might be for the evolutionist to talk for a while about the "degree" of probability. If evolutionary naturalism has a probability of, say, .8, then surely there is a very strong reason to accept it, he might say. But then we're pushed back to the presuppositions and assumptions *behind* such "degrees" informing the probability, assumptions which the Christian is under no pressure to accept and which, themselves, are unable to explain the obvious manifestation of God in all of creation.

So the "threat" of evolution, the "dangerous idea" of Darwin, turns out not to be so threatening or dangerous after all. Not surprisingly, evolutionary theory is simply an old argument in new clothes. It is the argument that God cannot exist because I refuse to see him, and since I refuse to see him, I'll need to find another way to try to make sense

---

[32] The point of this question is a point of persuasion; it is calculated to take the words of the evolutionist and challenge him to make sense of them on his own terms. In that way, it is similar to what Paul does on Mars Hill when he says, "Being then God's offspring, we ought not to think that the divine being is like gold or silver or stone, an image formed by the art and imagination of man" (Acts 17:29).

of things. But "sense" cannot be made when the *sensus* is suppressed; it cannot be made of things that God has made and through which he obviously and perpetually reveals himself, when God and his revelation are denied, ignored, and suppressed at the outset.

This should help us see that a "premeditated" application of biblical truth, including our ten tenets, can move us a long way in discussions of this sort, even if those discussions contain scientific (or philosophical or other) technicalities beyond our abilities.

There is, obviously, much more that we could say about this naturalistic evolutionary position, and much more that *should* be said. Hopefully, however, we can begin to see that the arguments given, no matter how technical or dense, really rest on quicksand; they cannot bear their own weight. They begin the discussion by a biased and prejudiced exclusion of what Christians believe. Such bias is anything but scientific; it is, in the main, rebellion against the true God who is known even before the scientific enterprise gets underway.

A Concluding Word to the Wise

Perhaps you are thinking that our previous discussion on evolution is possible only if one is intimately involved in and acquainted with some deep and technical philosophical or scientific literature. But let's think about that for a minute. Remember that I said at the beginning that apologetics is "premeditated evangelism." Let me reiterate here that what has been offered above as a possible response to evolutionary theory is an aspect more of premeditation than of any technical science or philosophy.

First, notice that we took Dennett's and Dawkins's own words seriously in order to respond to them. This is the positive approach; it is a legitimate use of an *ad hominem* argument. We acknowledged Dennett's own words in his affirmation of an "Argument from Authority" that itself is focused on persuasion. We also noted Dawkins's and Dennett's antipathy to anyone who doubts what they say. We acknowledged the search for truth and the emphasis on reasonable responses. Much, much more could have been said; we were only able to broach these topics.

On the negative side, we saw that Dennett's view was unduly biased toward his own assumptions. He offered to play the game, as long as his own autonomously erected "net" of rational judgment was in place. For him, either it was in place, in which case all that anyone said must conform to it, or it was dropped, in which case absurdity was the only option. This point might not have been obvious to everyone initially, but it was embedded in what Dennett said. Perhaps this is where it is important to engage in some biblical and theological meditation. It may be that we need to read such books on naturalistic evolution with a more biblically critical eye and with a view toward the assumptions behind what is being said. This may take some practice, but it is within the ability of most Christians to do.

The same can be said for the notion of plausibility. A little thought recognizes that a *plausible* conclusion has a high degree of subjective preference within it. One person's plausibility is another's incredulity. What we determine to believe is always and everywhere much more complex than a simple appeal to "the evidence." This is especially the case with respect to Christianity because "the evidence" will be seen in a foundationally different way by those who are in Adam than by those who are in Christ. So we train ourselves to be suspicious of any appeal to evidence *per se*, as if such things are as simple as opening our eyes.

On probability, discussions can become highly technical, and I am not able to enter all the technicalities of those discussions. But I need not be able to, nor do you. If we think about it, we can recognize that probability means, for the most part, a lack of certainty. So the conclusion can legitimately be drawn that an evolutionary argument from probability means that the position itself entails at least some level of doubt. How could it be then that anyone who doubts it is insane?

If, for example, we think about the probability of my pulling the ace of spades from a fifty-two-card deck, the probability turns out to be one in fifty-two. Could anyone legitimately think that I am ignorant or insane (but not wicked) if I believe I might pull the ace of spades from a given deck? I may be overly optimistic in some way, but surely the aspersions of ignorance and insanity (but not wickedness) cannot apply here.

Now suppose I actually pull the ace of spades from a given deck and I see it in my hand. Could anyone rightly protest that I am ignorant or insane (if not wicked) because I now believe I have an ace of spades? Even on the evolutionist's own terms, the probability of such things says little about their actual reality. I may believe that which is improbable—that I pulled an ace of spades from the deck—because of the evidence I have. For someone to call me insane because of its low probability is simply to ignore the obvious evidence in front of me, which is itself a kind of insanity. Such is the problem of the suppression of the truth.

But even if we have no or little knowledge of probability, we do know that probability has to assume certain things about "the way things are" (for example, the deck must be shuffled and not prearranged in a particular way, it has to have fifty-two cards, and so on). All of these things must be assumed if we are going to calculate what is probable or not with respect to them. And assuming these things requires some *background knowledge* that must always go into the calculation of what is probable and what is not.[33]

All of this might take a bit of "premeditation," but it centrally relies on what we already know about the status of unbelief. Unbelief cannot sustain itself; it is unable to make sense of the facts, many of which are the most obvious facts of the world; it assumes, rather than shows, that there is no God, that the world is not created by him, that his character is not obvious in creation, and so on. Then it proceeds to argue its case not by attempting to support those assumptions, but simply by assuming them and then arguing as if the assumptions themselves are, or must be, universal if one is to be "rational."

Given these (and other) basic biblical truths, which are part and parcel of our ten tenets, we are able then to begin to connect those truths with the arguments raised against Christianity. Once we connect those truths, we are in a position to discuss them without at any point pretending to be experts in areas (like science) where we may not excel. These discussions depend on and seek to make use of biblical wisdom. As we have seen, part of what that means is that we attempt to persuade. Persuasion means that we, when we can, take what our opponents say and use it, positively and negatively, to set forth our own case. It also means that we try to lay out the Quicksand Quotient. We

---

[33] Again, see Copi's example of this in *An Introduction to Logic*, 513.

try to show that the position being touted will crumble under its own weight; it cannot provide the sustenance needed to carry on.

We are then in a position to set forth the "Christian context" and to show how our foundational, biblical principles provide the explanation needed for things that cannot otherwise be explained, in science or in any other form of unbelief.

What might be Dennett's or Dawkins's response to our dialog above? There is no way to tell, really. Perhaps each would mock us; maybe one would want to hear more about this; or maybe, just maybe, some such skeptic would join us and believe (Acts 17:32–34). No matter what the response, if the truth of God is set forth and defended, then our covenantal apologetic has been "successful," at least from God's perspective. And that perspective is the only one that counts in the end.

Unbelief in all of its forms, scientific and otherwise, cannot carry its own weight. A habit of biblical "premeditation" will help us see how, where, and when that is true for any objection that might come our way.

When the world's sharp strife is nigh,
When they hear the battle-cry,
When they rush into the fight,
Knowing not temptation's might;
These thy children, Lord, defend;
To their zeal thy wisdom lend.[34]

---

[34] Frances M. Owen, "When Thy Soldiers Take Their Swords," ca. 1872.

7

You Are Very Religious

Instead of giving reasons why people believe Scripture to be the word of God, they answer that God has so given it to us to believe. By such an answer a Muslim can "prove" his faith in the Koran and every superstitious person his or her private superstition. The statement: "This is what I want, therefore this is what I command" takes the place of reasoning and proof. Let me grant, in the first place, that the believer cannot cite a deeper ground for revelation than its divine authority, which he or she recognizes by faith. But this is not to say that believers have nothing to say to the opponents of that revelation.[1]

Idol Worship

When a covenantal apologetic meets atheism or various other forms of obvious unbelief, the divide between the two positions (in Adam and in Christ) is as bright as the sun. It is obvious and it lights the way for clear avenues to travel as we try to show the futility of those positions. But when the position that we are dealing with is a specific *religion*, matters can become more complicated.

In a false religion (and here we're using the term *religion* in its usual sense), we are dealing with people who have committed themselves to a god, who spend their lives in service to this god, and who have divine direction, in some form or other, that tells them who they are and what they are to do. There is, therefore, in false religion, a *parody* or errant *copy* of Christianity at work. In every other religion, by definition, there are deep roots at work in a person that include ritual and worship, and normally a specific set of ideas and doctrines.

---

[1] Herman Bavinck, *Reformed Dogmatics*, vol. 1, *Prolegomena*, ed. John Bolt, trans. John Vriend (Grand Rapids: Baker Academic, 2003), 590.

Back in the early days of comic books, the creators of Superman decided it would be fun to have a villain that was just like Superman, except his opposite. They called him Bizarro. Instead of an *S* on his shirt, he wore a *B*, when he said "bad" it meant "good," and so forth. He depended on Superman in order to be who he was, but his intent was to turn much of what Superman was into its opposite.

False religions are "Bizarro" religions. They depend on the real thing for their basic identity, but they twist and turn all of what is right in the true religion of Christianity and make it into something false, confused, and wicked. False religions take what Christianity has and use it for their own superstitious purposes.

We will remember that Luke, in Acts 17, tells us that the apostle Paul was moved by idolatry he saw in Athens to such an extent that he was constrained to preach in the synagogue and the marketplace. It was his preaching in the marketplace that provoked his trip to Mars Hill. Paul knew what the plethora of idols in Athens represented. They represented a people who were "very religious," but whose religion was expressed by the *sensus/suppression* dynamic. They knew God, so they had crafted things to worship, and their knowledge of God was expressed (i.e., suppressed) in their idolatry. They had to worship *something* (Rom. 1:25), but they would not worship the true God, whom they knew. They would exchange the truth that God was giving them, what Paul calls "the glory of the immortal God," "for images resembling mortal man and birds and animals and creeping things" (Rom. 1:23). So knowledge of God was evident throughout the city, but so was the suppression of that knowledge.

The Greek word translated "very religious" (Acts 17:22) is itself a rhetorical device that Paul uses at the beginning of his address. The word in Greek, like our word *religious* in English, is ambiguous. It can be a compliment or a criticism. Paul uses this deliberately ambiguous word in order to gain the attention of his listeners. Positively, it means that one is devoted and loyal to a particular (supposedly "transcendent") cause. Negatively, it means that one is a slave of superstition.[2] So even as Paul begins his address on Mars Hill, he picks a word that

---

[2] The Authorized Version, for example, translates the Greek word as "too superstitious." This misses the persuasive reason that the word is used.

utilizes available avenues of persuasion in order, initially, to bring his audience into the context of what he wants to say.

We can imagine the reaction of the Athenians and philosophers there as Paul begins to speak. As soon as he says, "I perceive that in every way you are *very religious*," the philosophers might begin a quiet inquiry among themselves: "What does Paul mean by 'very religious'?" one of them might ask. "Does he mean to compliment us or is he criticizing us?" another might wonder. The use of the word itself, no doubt, gets their attention and arouses their religious and philosophical curiosity. They listen carefully in order to understand exactly what Paul means by "very religious." Paul is a master persuader.

What I propose to do in this last chapter is to think about how a covenantal approach to apologetics might address those who are "very religious." This task will be a bit different because of the uniqueness of false religions, as over against unbelief generally. False religions create questions with respect to apologetics that general unbelief might not.

One of the most persistent questions that has come to me, as one who seeks to stand on the authority of Scripture in apologetics, is why, for example, Muslims could not use the exact same approach that we are advocating in this book. Specifically, since our covenantal approach to a defense of Christianity has as its *principial* foundation the Bible as the word of God, could *any* religion that has and claims its own "Bible," or divine word, take the same apologetic approach? And is the best we can hope for with respect to other religions simply a "Battle of the Books"? Don't we just wind up quoting our respective authorities in our respective "Bibles" and thus engaging in nothing but an apologetic shouting match?[3]

We have already attempted to address some of these questions in previous chapters. We know that when we speak the truth found in Christianity, we are automatically "connecting" that truth with the truth that God has given through his creation.[4] No other religion makes that connection, since every other religion is a suppression of the truth. So even if all that is left *is* a "shouting match," the "shouting"

---

[3] This, for example, was the gist of the criticism of Van Til in John W. Montgomery, "Once Upon an a Priori," in *Jerusalem and Athens: Critical Discussions on the Philosophy and Apologetics of Cornelius Van Til*, ed. E. R. Geehan (Nutley, NJ: Presbyterian and Reformed, 1971).
[4] Recall tenet 5: "All people know the true God, and that knowledge entails covenantal obligations."

that comes from the Christian *gets through* to non-Christians in a way that theirs does not and could not, and it accomplishes exactly what God desires.

But in apologetics we are interested in more than simply shouting our position; as we have been at pains to affirm and demonstrate, we are interested in conducting ourselves with *wisdom*. We are interested in persuasion, and that means we would like to develop, as much as is in us, a rhetorical *argument* in response. This means, as we have seen, that we should, whenever we can, take into account the *pathos* of those to whom we speak, seeking to take and use whatever they say and believe that will help us to persuade them of their own errors and of the truth of Christianity.

This also means, at least, that we should take what they believe and show it to be in serious trouble, *trouble caused by their own system of (religious) belief.* This is the Quicksand Quotient that should be familiar to us by now. It further means that we should take what they believe and show how it can be what they propose it to be only if it is given its proper, Christian context. We move, then, between the Quicksand Quotient and the Christian context in our persuasive argument and discussion.

So, in all of these situations, we are dealing with the dynamic of the *sensus*, which means that they do know the true God and that knowledge will surface in various ways; and of *suppression*, which means that when that knowledge surfaces it will surface as a counterfeit—a "Bizarro"—of the real. The resulting counterfeit will inevitably take on the form of an idol.

This *sensus/suppression* dynamic is a hermeneutical tool in a covenantal apologetic. It is at least a partial grid through which we should interpret all unbelieving positions, including false religions. As such a tool, it gives us the ability to see aspects of another religion as the "welling up" of the knowledge of God that can never be annihilated.[5] It also helps us to see that "welling up" as a false belief or a false religion.

Paul was addressing another religion, or more than one, in his speech on Mars Hill. The Athenians had a plethora of gods. So Paul was

---

[5] This is what tenet 8 is designed to highlight: "Suppression of the truth, like the depravity of sin, is total but not absolute. Thus, every unbelieving position will necessarily have within it ideas, concepts, notions, and the like that it has taken and wrenched from their true, Christian context."

able to quote from the Greek poets because what they had written was a product of this *sensus/suppression* dynamic. Their statements said true things about God (*sensus*), provided the God to whom the statements referred was the true God. *As stated*, however, the statements were false (*suppression*), given their faulty reference point and meaning.

So also for all other religions. Our biblical principles will not let us affirm anything that another religion ultimately says or believes, given that such statements always have a false god as their overall reference and context. If we are aware of what those religions have taken from Christianity, we can then use those "copied concepts" in the context of the truth of Christianity. But we dare not assume that what they say is true (even true as far as it goes). "In him we live and move and have our being," when initially written, is *not* true "as far as it goes" because it could only go as far as that to which it referred—Zeus. It was a false statement because it referred to an illusion, a false god. But it became a true statement when biblical content was poured into it.[6]

In a covenantal approach to apologetics, just as with unbelief generally, we cannot suppose that there are ideas, concepts, notions, affirmations, and the like that we have in common with those who remain in Adam. Just because a statement or religion uses the term *God* does not mean that we stand in the same sanctuary. Everyone has at least one god (Rom. 1:25); the question is whether or not it is the true, real, and triune God or an illusory idol.

Though we cannot set up Paul's address on Mars Hill as the only definitive model for approaching other religions, it is instructive to recall how Paul determined to speak to the Athenians. He began his discussion by explaining what they claimed not to know. He told them who the "unknown God" is. Paul knew that his audience was theistic, so he began by proclaiming the true God. But his proclamation was set in contrast to what they themselves believed.

For example, Paul did not simply say that God is infinite, but he spoke of God's infinity in contrast to a god who would *need* a place to

---

[6] As far as I can tell, this is what is meant when other religions are said to be "subversively fulfilled" in the gospel. See, for example, Daniel Strange, "Perilous Exchange, Precious Good News: A Reformed 'Subversive Fulfillment' Interpretation of Other Religions," in *Only One Way? Three Christian Responses on the Uniqueness of Christ in a Religiously Plural World*, ed. Gavin D'Costa, Paul Knitter, and Daniel Strange (London: SCM, 2011).

dwell (as Greek polytheism affirmed), or would *need* people to serve him. Immediately, Paul contrasted the true God with their false gods. He then made clear that his audience was utterly dependent on this God—this God whom Paul had just proclaimed to be the Creator and sovereign Lord (Acts 17:24). This God gives to all mankind life and breath and everything.

The Athenians and philosophers there would have understood that Paul was claiming that everyone present depended at every moment on the true God. Paul then supported his declaration that God is sovereign Lord by quoting Epimenides, and he supported his declaration that God is Creator by quoting Aratus.

Thus, Paul's focus among the religious people of Athens was on God's character, and specifically on his *aseity*, his utter independence from everything created. With that aseity comes God's sovereignty, which, for Paul, included God's meticulous sovereignty even over each breath that we take. The God whom Paul proclaimed is both transcendent and immanent. He is in need of nothing, thus completely self-sustaining, and he is "not far from each one of us" (Acts 17:27), giving every one of us the life we have and our every breath.

As Paul concluded his address, he reminded his audience that God has appointed a day of judgment, and on that day the One who was dead and now lives will judge the living and the dead. This One, obviously, has all authority to judge. No one without such authority could judge the entirety of mankind. So Paul's conclusion pressed home the reality of Christ's lordship. Paul did not shrink from proclaiming "foreign divinities" on Mars Hill, nor did he leave out the controversial notion of the resurrection, even though it was those very things that provoked the scorn of the philosophers. He told them exactly who this "foreign divinity" is and that they themselves were accountable to him.

There is no one recipe for covenantally defending the faith among and with other religions. All religions have their own specific dogmas, codes, rituals, and worship. However, it does seem that, at least initially, three basic categories can help us to focus our analysis of those religions and our conversations with those who hold them.

First, with Paul, we must be acutely aware of exactly who the god of the other religion is. Because other religions exist in order to avoid the true God, they will inevitably interject another god, and that god will have distinct characteristics. This is more difficult to recognize, for example, in Buddhism than in Islam, but it is useful if we can focus, first, on the doctrine of god on which the false religion depends.

Second, it will help us to see how the false religion deals with its god's relationship to creation. Whatever that relationship, every false religion will inevitably posit either something like a god who is too far off to really relate to creation, as in Islam, or something like a god who is so close that we become gods ourselves, as in Mormonism. In any case, it is useful if we can pinpoint how the proposed god is thought to relate specifically to his creation and to us. What are the attributes or characteristics that allow (or do not allow) this god to relate to us?

Third, if we can understand something of the false religion's theory of revelation, that understanding may serve us well. This might require that we read the actual books, if there are such books, to which the false religion is committed. But such things can also be brought out in conversation with its followers.

It might also mean attempting to find out just *how* those books are what the religion claims they are. In almost every case, the books in false religions came to exist in some isolated, unobservable, and un-verifiable way—for example, through Muhammad, by himself, over a period of twenty years or so; or through Joseph Smith, by himself in a barn. In understanding this, we have the opportunity to highlight the public and historical roots of Christianity in redemptive history. It helps, at times, to be able to point out that Christianity did not have its beginning in a private room or with only one prophet, or even simply at the time of Christ. Rather, it began "in the beginning," and it reached its climax in history in the coming of the Son of God himself in the flesh.

These three things often prove useful in discussions with other religions. They are not the only things to be aware of—certainly not all that we may need to understand—but they could be a good starting place.

Finally, before we move to our Muslim-Christian dialog, one more anecdotal point is worth mentioning. When I was a first-semester seminary student, a Jehovah's Witness came to my door one Saturday morning by himself (which was unusual, because they usually travel by twos). His name was Lawrence, and as he began to talk to me about his religion, I told him that I was a Christian and therefore believed that Jesus Christ is fully God, as Scripture teaches. Lawrence then told me that the verse in John 1:1 actually, in the Greek, said that the Word was "a god."

As a young and brash seminary student, I told him to hold on a minute. I went to my study and got my Greek New Testament. I then pointed him to John 1:1 and asked him to tell me exactly how he thought the Greek should read "a god" instead of "God." Lawrence lowered his head, looking ashamed, and said he did not know how to read Greek. (Of course, as a first-semester seminary student, I didn't know much Greek either.) As I watched Lawrence, it was clear to me that he saw himself at that point as a failure. I felt compassion for him, especially because, truth be told, about all I could read in the Greek New Testament at that point was John 1:1!

So, in the midst of the awkward silence, I decided to change the subject. I asked Lawrence if he thought that God is holy, perfect, and without blemish. Surprisingly, he said yes. Then I asked him how he thought this holy and perfect God was going to accept the likes of us when we are so unholy and sinful. Lawrence looked at me and said, "No one has ever asked me that question before."

Maybe Lawrence was new at this. Maybe his heart was not into what he was told to do at Kingdom Hall. Whatever the case, Lawrence and I had a great discussion about the gospel of Jesus Christ and how only in Christ can we be acceptable, and accepted, by a holy God. I watched as Lawrence walked away. He did not stop at any other door; he just walked and walked.

I don't know what finally happened to Lawrence. The point of recounting this is to remind us that what anyone needs, and this includes those who have been deceived into other religions, is the gospel of Jesus Christ. Had I been able to argue the fine points of Greek with Lawrence, I may have succeeded in showing him that I knew Greek better than he did—maybe even in showing him that his own translation of John 1:1 was questionable. But if I had discussed only that, I would have done him a disservice.

It is only the gospel of Christ that can change hearts. It may be that other religions are a fertile seedbed in which that gospel can be effectively planted (as God, in his sovereign wisdom, gives the increase). If so, then evangelism can often be the proper response to false religions. The gospel is the "power of God for salvation to everyone who believes" (Rom. 1:16). But that power must be communicated in order to be activated. We should never lose sight of that fact in our discussions.

But there are times when what is needed is a little "premeditation" in the context of our communication of the gospel. In those cases, it might be useful to employ a covenantal apologetic, to defend Christianity in the context of problems and issues that false religions bring to the fore. In the dialog below, we will seek to do just that.

God Is (Not?) Great

Before we move into a sample dialog between a Muslim and a Christian, a word or two of explanation is in order. First, the most persistent question that I receive when I am teaching or explaining the covenantal approach to apologetics is, "What about a Muslim? Couldn't a Muslim stand on the Qur'an as his *principial* ground and defend his faith in the same way that you say Christians should? Doesn't a Muslim presuppose his own Bible and defend Islam by the same method?" Those are good and fair questions, and I propose to address them by way of the dialog below.

Also, to this point, you may think that our dialogs have become increasingly complex as we move from chapter to chapter. This has been intentional. Since apologetics is "premeditated evangelism," I am assuming all along that premeditation is moving forward as well. But if it is not yet possible to engage in any significant premeditation on many of these issues and their relationship to Christianity, that is understandable. As we began the dialog in the previous chapter, you may not have had the opportunity yet to give much attention to notions of probability and plausibility and their relationship to the Dawkins/Dennett proposal of evolution. So that dialog was meant to point to one of the premeditative ways that you could go in such discussions.

Likewise, the dialog below. There may be areas of thought and theology that have not yet been engrafted into your theological and apologetic arsenal at this point. So let me introduce here a couple of theological concepts that will inform our dialog and are an integral part of our theology, and thus of a covenantal approach to apologetics.

In certain versions of Islam, as in Christianity, there is a good bit of discussion about the relationship of necessity and contingency. Put simply, anything *necessary* is something that *must* be, and anything *contingent* is something that *might* be but does not *have to* be. For Christians, only God is absolutely necessary, and everything else is contingent. That is, it is impossible—*absolutely* impossible—that God not exist. Not so for anything else. Anything else might not have existed, but God freely determined that it would.

When God created, he brought into existence the universe and all that is contained in the heavenlies. The universe did not have to exist; its existence is not necessary. But God freely determined to bring the universe into existence. His commitment to create, as we have seen, assumes that God condescended and that he bound himself to what he had made, so that what he had made would bring glory to him. This commitment is his covenant, and it is active from the point at which he—Father, Son, and Holy Spirit—determines "whatsoever comes to pass."

But as we have seen throughout this book, even as he condescended and bound himself to what he had made, he in no way ceased to be who he is in himself. He continued to be, as he must always be, fully and completely the one true triune God.[7] So Christianity has always believed that God remains who he is (as he *must*, since he cannot deny himself) even while he relates and commits himself to creation, and specifically to man, who alone is made in his image. That relationship that God unilaterally initiated included the fact that God reveals himself in various ways (e.g., grace, wrath) that he would not have been revealed had there been no creation. If he had not created, he would not have occasion to be gracious or wrathful toward us.

In revealing himself in this way, he did not cease to be who he is; he did not change into something less than God; indeed, he cannot do

---

[7] A discussion of these issues can also be found in K. Scott Oliphint, *The Majesty of Mystery: Celebrating the Glory of an Incomprehensible God* (Bellingham, WA: Lexham Press, 2016), chap. 7.

that. What he did instead was express himself through characteristics that are what they are by virtue of his real and covenantal relationship with creation. The incarnation is the paradigmatic example of this. The Son of God takes on a human nature, but that does not mean that he in any way ceases to be fully and in every way God.

Moreover, God's (necessary) character, *as God*, and his (contingent) relationship to creation are not at odds with each other. These two aspects of God's character are not fighting against each other, but they are brought together and unified by God himself, specifically, by the Holy Spirit (again, think of the incarnation). So, in God, there is no contradiction or incompatibility between his character *as God* and his revelation to us as God *with us*.

These theological truths will be crucial to understand as we look at a specific instance of Islam. Because there are as many permutations of Islam as there are of Christianity, it is necessary for us to focus our dialog. So, given that a covenantal apologetic is "occasional," in that it must take into account the *pathos* of the one(s) to whom we speak, we will set our sights on a convert to Islam, whom we will call by his newly adopted name, Ish·āq Muhammad (IM) as he enters into a dialog with a covenantal apologist (CA).

As in all of our dialogs, there are things that could have been said that are not, and other things that are said to which different responses could be given. So it is incomplete, but should at least point out *a way* one might begin covenantally to defend Christianity with a Muslim.

> IM: I am anxious to talk with you about my faith. I was raised in a nonreligious home. A friend in college introduced me to the Islamic faith. The more I spoke with him, the more what he said resonated with me. He gave me a book entitled *Theology of Unity*.[8] That book provided for me, as it had for so many others,[9] the best current explanation of Islam and how best to defend it. In the words of its introduction, "It embraces all that Islamic thought has broadly taken

---

[8] Muhammad 'Abduh, *The Theology of Unity*, trans. Ish·āq Musa'ad and Kenneth Cragg (London: George Allen & Unwin, 1966). Because it is impossible to represent all the differing approaches to Islam, and because every *pathos* will have its own specific character, I have designed a dialog around the emphases and tenets contained in 'Abduh's book. This will help focus the discussion, but we should also be aware that the book itself seems to be a central resource of many contemporary doctrines of Islamic theology.

[9] In his introduction to *The Theology of Unity*, Cragg notes that in the book "it will be seen that Muhammad 'Abduh is the unfailing mentor of all subsequent apology." Cragg, introduction to 'Abduh, *The Theology of Unity*, 22.

to be the shape and argument of its renewal."[10] It has become almost as important to me and to many other Muslims as the Qur'an itself.

So in reading the Qur'an, and 'Abduh's apology for its truth, I decided to become a follower of Allah. May I tell you why you must become a follower of Allah as well?

CA: Yes, I want to hear what you have to say. As you know, Ish·āq, I am a Christian. Because I am a Christian, I must confess to you that you and I do not worship the same God. There is only one God, and he is not the God of Islam. But I will listen to your arguments, if you will allow me to respond in kind.

IM: Of course. That is only fair. But let me first say that one of the things that drew me to Islam was the tremendous amount of overlap I found between the God of Christianity and Allah. It seems to me that if you are a Christian, there is much about Islam that you already believe. Christians and Muslims have much in common, and that is one reason why my conversion seemed so natural.

As a Christian, you believe, as I do, that there are two sources of theology. There is reason, on the one hand, and revelation, on the other. As far back as your theologian Thomas Aquinas, who borrowed much from our Muslim philosophers, it has been agreed that you and I, and anyone else, can learn much truth about God simply by reason alone, without the aid of revelation.

So you and I together can begin to understand who God is by a process of natural theology. In fact, "there is nothing in the whole range of Islam which transcends reason's discovery."[11] It is incumbent on reason to understand and affirm even those things which reason cannot penetrate.

You and I can affirm, therefore, that God is a transcendent and necessary being, that he is one, that he is simple and without composition, and that he is the first cause of everything else that exists. Your own philosophers have taken from our philosophers in order to prove and affirm these theological truths.[12]

CA: You are quite right, Ish·āq, that many of our church fathers sought to establish much about God from reason alone, and they were convinced that, based on reason, we all believed the same thing about God. But I should tell you that such a method has been detrimental to

---

[10] Cragg, introduction to 'Abduh, *The Theology of Unity*, 22.

[11] Cragg, introduction to 'Abduh, *The Theology of Unity*, 15.

[12] Aquinas referred numerous times to the Muslim philosopher Al Ghazālī (1058–1111) and freely borrowed from his natural theology. The "five ways" of Thomas Aquinas were dependent on, and adopted, these Muslim philosophical discussions of previous centuries.

a proper defense of Christianity. I cannot abide by that method and so must disagree with you about our supposed mutual theological agreement. To agree with you on that, I think, would be to give away our only source of authority about God and creation.

Allah and the God of Christianity do not share the same characteristics. The very characteristics that you say Allah has, if they truly are characteristics of God, can only properly be ascribed to the Christian God. I hope to explain that more as we continue this conversation.

IM: That does not seem to agree with so much of the philosophical theology that I have heard from you Christians. But very good; let's see if we can find some common ground by considering this for a moment.

I know that you agree with me, and with Islam, that God is a necessary being. It seems to me that reason requires such a being. Everything that we see around us is accidental and contingent. There is nothing in our experience that *must* be; everything *might or might not* be. Are you saying to me that there is no rational principle that requires us to postulate something necessary as an explanation of all that is contingent? 'Abduh has convincingly argued that without something necessary, we have no way to explain the contingent at all.

CA: Let me respond to you with a question. Your own philosophers argue that the contingent requires something necessary. The "necessary" is what you call Allah, or God. Is that correct?

IM: Yes. Allah is the only explanation for everything else, and *everything else* is contingent. So Allah is necessary, eternal, infinite, simple, and much more. He is absolutely transcendent; he alone is one, and only one. This unity of Allah is not something abstract; "it means 'unity' intolerant of *all* pluralism."[13]

This absolute "oneness" of God is, I think, where you and I will disagree, but I am first trying to establish common theological ground for our discussion, so I would prefer to look to your own philosophers, who took their cue from our Muslim religion, so that we might make room for further discussion.

CA: I understand why you want to do that, Ish·āq, but you must understand why I cannot do it.[14] Let me put it to you this way. Say your argument from contingency to necessity is true. *On what basis* can you posit a necessity that is transcendent, eternal, infinite, and

---

[13] 'Abduh, *The Theology of Unity*, 12, my emphasis.
[14] Samuel P. Schlorff, "Theological and Apologetical Dimensions of Muslim Evangelization," *Westminster Theological Journal* 42, no. 2 (1980): 335–66, following Harvie Conn, argues rightly that an apologetic to Muslims must move beyond Thomism in order properly to defend and present the Christian faith.

one? Can you point me to an *empirical* principle that allows for such categories? Or, if not, can you define for me the *rational* principle that requires such a thing?

I can agree with you that if there is a necessary being, he must exist necessarily, but that truth, in and of itself, does not require that a necessary being actually exist. What I cannot see from your own argument, based as it is on our experience of the contingent, is how you can posit the transcendent, the eternal, and the infinite.

What if I have no experience of such things as eternity, infinity, and the like? Do you have any such experiences? And there is nothing available to reason *alone* that itself shows us how to define and delimit the eternal and the infinite. All that reason has available to it are things that are always time-conditioned. I experience things and think about things in a temporal world.

IM: Of course I, as a follower of Islam, can supply the rational component that you ask for. Let's think about it in terms of the contrary. Suppose all that is contingent were dependent on something necessary, but that this necessary thing were not eternal or infinite. Would this necessary thing not itself be dependent on time and space? And if so dependent, wouldn't it be not necessary, but *contingent*?

CA: Yes, it would be dependent on time and space. But that is exactly my point. Since, in your argument, you propose to start with our mutually agreed upon experience (of contingent things), I cannot see how you are able to leap beyond that experience, given that it is your own admitted starting point. You want to posit something that is no part of your experience, and therefore that is no part of your rationality, but I need to know the experiential or rational *principle* that requires what you posit as transcendent, eternal, and infinite. The principle cannot simply be, "Well, it has to be necessary and not contingent."

Your notion of eternity requires that there be no process, no movement, of thought or anything else. Your notion of infinity requires that there be no constraint of space. Can you point me to a rational principle or an experience that is, itself, eternal and infinite?

The question that perplexes me is this: when you begin with our supposedly common experience and then, *on that basis*, move from that to something that is, by definition, unable to be experienced at all, what principle is it that requires that I affirm such a thing? I certainly cannot affirm it based on a common experience that you and I have. Neither can I conjure up a rational principle that requires something of which I have no experience. Such a principle itself, *based on your argument*, would need experience as its foundation.

So while you may want to assert something transcendent, necessary, eternal, infinite, and one, you are unable to provide a foundation, a *reason* or rationale, for such an assertion.

IM: I see what you mean. But if there is no such thing, then do we have any explanation for the contingent world around us? Are we meant simply to be content that everything is contingent?

CA: No, we're not meant to be content at all. As a matter of fact, no one is content with only the contingent. But the *reason* or rationale for this discontent is not that we are so rational, nor is it that our experience, in and of itself, moves us to transcend experience. It is, rather, that everyone, including you, knows the true God. There is a built-in and constant pressure on every one of us; a pressure that all of us continually *experience*, and it moves us beyond the contingencies of this world to the true and eternal God.

The movement, therefore, from the contingent to the necessary is a movement that has its foundation in God's "movement" from eternity to history; in other words, it is a movement that has its foundation in God's *revelation*, not in some notion of neutral experience or rationality.

IM: Okay. Now we're getting somewhere. I agree with you on some of this. Islam, as well, teaches that all people, internally, know Allah. That knowledge is a knowledge of his will, but it includes knowledge of his transcendent, eternal, and infinite oneness.

It is this oneness that is nonnegotiable in Islam. No matter what "brand" of Islam one chooses—be it Sunni, Shiite, or some other— we all agree that God is *absolutely* one and *only* one. I had hoped to move to this contentious point later, but it appears we must deal with it now.

CA: Yes, we must, because, as you know, Christianity holds, as well, that God is one. But included in his oneness is the fact that he is three persons, each of whom is fully God, yet the three do not make up three gods; they are themselves the one God. So the oneness of God includes the attributes of necessity, eternity, infinity, and others, but it also necessarily includes three persons—Father, Son, and Holy Spirit.

IM: Well, I can see now why you did not want to reason together with me. You have discarded reason altogether! There is no way to make sense of this kind of "three Gods–one God" idea that you have. "Muslims are of one mind that though there may be in religion that which transcends the understanding, there is nothing which reason finds impossible."[15] The oneness of God may surpass our understanding, but it is not impossible for reason to understand, as your "three in one" is.

CA: I see. Could you tell me the nature of this transcendent oneness of Allah? I am having a difficult time understanding what his relationship is to everything else, given that such absolute oneness is not found in all of creation.

IM: Good question. "Islamic religion is a religion of unity throughout. It is not a religion of conflicting principles but is built squarely on reason, while Divine revelation is its surest pillar. Whatever is other than these must be understood as contentious and inspired by Satan."[16] So, I regret to say to you, what you propose is satanic to a Muslim; it defies reason and denies the pillar of revelation, the Qur'an. We believe that reason discovers this transcendent oneness, and we affirm both *that* it is and *what* it is in the Qur'an.

The oneness of God, called the *Tauh·īd*, is the foundation of everything else in Islam. Without it, there is no Islam. This oneness of God, according to the Qur'an, is something we can acquire by rational judgment, but it is further understood and defined in the Qur'an itself. But nothing that is said in the Qur'an about oneness defies reason, as your "three Gods–one God" does.

So, for example, for God to be one means that everything that he is, is identical with his oneness; this is what we mean by Allah's "simplicity," and many of your philosophical theologians have agreed with that. That oneness is necessarily and absolutely transcendent. If it were not, then it would not be necessary. Necessity, by definition, is not related to anything, except what is necessary. This is what I mean by transcendence.

So whatever the One is related to must itself be necessary, and one with him. If it were related to something not necessary, it would need that relationship in order to be what it is. But that cannot be the case. If necessity is going to be necessary, it must not be in need of anything contingent.

Therefore, it cannot be related to anything other than itself. Allah, therefore, due to his transcendent oneness, "never takes human relations into itself."[17] He could not do that and remain transcendent, necessary and one.

[15] 'Abduh, *The Theology of Unity*, 31.
[16] 'Abduh, *The Theology of Unity*, 48.
[17] Cragg, introduction to 'Abduh, *The Theology of Unity*, 18.

CA: That is a fascinating idea. But I am having trouble seeing how this is consistent with reason. I recognize that you claim that there are Islamic truths that transcend reason, but you also want to maintain that they are not impossible for reason to affirm. It seems to me, though, that what you propose is manifestly *un*reasonable.

IM: Really? How so?

CA: Maybe we can get at it this way. When you say that Allah never takes human relations into himself, does that mean that all that he is and does is, by definition, both transcendent and necessary? Was it necessary for him to reveal himself to Muhammad, his prophet? If so, then it seems his necessity is, in some sense, at least, dependent on Muhammad, or on Allah's act of revelation.

IM: Ah, this is a common misunderstanding of outsiders. To say Allah is a necessary being does not mean that everything that he does is necessary. Quite the opposite. This too is eminently reasonable, and you Christians affirm something similar.

If Allah's revelation to Muhammad were itself necessary, you would be correct. He would be dependent on something that was not necessary in order to be who he is. But this cannot be. In Allah there is nothing but oneness. Included in this oneness is that he alone is *absolutely free*. And I must emphasize that his freedom is *absolute*. There is *no constraint* in him whatsoever; indeed, there could not be, or he would be dependent. Whatever he does, he does freely.

In other words, his oneness and his necessity guarantee that he must be free. There is nothing that constrains him at any point—*nothing at all*! Surely the fact that a necessary being is absolutely free does not defy reason.[18]

As a transcendent and necessary being, in other words, he cannot be constrained by anything—not by creation, not by people, *not by anything*. So, because Allah is necessary there can be nothing that otherwise constrains him.[19] Whatever comes from Allah's knowledge and will must always be something that is freely chosen by him. And he is eternally free to choose *whatever* he wants at any "time."

CA: That does help clarify your position. God's revelation is free and freely chosen. He was not obligated to reveal anything. We Christians believe that as well with respect to the triune, Christian

[18] This notion might be a good and proper point to pursue in a dialog, but things could become quite technical. For an analysis of the relationship of necessity and freedom in God, see the discussion in Oliphint, *The Majesty of Mystery*, chap. 7. That discussion includes a biblical distinction between the necessary and the contingent in Scripture.

[19] Cragg, introduction to 'Abduh, *The Theology of Unity*, 19.

God. But let me ask you this. Since Allah decided to create the world and to reveal himself to men, doesn't that mean that he is now in some way *with* his creation and in a relationship *with* his people? How can one both create and then not in any way *relate* to that creation?

IM: This question surprises me; even some of your own philosophical theologians have affirmed this. It is not that Allah does not relate to his creation at all; rather it is that his relationship is one of *absolute* transcendence. He is above and beyond all that is contingent and accidental. He cannot involve himself in such things, or he would not be the one and transcendent Allah. Nothing, not even his creation, can constrain him in *any way* whatsoever. Allah is so far above everything that exists that there is nothing—and by that I mean *absolutely nothing*—that can, will, or could obligate him at *any* point. To summarize, then, since he is the only transcendent and necessary being, he alone is truly and absolutely free.

CA: May I ask you then about this revelation, the Qur'an? Since Allah revealed himself to your prophet, Muhammad, over the course of a couple of decades, is he not now constrained to be what that revelation says he is, since that revelation is his divine word, and to do what that revelation, what *he*, says he will do?

IM: This is a common idea in the West, and especially among Christians. But here is what you need to understand. The revelation that Allah gave to Muhammad was not a revelation of *himself*. Rather, it was a revelation of his *will*. What he gave to Muhammad in those years, and what we have in the Qur'an, is what he *requires* of all people. If we are able to meet those requirements, then we have hope that he will reward us in heaven. But hope is all that we can have, because Allah cannot be bound by anything, but is, always, absolutely free.

CA: But isn't the revelation of his will something that carries within it a *guarantee* of your reward? How can it be that you could follow the will of Allah and fail to reach your reward?

IM: What we must follow is the will of Allah, *in hopes* that we will reap our reward. But that reward cannot be a reward of necessity, because then Allah would be constrained by something contingent— *by our own actions*—which is a wicked thought.

As I'm sure you can understand as a Christian, what I am saying about Islam is that in all things, we depend on Allah; he alone is most free and will do whatever he wills. Even those things that he commands are, in the end, left up to him freely and without constraint to judge. He has no duty to reward or to punish. "To speak of duty resting upon God suggests obligation and constraint."[20]

As I have already said, Allah is so transcendent that duty is completely foreign to him. He is necessary, and so he alone is most free. As that greatest of Muslim apologists, Muhammad 'Abduh, has said, "The power of God transcends all human competence and has alone the supreme authority over all the desires of men and their realization, whether by voiding the obstacles or ordering the operative factors which elude either the knowledge or will of man."[21] In other words, while we admit that there is no assurance for any of us, we praise Allah that he alone does whatever he wants to do, and that nothing, *not even his revealed will*, can obligate him to do something.

CA: That is interesting and I will want to respond to it shortly. But first let me ask you one more question. Since you claim that the Qur'an is the word of Allah, that it came miraculously to Muhammad, who himself was supposedly illiterate and thus unable to construe such a book, how can it be that the Qur'an is a *reliable* guide for you?

IM: The question you ask highlights what is mysterious for Muslims. What Allah has revealed is his *will* for man. It is not for us to probe the relationship of that *will* to the *being* of Allah; that will remain a mystery. But the Qur'an is nothing other than a divine gift to his prophet. It is the very speech of Allah himself.

CA: But wait a minute. I thought you said that Allah is transcendent, one, and simple. He is in no way composed of parts. How could it be, then, that this one God spoke? Is not the very *act* of speech itself a participation in that which is plural and not one? By your own reckoning, that which is one can only refer, always and everywhere, to *itself*, if it is to remain one. But speech, by definition, says more than one thing and refers to other things. It *requires* plurality. When Allah speaks, does he not also, by using subjects, predicates, and so forth, deny his essential unity?

IM: You ask a question that is still a matter of great debate among Muslims. My own understanding, with which many Muslims agree, is that the Qur'an itself is eternal. It is the eternal speech of the one Allah. "The source of this speech to which man hearkens from God most high is undoubtedly eternally of His essence."[22] So, unlike you Christians, we will not reduce Allah to a dependence on

[20] 'Abduh, *The Theology of Unity*, 61.
[21] 'Abduh, *The Theology of Unity*, 64–65.
[22] 'Abduh, *The Theology of Unity*, 53.

man for his revelation. The prophet Muhammad was only a medium through whom Allah's eternal, divine revelation came. Like him, Allah's revelation is eternal. This, as I have said, is perfectly amenable to rational judgment, even if it requires the faith of a Muslim to believe it.

CA: Thank you for your kind and informative responses to my questions, Ish·āq. I would like, if I could, to address some questions that still remain. I would also like to address your responses from the perspective of Christianity, if you would allow me the opportunity.

IM: Yes. We have agreed to this; please do.

CA: I need to try to clarify what you have said. You say that the transcendent oneness of Allah surpasses our understanding, but that it is not impossible to grasp by reason, as my view of the Trinity is. I wonder, though, how you can know this.

Let's suppose that Allah is absolute oneness, as you say. That means that there is no differentiation *in him* whatsoever. This means, as you say, that even the revelation of his will, the Qur'an, is his *eternal* speech. But I remain puzzled as to how the transcendent One can have speech at all? If it is identical to him, it cannot be differentiated.

Just what *is* speech that contains no difference at all? How can there be meaning in speech that is one and not differentiated? I can't imagine that we humans could have *experience* of such a thing. And if it *is* something that is differentiated, then it cannot relate to the one of Allah, since nothing that is a plurality relates to him.

You will say to me that this is a great mystery. On that we can agree. But it seems to me that mystery, for you, has its foundation not in any real content, but only in utter and blind darkness.

IM: Wait a minute! Are you telling me that there is no mystery in Christianity? Surely, if there were such a thing as your "Trinity," you would be compelled to speak of it as a mystery. How is my mystery, as you say, of "utter darkness" different from your own mystery?

CA: I'm glad you asked. Let me explain what I mean by a mystery of "utter darkness." As far as I can tell from what you have said, Muslims (and many Christians, I should reiterate) affirm what is according to reason concerning Allah—that he is transcendental, eternal, infinite, one, and the like—but then they must also affirm that Allah has speech as one of his attributes.[23] The speech that Allah has is eternal,

---

[23] "Among the attributes of which the law tells are those which reason, though able to hold them compatible with the necessary Being, cannot of itself guide us to their recognition. . . . Among these is the attribute of speech." 'Abduh, *The Theology of Unity*, 53.

but then it comes to the temporal through the prophet Muhammad and composes the Qur'an. Correct?

IM: Yes, that is my position.

CA: The question then is, how can the eternal be temporal or related to the temporal in that way? Is this not a blatant contradiction, based on your own commitment to reason? Is not the eternal, which belongs alone to Allah, incompatible with the temporal, which is the Qur'an?

IM: Indeed it is, and that is the mystery. Reason cannot guide us in this.

CA: But can you not see that this mystery has no real content? It is simply the assertion of a contradiction, which reason can neither understand nor grasp. In that sense, I think, it seems to be "utter darkness," mystery with no real content. It is the affirmation of that which, on the basis of your own supposition of reason, *cannot* be. Mystery, for you, is the default position for that of which there is or could be absolutely no rational explanation, no experience or thought. Mystery, it seems, for Islam, is just another word for manifest absurdity.

IM: Well, I have said to you that Muslim scholars disagree about the status of the Qur'an. What you point out is one of the tensions that we all recognize in Islam. It will not, however, shake our faith in Allah and his divine will, revealed to us in the Qur'an.

CA: Okay, but there are other questions I would like to pursue for a moment. You have said that Allah is absolutely transcendent and that he is a necessary being and is one. As absolutely transcendent and necessary, he can have no relationship to anything contingent. This means, in part, that "there is nothing good for the universe which is incumbent upon him."[24] Your understanding of Allah's transcendence is, as you have said, such that "despite creation, revelation, law and prayer . . . it never takes human relations essentially into itself."[25]

This brings me to a question. Can you be sure that what Allah says is his will *is* actually, when all is said and done, his will? Is the will of Allah, revealed in the Qur'an, something to which he himself is bound, or is it just one more contingent thing that cannot bind him?

IM: Well, if you mean by "bound" that Allah must do what he says he will do, no. The Qur'an "affirms the reward of good deeds and the retribution of evil deeds and *leaves the recompense of approbation and punishment to the arbitrament of God.*"[26]

---

[24] Cragg, introduction to 'Abduh, *The Theology of Unity*, 19.
[25] Cragg, introduction to 'Abduh, *The Theology of Unity*, 18.
[26] 'Abduh, *The Theology of Unity*, 31, my emphasis.

I have already explained to you that reason dictates that Allah be both necessary and one. As such, he is also utterly transcendent. If he were bound by his revelation, then he could not be necessary, nor could he be transcendent. He would be dependent on something that is in this world. And that would destroy Allah, which is impossible.

We give all praise to him because he alone is absolutely transcendent and free. If he were bound, he would not be worthy of our praise.

CA: But you see, Ish·āq, Allah is not free at all.

IM: You recognize that to say such a thing is, in my religion, not only satanic, but *shirk*; it is not letting God be God. If there is anything that is anathema to a Muslim, it is *shirk*. We must let God be God, even if we cannot understand all that he is. What we do understand, however, is amenable to rational judgment, as I have said.

CA: But that is exactly my point, Ish·āq. You have shown, by reason, that Allah is a transcendent and necessary being. You have then drawn out the "reasonable" implications of this transcendence and necessity. One of those is that he must be most free. He cannot be constrained, because that which is constrained is dependent on something outside itself, and thus it cannot transcend all things and it cannot be necessary.

But here is my problem. For you, Allah is *not free* to have a relationship. He *cannot* have a relationship because if he did, he would not maintain his own transcendent necessity. His necessity, which you have posited as a rational principle, constrains him in such a way that all that he creates and all that he reveals can in no way determine what he does. Because he cannot commit himself to his followers, or even to his own word, Allah cannot be *most free*; he is a slave to his own transcendent necessity.

IM: Ah, but there you also have a problem as a Christian, don't you? You too will agree that your God cannot do some things. He cannot deny himself. To deny himself would mean that he could become something less than himself. Your God cannot lie. Doesn't that mean he is bound by his own transcendent and necessary character as well? Surely you will not hold, as some of your liberal and process theologians hold, that God denies and gives up his necessity in order to become who he is in the process of history, will you?

CA: No, you are correct. The triune God of Christianity necessarily exists and is necessarily who he essentially is; he cannot deny his essential deity, his "God-ness." I will get to that in a moment. Before I do, I would like to ask you one more thing.

IM: Go ahead.

CA: If it is true that Allah must not be constrained, then you have no real *assurance* of your eternal destiny. Is that correct?

IM: If you mean by assurance that I am guaranteed that Allah will bring me to heaven, yes, you are correct; I have no assurance of that. I cannot have such assurance, because—Allah be praised—his will cannot be constrained or in any way certain.

CA: How then, Ish·āq, do you *know* that the Qur'an is his will?

IM: We know because the Qur'an, as I have said, is Allah's eternal speech, which always was, but which has come-to-be through the Great Prophet, Muhammad.[27]

CA: But if I have heard you correctly, Allah's will does not in any way *constrain* him. Allah does now, and will always do, whatever he wants to do. And what he wants to do later could be the opposite of what he has revealed through Muhammad. This is why you can have no guarantees with respect to Allah's *will*, which is the sum and substance of Islamic religion. Is that correct?

IM: Yes, theoretically, that is correct. He cannot be constrained because he transcends all. But Muslims have hope that Allah will delight in our deeds and so bring us to heaven.

CA: I understand. But that hope is only an empty hope. And, like your understanding of mystery, it has no basis in *knowledge*. It is, as we like to say, a blind faith.

Since the Qur'an is a revelation of Allah's will, and what Allah may do is in no way constrained by the Qur'an, what he *wills* to do in the end may be the opposite of his will revealed in the Qur'an. Correct?

IM: Yes. Allah be praised. That is correct.

CA: Well, Ish·āq, if that is true, then it just may be that what I believe and what you believe are the same thing, though you could never *know* that.

IM: What? This is blasphemy. I do not believe that Allah is three gods; I do not believe that he has a son. I reject all that you hold to be true.

CA: Yes, I know. I did not say that you believe what I believe. What I said is that *it may be the case* that what you believe and what I believe are the same. Allah is free to *will* such a thing.

---

[27] "Whatever we may say about the mystery of God's eternal attribute of speech, there is no necessity about the 'incidence' thereof in the [Qur'an] of which Muhammad . . . begins to be the recipient. God cannot be held eternally under the obligation of that initiative. From this angle it must be seen to-come-to-be within the freedom of His will, though it is eternally in His knowledge." Cragg, introduction to 'Abduh, *The Theology of Unity*, 20.

You will have to admit, Ish·āq, that Allah is free enough to decide and to will that he will bring all Christians to heaven and reject all Muslims. You will also have to agree that he may determine to have a son. He may, if he so wills, determine that Christian belief is to be rewarded eternally and Muslim belief is to be condemned. If this were true, would you say, "Allah be praised"?

This, it seems to me, is the only "reasonable" conclusion to your own religion. There is nothing in the transcendent necessity of Allah, since that necessity includes his absolute freedom (except, as I have said, not the freedom to relate to anything), that hinders him from accepting all Christians. So it just may be, based on what you have told me, that Christianity is the true religion and Islam is not, at least from the perspective of Allah's absolutely free *will*.

IM: Why does it seem as though you are trying to trick me? Muslims have never allowed that Allah could accept Christianity. At least Muslims, unlike you Christians, attempt to be reasonable. What you have said to me seems completely *un*reasonable. That is no surprise, since your own religion sacrifices reason on the altar of absurdity.

CA: I know it seems unreasonable to you, but if you think about it, it is consistent with what you have told me about your own faith. Because your faith is, in the end, blind, anything goes when it comes to Allah's will.

Will you allow me to address your charge of absurdity?

IM: Please do. I suspect that what you see as absurd in Islam will pale in significance compared to your absurd notion of "three Gods—one God."

CA: It may seem so to you, given your own commitment to reason as your standard of truth. You have explained to me a religion that holds reason to be an all-determinative guide. But I have tried to show you that to have such a view of reason leads to conclusions that your rational religion cannot tolerate. It seems you might need another foundation than reason if you want to make sense of yourself and your world. And that foundation cannot be the "pillar" of the Qur'an, since, by your own testimony, the Qur'an can in no way bind Allah.

That is why, for the Christian, our foundation is in God's own revelation. That revelation comes to us in creation and in his Word, the Bible. But notice the initial difference between us on this. God's revelation is a revelation of *himself*. It includes a revelation of his will, but that will is inextricably linked to his *character*. God not only tells us what he requires of us, but he also tells us *who he is*.

I suspect, Ish·āq, that the main reason Islam is so fraught with rational difficulties is that, from the Christian perspective, it has tried to take, by way of reason alone, God's revelation in creation *by itself*, and then Islam attempts to exalt that ("reasonable") revelation above all else.

In Christianity, we affirm that God's invisible attributes, including his eternal power and divine nature, are clearly seen and understood by all men through what has been made (Rom. 1:20). Being "clearly seen" and "understood" is something that obtains for all people not because they are so eminently "reasonable," but rather because they are all created in God's image.

But not only is God's *character* given in natural revelation; God's "righteous requirements" are known through creation as well. So clear are those requirements that all people know that if they do not abide by them, they deserve to die (Rom. 1:32). Your religion affirms as much. The deep and abiding universal problem, however, is found in what people *do* with this clear and understood natural revelation of God.

If they remain in rebellion against the true and triune God, they spend their lives exchanging the truth that they receive from him for a lie (Rom. 1:25); they always and everywhere suppress the glory of that truth about God by substituting other gods in his place, so that they will worship something that is man-made, rather than their God and Creator (Rom. 1:23).

The genesis of Islam, if I may put it this way, is its unrighteous suppression of the truth that God constantly gives. The worship of Allah is the worship of a man-made idol. Islam itself is an example of the suppression of the righteous requirements of the true God. God's revelation says that even though all people know God's requirements, and even though they know that violating God's requirements will bring certain death, they not only continue to violate them, but also gather to themselves others who violate them (Rom. 1:32).

This sounds like a description of Islam to me, Ish·āq. The law of God, which is his will, is written on every heart, including yours, and including all Muslims. Islam is an attempt both to suppress that law and to make it something that will end with reward and punishment. This is all you have when God's clear natural revelation is perfectly understood, but wrongly manipulated.

IM: I understand that you are explaining to me your position as a Christian, but these are strong, even satanic, words. I think, though, that you have trapped yourself. If God's revelation in nature produces the likes of Islam, how then can you avoid being Muslim? Don't you receive the same revelation that we do?

CA: Yes, all people receive it. The difference, however, goes back to the beginning of our discussion. You remember that you wanted to establish common theological ground with me. And you wanted to do that by an appeal to our theologians who have argued that the characteristics of Allah, which we understand by way of natural theology, are the same characteristics that we attribute to God.

I told you then what I must reiterate now. You and I cannot have "what is rational" as our common foundation. What you think is "rational" is, as I have already indicated, actually a product of your Islamic religion. That is why you thought you could leap from the finite to the infinite, from the temporal to the eternal, with no principle available, thus no foundation in experience or in rationality. What you thought to be "rational" was actually interpreted through your Islamic grid. You have "read" Islam into what you deem to be rational.

The foundation on which I understand God's natural revelation has to be what he has revealed to me in his Word. It is through his Word alone that his works can be properly understood. There is no true natural theology apart from an acceptance and understanding of "supernatural" theology, in God's Word. Apart from that Word, there is no *certain* understanding, as your own religion illustrates. With that Word, there is *real* and *certain* assurance.[28]

IM: *Real* and *certain* assurance? Are you telling me now that your God is *not* transcendent and necessary, but is bound to do what you say he must do? This makes your God something contingent and surely not worthy of praise.

CA: No. I am saying that the triune God has *committed himself* to what he has said. I believe what he has said, so I can now have assurance. His commitments are strong; in fact, they are absolute and thus binding.

---

[28] Note, for example, the Westminster Confession of Faith 18.1–2: "Although hypocrites and other unregenerate men may vainly deceive themselves with false hopes and carnal presumptions of being in the favor of God, and estate of salvation (which hope of theirs shall perish): yet such as truly believe in the Lord Jesus, and love Him in sincerity, endeavoring to walk in all good conscience before Him, may, in this life, be certainly assured that they are in the state of grace, and may rejoice in the hope of the glory of God, which hope shall never make them ashamed.

"II. This certainty is not a bare conjectural and probable persuasion grounded upon a fallible hope; but an infallible assurance of faith founded upon the divine truth of the promises of salvation, the inward evidence of those graces unto which these promises are made, the testimony of the Spirit of adoption witnessing with our spirits that we are the children of God, which Spirit is the earnest of our inheritance, whereby we are sealed to the day of redemption."

IM: Ah, now I see. This is why you could not follow me in affirming that God is necessary. Your God is *not* necessary at all; he has bound himself to creation and now must depend on creation in order for his will to be accomplished.

This is no transcendent God. This is nothing more than a man. No wonder you want to posit a "three Gods–one God" being. If God is a man, then three can be one, black can be white, and, if I may borrow your criticism, Islam can be Christianity. Maybe, according to your scheme, we both do have the same religion after all. Absurdity knows no bounds.

CA: I'm glad you brought that up. Here is where the mystery that we confess is so different and antithetical to yours. We do believe that God is one God in three persons. That is indeed a mystery. We do not know *how* God can be the kind of tripersonal God that he is. We have no experience of such things, neither do we have a rational principle that can exhaustively comprehend it. But we need not have such if we base what we know on his revelation to us.

You see, since God's revelation reveals *himself*, and his will is a part of that self-revelation (not, as in Islam, disconnected from him), we can, therefore, affirm God's *character* as triune (as well as his will) without destroying the rational or the empirical. It is the rational and empirical that are, themselves, *revelatory* of that character. And it is his spoken Word that tells us what his character is like. We see, then, the rational and the empirical through the lenses of what he has spoken in Scripture.

IM: But how is this mystery of the Trinity not the same thing as what you call the "utter darkness" of the mystery of Allah and Islam?

CA: It is not the same because the mystery that we hold is *based on* what God has said about himself, and on what he reveals about himself. It is not, as with Islam, based simply on the limits of our rational faculty or our experiences. So we can affirm that it is true, even though we cannot rationally explicate its depths, and even though we have no experience of such things, because he has told us that this is who he is. It is mystery, then, but it is not "utter darkness" because it has real, true, revelatory content.

IM: So it seems to me that this triune God of yours, who has bound himself to his creation, *cannot be* transcendent and necessary, because he has bound himself to his creation. This seems to me to be no more mysterious than quantum physics. It's just something in creation that we have not yet discovered. But it is not transcendent!

How can something like that be praised? At least Allah transcends all of this contingency, *including his will in the Qur'an*. At least he retains characteristics that have normally been ascribed to what is called God. Your God is nothing more than another aspect of creation. It doesn't matter, then, whether he is three or one or both at the same time!

CA: This is where Christianity, rooted in the revelation that God gives to us, is the only way to make sense of God and of anything else. You see, Ish·āq, Christianity has always held that God's special revelation of himself has come to people, specifically his people, by way of God's condescension.

We hold, as you do, that since God is transcendent, he transcends space and time. So, like you, we say that God is infinite, eternal, and so forth. As infinite, however, he does not remain aloof from his creation. Neither is he "constrained" by those attributes. Instead, he is so free, so majestic, and so utterly praiseworthy that he is able to come down, to condescend, to his creation. Unlike Allah, he is not a prisoner of an abstract and rationalistic understanding of transcendence or necessity.

The triune God of Christianity can remain who he is—infinite, eternal, independent, necessary—even while he condescends to reveal himself in ways that show him to be with and in his creation in order to interact with it.

IM: And you accuse me of contradiction? How can this not be utter and meaningless absurdity? You're telling me that the necessary is contingent, that the transcendent is immanent, that the one is three, that the eternal is temporal, that the infinite is finite. No wonder you think that Islam can be Christianity!

CA: Well, you're partly right. But remember, my criticism was not that Islam can be Christianity based on *my* beliefs, but rather on the basis of your own principles and religion. That needs to be clear. However, I am not simply saying these things in order to affirm crass contradictions. Think of it this way. Before there was creation, there was nothing but God. You yourself believe that, don't you?

IM: Indeed I do.

CA: When God determined to create, he also determined to *bind himself* to that creation. He determined that he would, from that point on, be in a real, dynamic relationship with all that he created, and especially with man (male and female), since he created them in his image.[29] To be "image of God" means, in part, that there will be, from

---

[29] That God is the "I Am" (Greek, *eimi*) and man is image (Greek, *eikon*) has deep and abiding implications for a Christian view of reality. See Oliphint, *The Majesty of Mystery*, chap. 5.

then on, an eternal relationship with man. The end result of that relationship will be either a new heaven and new earth eternally with him or eternal punishment under his wrath. In either case, there is a *relationship*. A relationship characterized by his grace, in Christ, or one characterized by his wrath, in Adam. We call this relationship God's covenant.

In order to have this covenant relationship, God freely decided that he would enter "our" world (which is really his world), interact with us, walk with Adam in the garden, and, when Adam decided to rebel against him, condescend to redeem a people for himself.

IM: Hold it! Islam is built on the firm belief that it is we who must try to gain the favor of Allah. For Allah to gain that for us is beneath him and destroys his transcendent character. He could not be Allah if he stooped to do such a mundane and menial task.

CA: Of course he couldn't, because you have defined Allah according to your own rationalistic notion of transcendence, of necessity, and of unity, rather than according to what God has said in his Word. But if we define God according to what he has said, we affirm that he continues to be who he is in all of his transcendence, even while he comes down to accomplish what we ourselves are not able to accomplish.

Ish·āq, you are correct to assert that your own obedience to the will of Allah cannot garner assurance. It never could. There is no way to meet the standard that you have set for yourself. The best your rational view of Allah can give you is a "maybe, maybe not" judgment in the end.

But God came down, in the person of his Son, and took on a human nature, even while he remained fully God, and accomplished what you and I could never accomplish. *He gained the reward that we could not gain*, so that we can have assurance based on *his* obedience, not ours.

IM: Hold it again! I have agreed to listen to you, but at this point I must protest. Now you are telling me that this Son of God, who is God—eternal, infinite, etc.—came down to earth and became temporal and finite? How am I supposed to believe that?

CA: Well, if I may say so, it should not be that difficult, since you already have such ideas embedded in your own religion. Perhaps you can think of it like this. The Bible calls the Son of God "the Word." This Word always was, and was present before creation. Through him, all things were made, and apart from him nothing was made that has been made (John 1:3). This Word of God is *with* God, so that he is distinct, and he *is* God, so that he is identical to God, with all the attendant attributes of God himself (John 1:1). This Word, we are told in Scripture, became flesh and dwelt among us. But his becoming flesh in no way undermined or cancelled out his essential deity.

Now, the "word" that you have in your religion is the Qur'an. As you said, debates still rage as to whether the Qur'an came to be or is eternal, or both. Those debates, I am sorry to tell you, will never be resolved. They cannot be resolved based on your own rational principle. But here is the answer to your question: what you have in Islam is something that is eternal—the speech of God[30]—and that has "come-to-be within the freedom of his will."[31]

So, in reality, what you have in Islam is a parody, a suppressed *copy*, of the truth that is in Christianity. The true Word of God is both eternal—in that he is and remains fully, completely, and truly God—and temporal—in that he took on a human nature. You grant this kind of tension within your own religion, in the Qur'an. Surely you have no basis on which to discount it in Christianity.

So, if I may continue, the Word of God, who is Jesus Christ, accomplished the redemption that is necessary if we are going to see God in all of his glory. The reason I can have *assurance* about that is the same reason you can have assurance if you trust in what I trust in—because God is the One who has accomplished all that you and I need. In Christianity, unlike Islam, we do not and cannot trust our own deeds, even if those deeds are in response to God's revealed will! By trusting *him* in the person of his Son, instead of ourselves, I can be assured of his commitment to me, not because I have done what is needed, but because *he himself* has.

IM: But you have not addressed the basic problem with all of this. How am I to accept a God who is both one and three, or a God who is both necessary and contingent? Such things seem patently absurd to any rational mind.

CA: Not to *any* rational mind; only to those who will not acknowledge the truth that they know. The way to accept such things is to replace your notion of a supposedly neutral "rational mind" with the Christian notion.

IM: So Christians now have their own logic?

---

[30] 'Abduh, *The Theology of Unity*, 53.
[31] Cragg, introduction to 'Abduh, *The Theology of Unity*, 20.

CA: Not at all. And here issues can become very complex, but let me try to restate it this way. Islam has erected a notion of transcendence, unity, necessity, and so on that has its foundation in an abstract rationality. Because of that, it cannot find a way to relate the necessity that is Allah's with the contingency of creation. To put it in logical terms, Allah = Allah and that is all that can be said for certain. Nothing else can impinge on that blank identity that is supposedly his.

Aristotle had this same idea, I'm sure you know from your own Muslim philosophers, when positing his notion of the "absolute." For him, that which is ultimate has to be "thought thinking itself," since if "thought" thought anything but itself, it would be dependent on that thought to be what it is, and thus it would not be transcendent, necessary, and absolute.

Islam's god is the same as Aristotle's absolute. That is why I have shown you that it is your view of transcendence, unity, and necessity that "traps" Allah and predetermines that he can have no relation to creation and can have no obligations to anyone, even to those who earnestly seek to do his will. It is these rational notions that you ascribe to Allah that are the real gods in Islam, so that even Allah cannot in any way move beyond them. He who is said to be most free is *not* free after all, since he is not able to relate to what he has made. That relationship, you think, would destroy him.

IM: But I thought you Christians agreed that your God is transcendent, one, and necessary.

CA: Yes, we do. But the necessity that is God's is not an abstract necessity that some notion of rationality defines, and to which our God must adhere. Necessity, for Christians, is first defined and delineated in terms of who God has revealed himself to be. So, we believe that God is necessary in that he must exist. There is no possibility that he could not exist. And everything that he is, in himself, is identical with him, even when properly distinguished.

Because God is one God in three persons, the Father, Son, and Spirit are all identical with the one God, though the Father is not identical with the Son who is not identical with the Spirit. There is, then, in God, the necessity of the one and the necessary distinction of the three. The necessity of the one is the necessity of the triune God as God. So, in God, both unity and diversity are equally ultimate. The one does not take precedence over the three; neither are the three primary over the one.

Because of this equal and absolute ultimacy of unity and diversity, the triune God is not bound by an abstract notion of unity, transcendence, or necessity. His necessity is triune necessity. His unity is triune unity. His transcendence is triune transcendence.

What does all of this mean? It means that God can remain who he is in his oneness, his transcendence, and his necessary character, even while, when, and if he condescends to reveal himself because he has graciously bound himself, in covenant, to creation and to his human creatures, without in any way denying or destroying those essential attributes.

An abstract "oneness," by definition, can admit of no such thing; this is why you have trapped Allah in his necessity, transcendence, and oneness. A triune oneness can allow for a "both–and" that is not contradictory because he is, at one and the same time, *both* one *and* three. In other words, built into the essential character of God is both his oneness and his *relationship* among the three persons, each of whom is the one God. The relationship that each of the persons has with the other in no way undermines or destroys the fact that he is one God.

IM: Tell me this. How in the world do you dare to charge me with the mystery of "utter darkness" when you speak of such things? If what you say is true, then, short of absurdity, the nature of God must be *nothing but* utter darkness. There can be no real, intelligible content to what you are saying.

CA: This is the most exciting aspect of Christianity, of which your religion has no idea. I have agreed with you that there is indeed mystery in our understanding of God. His ways are not our ways. No one has known the mind of the Lord in any exhaustive way. But here's the good news for you and for me.

This God, who is one and three, has come down. He has revealed not simply his *will*, but *himself* to us and to any who have eyes to see. He has revealed himself in his Son, who took on a human nature. The Son was sent, and agreed to come, to accomplish what we could not. He fulfilled his task perfectly. After completing his work on earth, he ascended into heaven and sent the Holy Spirit. It is this Spirit who is drawing the Lord's people to himself. And in doing so, he unites us to his Son forever.

So the mystery that is God's character is not utter darkness at all. It is a mystery that has as its expression, for us, the revelation of God's character and the work of God in creation and in redemption. What God has revealed himself to be, in creation and redemption, in his Son and in his Word, is exactly who he is in himself. He is *more than* what he has revealed, but he is not contradictory to what he has revealed. There is *mystery*, but there is also real *knowledge* and not utter darkness. To be sure, the triune God is and will always remain incomprehensible. But what he has made known to us is exactly (though not comprehensively) *who he is.*

So mystery, for the Christian, is a confession that God, though knowable and known, is never in any way exhausted by our knowledge of him. How could he be when he remains transcendent, eternal, infinite, immutable, and more? But we do know him, and what we know of him will not and cannot be false. Neither can it completely define him. What we know is true, though never (in this life or the next) exhaustive.

You see, Ish·āq, if I may say this with respect, as much as you proclaim, "Allahu Akbar," "God is Great(er)," it seems plain to me that Allah is not so great as you have been led to believe. He is not able, freely, to choose to relate himself to you, to the Qur'an, or to his world. He is not so great as to freely reveal *himself.* He is a prisoner of Islam's rationalism. He is trapped, by virtue of a rationalistic view of oneness, so that he cannot relate to you, to me, or to anything else. He is nothing more than Aristotle's "thought thinking itself."

The Christian God, however, is *truly* great. He is and will eternally be one God—simple, transcendent, necessary, and eternal. But he is also able, freely, to choose to be in a relationship with his creation, for eternity, all the while remaining who he is and has always been.

Now you can see that many of those attributes that you want to ascribe to Allah truly belong to the triune God. But more than that, the true and triune God has freely and specially chosen to bind himself to all who will come to him in repentance and faith, and they will live with him, most *certainly* and *assuredly*, in the new heaven and the new earth forever. This is true and eternal *greatness.* There can be no other God; there can be no assurance without this God.

IM: Okay. You have convinced me, at least, that you and I cannot *in any way* agree on who God is. Yours is defined by your own revelation. Even your view of unity, of transcendence, and of necessity have to have God's triunity as a foundation in order to be properly understood.

I must leave now; it is prayer time. But I would like to hear you more concerning these things.

As we have said, there is more to this discussion that could have been pursued. We did not get into the history of Islam or the historic alterations of the Qur'an, and other matters that are important and debated in Islam.

What we did do, however, is seek to show how the religious system of Islam cannot stand of its own rationalistic weight. We then argued that only Christianity answers the questions and needs that are an integral part of the Islamic religion. This sample dialog can at least point a way forward as we think about how best to answer those whose religions can seem, in places, to align closely with Christianity. In reality, however, they are as far away from Christianity as is unbelief itself.

Vain are the heathen gods, idols and helpless;
God made the heavens, and his glory they tell;
Honor and majesty shine out before him,
Beauty and strength in his temple dwell.[32]

---

[32] "Sing to the Lord, Sing His Praises," *The Psalter*, 1912, from Psalm 96.

Conclusion

> If we drop to the level of the merely probable truthfulness of Christian theism, we, to that extent, lower the claims of God upon men. Accordingly I do not reject "the theistic proofs" but merely insist on formulating them in such a way as not to compromise the doctrines of Scripture. That is to say, if the theistic proof is constructed as it ought to be constructed, it is objectively valid, whatever the attitude of those to whom it comes may be.[1]

What I have proposed throughout this book are principles and practices of a covenantal apologetic. I have attempted to lay out what theological tenets have to be in place in order to think properly about a defense of Christianity. I have also attempted to show, by means of sample dialogs, how those principles and tenets might be applied. My goal throughout has been to elaborate on a covenantal apologetic as the consistently Reformed approach to a defense of Christianity. In so doing, I have argued that persuasion is the best means by which we might defend the faith.

There are a couple of points that may not have received the attention they deserve and that I would like to emphasize before we finish.

If persuasion is the means by which we are to defend the Christian faith, then this requires, in the end, that we must be people who pursue holiness, without which no one will see the Lord (Heb. 12:14). It means, in the first place, that we cannot expect to imbibe the spirit of the age and at the same time to present a credible defense of Christianity. This is the *ethos* of persuasion, and we have not given that central and crucial factor its due in this book. This lack of attention should not, however, take away from its *necessary* role in apologetics.

---

[1]Cornelius Van Til, *The Defense of the Faith*, 4th ed., ed. K. Scott Oliphint (Phillipsburg, NJ: P&R, 2008), 255.

It has to be emphasized here, therefore, at the conclusion of our discussion, that a defense of Christianity must not be wrongly defensive. If we lose our focus and begin to think that our goal is to "out-argue" or intellectually batter those to whom we speak, we have lost the proper *ethos* for a Christian defense. Having the *ethos* of holiness does not mean that we have to be without strong conviction or be soft in our presentation of the gospel's defense. One of Van Til's favorite phrases was that we are to be *suaviter in modo, fortiter in re*—mild in manner, strong in matter.

What this means for us is that we must remember all along that the Lord God will do *his own* sovereign work, but that he has chosen to do that work *through us*. It is not ours to convert; it is not even ours to "win" an argument. Ours is to show forth the gentleness and respect that Christ himself had, even as we fight the good fight of contending for the faith once for all given to the saints (Jude 3).

We must contend. We must fight. We must not lose sight of the fact that we are in a real "holy war." But we must also constantly remind ourselves that the Lord of hosts is the commander of the army, and not we ourselves. As his loyal subjects, we fight in full recognition that he alone is in charge, and he alone will procure whatever victory he deems fit and appropriate. As his subjects, we must be vigilant to use only his weapons, and content that those weapons always accomplish the perfect will of our commander in chief.

A very helpful and instructive passage in this regard is Joshua 5:13–15:

> When Joshua was by Jericho, he lifted up his eyes and looked, and behold, a man was standing before him with his drawn sword in his hand. And Joshua went to him and said to him, "Are you for us, or for our adversaries?" And he said, "No; but I am the commander of the army of the LORD. Now I have come." And Joshua fell on his face to the earth and worshiped and said to him, "What does my lord say to his servant?" And the commander of the LORD's army said to Joshua, "Take off your sandals from your feet, for the place where you are standing is holy." And Joshua did so.

Notice, first of all, that Joshua asks the wrong question. He wants to know whether the man in front of him is "with him or against him." Without impugning any motives of Joshua here, it is helpful to recognize that, for Joshua, these are not the only two options available. So even as Joshua expects a "for" or "against" answer, what he receives is a "No." But his question is not a "yes or no" question. In other words, the assumption behind the question is wrong.

In our holy warfare, it is not "us versus them" only, as Joshua apparently surmises, but it is, in a Christian context, the Lord of hosts and those he has called to himself versus those who oppose him. What we do when we defend the faith that God has graciously bestowed on us is move out as servants and soldiers—*warriors*—under this commander, this divine warrior, the Lord. The *real* question to ask is, are you for the Lord or are you for his adversaries? When we defend the faith against opponents of Christianity, the opposition, we must always remind ourselves, is against Christ and his Word, not mainly against *us*.

Notice also that once Joshua recognizes who is standing in front of him, he falls on his face and worships. Having worshiped, he is then moved to ask the proper question, "What does my Lord say to his servant?"

This, as ought to be clear to us by now, is the question that we should ask and answer as we "premeditate" regarding our Christian defense. We have nothing to say to unbelief, in whatever form, unless it is what the Lord himself says to us in his Word. What we hope to offer our opponents is of eternal value. We hope to present the context and content in which alone is the eternal life found only in Christ. This can only be done if we know what the Lord has said to us, his servants, in his Word. In any apologetic encounter, we must ask, with Joshua, "What does my Lord say to his servant?" In recognizing that the Lord of hosts is the commander of his army, in agreeing that we must know and communicate his Word to those who oppose him, we are then in a position to do what the Lord commands.

Like Moses on Mount Sinai, Joshua stood on holy ground. He bowed and he worshiped the One who alone is worthy of worship. Once Joshua's perspective was "redeemed," so that he understood himself to be fighting as a servant, not as a sovereign, only then was he fit to fight the battle of Jericho in the name and for the glory of the Lord of hosts.

So also with us. A covenantal apologetic is not an isolated or abstract "system" or "structure" that need only be uniformly and firmly applied to any and every unbelieving position. Rather, it is infused with the principles of Scripture itself, the Lord's principles, so that he might use such things, and the likes of us, to continue to build a footstool for the feet of Christ. It is a defense that requires our unwavering commitment to him, and to be *like* him. It requires, as well, that we know what the Lord has said and how what he has said can help us to fight his battles in his way.

In the midst of those battles, the enemies of Christ are being subdued, even now. Some are subdued by a proper and biblical defense of the Christian faith. Some are subdued by a proper and biblical preaching of the gospel. So in preparation to fight his battle, we say, "What does my Lord say to his servant?"

Perhaps the Lord will see fit to use you in a holy, persuasive, gentle, and respectful response to unbelief, to help build that footstool. Once that footstool is complete, and the last enemy is destroyed, then the perishable shall put on the imperishable, the mortal shall put on immortality. "For he must reign until he has put all his enemies under his feet. The last enemy to be destroyed is death. . . . When the perishable puts on the imperishable, and the mortal puts on immortality, then shall come to pass the saying that is written: 'Death is swallowed up in *victory*.' . . . But thanks be to God, who gives us the *victory* through our Lord Jesus Christ" (1 Cor. 15:25–26, 54, 57).

The church shall never perish!
Her dear Lord to defend,
To guide, sustain and cherish
Is with her to the end;
Though there be those that hate her,
And false sons in her pale,
Against or foe or traitor
She ever shall prevail.[2]

---

[2] Samuel J. Stone, "The Church's One Foundation," 1866.

Bibliography

'Abduh, Muhammad. *The Theology of Unity*. Translated by Ish·āq Musa'ad and Kenneth Cragg. London: George Allen & Unwin, 1966.

Aquinas, Thomas. *Summa Theologiae: Latin Text, English Translation, Introduction, Notes, Appendices and Glossary*. 60 vols. Edited by Thomas Gilby. London: Eyre & Spottiswoode; New York: McGraw-Hill, 1964.

Aristotle. "Rhetorica." In *The Basic Works of Aristotle*, edited by Richard McKeon, 1325–1451. New York: Random House, 1968.

Athanasius. *The Incarnation of the Word, Being the Treatise of St. Athanasius (De Incarnatione Verbi Dei)*. Translated by C.S.M.V. St. Th. London: Geoffrey Bles, Centenary, 1944).

Bavinck, Herman. *Reformed Dogmatics*. Vol. 1, *Prolegomena*. Edited by John Bolt. Translated by John Vriend. Grand Rapids: Baker Academic, 2003.

_____. *Reformed Dogmatics*. Vol. 2, *God and Creation*. Edited by John Bolt. Translated by John Vriend. Grand Rapids: Baker Academic, 2004.

_____. *Reformed Dogmatics*. Vol. 3, *Sin and Salvation in Christ*. Edited by John Bolt. Translated by John Vriend. Grand Rapids: Baker Academic, 2006.

Bunge, Mario Augusto. *Critical Approaches to Science and Philosophy*. Piscataway, NJ: Transaction, 1998.

Calvin, John. *Institutes of the Christian Religion*. Edited by John T. McNeill. Translated by Ford Lewis Battles. 2 vols. The Library of Christian Classics. Philadelphia: Westminster Press, 1960.

Clifford, W. K. "The Ethics of Belief." In *Philosophy of Religion: An Anthology*, edited by Charles Taliaferro and Paul J. Griffiths, 196–99. Blackwell Philosophy Anthologies. Oxford: Blackwell, 2003.

Copi, Irving M. *An Introduction to Logic*. 7th ed. New York: Macmillan, 1986.

Cragg, Kenneth. Introduction to *The Theology of Unity*, by Muhammad 'Abduh, 9–23. London: George Allen & Unwin, 1966.

Cunningham, David S. *Faithful Persuasion: Theology*. Notre Dame, IN: University of Notre Dame Press, 1992.

Dawkins, Richard. *The Blind Watchmaker: Why the Evidence of Evolution Reveals a Universe without Design*. New York: Norton, 1996.

_____. *The God Delusion*. New York: Houghton Mifflin, 2008.

Dennett, Daniel C. *Breaking the Spell: Religion as a Natural Phenomenon*. New York: Penguin, 2007.

_____. *Darwin's Dangerous Idea: Evolution and the Meanings of Life*. New York: Simon & Schuster, 1995.

DeYoung, Kevin. *The Hole in Our Holiness: Filling the Gap between Gospel Passion and the Pursuit of Godliness*. Wheaton, IL: Crossway, 2012.

Edey, Maitland A., and Donald C. Johanson. *Blueprints: Solving the Mystery of Evolution*. Boston: Little, Brown, 1989.

Edgar, William, and K. Scott Oliphint, eds. *Christian Apologetics Past and Present: A Primary Source Reader*. Vol. 1, *To 1500*. Wheaton, IL: Crossway, 2009.

_____. *Christian Apologetics Past and Present: A Primary Source Reader*. Vol. 2, *From 1500*. Wheaton, IL: Crossway, 2011.

Flint, Thomas P. *Divine Providence: The Molinist Account*. Cornell Studies in the Philosophy of Religion. Ithaca, NY: Cornell University Press, 1998.

Harris, Sam. *Free Will*. New York: Free Press, 2012.

Henry, Matthew. *Matthew Henry's Commentary on the Whole Bible: Complete and Unabridged in One Volume*. Peabody, MA: Hendrickson, 1996.

Hodge, Charles. *A Commentary on the Epistle to the Romans*. Rev. ed. Philadelphia: Claxton, 1866.

Hume, David. *Dialogues Concerning Natural Religion*. 2nd ed. London: 1779.

Israel, Jonathan Irvine. *Radical Enlightenment: Philosophy and the Making of Modernity, 1650–1750*. New York: Oxford University Press, 2001.

Kant, Immanuel. *Critique of Pure Reason*. Translated by Norman Kemp Smith. New York: St. Martin's, 1958.

Kenny, Anthony. "Omniscience, Eternity, and Time." In *The Impossibility of God*, edited by Michael Martin and Ricki Monnier, 210–19. Amherst, NY: Prometheus, 2003.

Martin, Michael, and Ricki Monnier, eds. *The Impossibility of God*. Amherst, NY: Prometheus, 2003.

Montgomery, John Warwick. "Once Upon an a Priori." In *Jerusalem and Athens: Critical Discussions on the Philosophy and Apologetics of Cornelius Van Til*, edited by E. R. Geehan, 380–403. Nutley, NJ: Presbyterian and Reformed, 1971.

Moo, Douglas J. *The Letters to the Colossians and to Philemon*. The Pillar New Testament Commentary. Grand Rapids: Eerdmans, 2008.

Moore, Brooke Noel. *Making Your Case: Critical Thinking and the Argumentative Essay*. Mountain View, CA: Mayfield, 1995.

Muether, John R. *Cornelius Van Til: Reformed Apologist and Churchman*. Phillipsburg, NJ: P&R, 2008.

Muller, Richard A. *Post-Reformation Reformed Dogmatics: The Rise and Development of Reformed Orthodoxy, ca. 1520 to ca. 1725.* Vol. 1, *Prolegomena to Theology.* 2nd ed. Grand Rapids: Baker, 2003.

_____. *Post-Reformation Reformed Dogmatics: The Rise and Development of Reformed Orthodoxy, ca. 1520 to ca. 1725.* Vol. 3, *The Divine Essence and Attributes.* 2nd ed. Grand Rapids: Baker, 2003.

Oliphint, K. Scott. *The Battle Belongs to the Lord: The Power of Scripture for Defending Our Faith.* Phillipsburg, NJ: P&R, 2003.

_____. "Because It Is the Word of God." In *Did God Really Say? Affirming the Truthfulness and Trustworthiness of Scripture,* edited by David B. Garner, 1–22. Phillipsburg, NJ: P&R, 2012.

_____. "The Irrationality of Unbelief." In *Revelation and Reason: New Essays in Reformed Apologetics,* edited by K. Scott Oliphint and Lane G. Tipton, 59–73. Phillipsburg, NJ: P&R, 2007.

_____. "Is There a Reformed Objection to Natural Theology?" *Westminster Theological Journal* 74, no. 1 (2012): 169–204.

_____. *The Majesty of Mystery: Celebrating the Glory of An Incomprehensible God.* Bellingham, WA: Lexham Press, 2016.

_____. "The Old New Reformed Epistemology." In *Revelation and Reason: New Essays in Reformed Apologetics,* edited by K. Scott Oliphint and Lane G. Tipton, 207–19. Phillipsburg, NJ: P&R, 2007.

_____. "A Primal and Simple Knowledge." In *A Theological Guide to Calvin's Institutes: Essays and Analysis,* edited by David Hall and Peter A. Lillback, 16–33. Phillipsburg, NJ: P&R, 2008.

_____. *Reasons for Faith: Philosophy in the Service of Theology.* Phillipsburg, NJ: P&R, 2006.

_____. "Something Much Too Plain to Say: A Systematic Theological Apologetic." In *Resurrection and Eschatology,* edited by Lane G. Tipton and Jeffrey C. Waddington, 361–82. Phillipsburg, NJ: P&R, 2008.

_____. *Thomas Aquinas.* Great Thinker Series. Phillipsburg, NJ: P&R, 2017.

_____. "Using Reason by Faith." *Westminster Theological Journal* 73, no. 1 (2011): 97–112.

Oliphint, K. Scott, and Rod S. Mays. *Things That Cannot Be Shaken.* Wheaton, IL: Crossway, 2008.

Owen, John. *The Works of John Owen.* Edited by W. H. Gould. Ages Digital Library CD edition. 16 vols. Edinburgh: Banner of Truth, 1977.

Perelman, Chaim, and Lucie Olbrechts-Tyteca. *The New Rhetoric.* Rev. ed. Notre Dame, IN: University of Notre Dame Press, 1991.

Plantinga, Alvin. *God, Freedom, and Evil.* New York: Harper & Row, 1974.

_____. *Where the Conflict Really Lies: Science, Religion, and Naturalism.* New York: Oxford University Press, 2011.

Postman, Neil. *Amusing Ourselves to Death: Public Discourse in the Age of Show Business.* London: Methuen, 1987.

Poythress, Vern Sheridan. *In the Beginning Was the Word: Language—a God-Centered Approach.* Wheaton, IL: Crossway, 2009.

_____. *Logic: A God-Centered Approach to the Foundation of Western Thought.* Wheaton, IL: Crossway, 2013.

_____. *Redeeming Science: A God-Centered Approach.* Wheaton, IL: Crossway, 2006.

Ryle, J. C. *Holiness: Its Nature, Hindrances, Difficulties, and Roots.* Various editions.

Schaeffer, Francis A. *Death in the City.* Downers Grove, IL: InterVarsity, 1969.

Schlorff, Samuel P. "Theological and Apologetical Dimensions of Muslim Evangelization." *Westminster Theological Journal* 42, no. 2 (1980): 335–66.

"Secular Humanism." *The John Ankerberg Show.* Complete program transcripts. Chattanooga, TN: John Ankerberg Evangelistic Ministries, 1986.

Strange, Daniel. "Perilous Exchange, Precious Good News: A Reformed 'Subversive Fulfillment' Interpretation of Other Religions." In *Only One Way? Three Christian Responses on the Uniqueness of Christ in a Religiously Plural World*, edited by Gavin D'Costa, Paul Knitter, and Daniel Strange. Kindle edition. London: SCM, 2011.

Sudduth, Michael. *The Reformed Objection to Natural Theology.* Ashgate Philosophy of Religion Series. Burlington, VT: Ashgate, 2009.

Tipton, Lane G. "Resurrection, Proof, and Presuppositionalism." In *Revelation and Reason: New Essays in Reformed Apologetics*, edited by K. Scott Oliphint and Lane G. Tipton, 41–58. Phillipsburg, NJ: P&R, 2007.

Van Til, Cornelius. *Common Grace and the Gospel.* Edited by K. Scott Oliphint. Phillipsburg, NJ: P&R, 2015.

_____. *The Defense of the Faith.* 4th ed. Edited by K. Scott Oliphint. Phillipsburg, NJ: P&R, 2008.

_____. *A Survey of Christian Epistemology.* Nutley, NJ: Presbyterian and Reformed, 1969.

Versteeg, J. P. *Adam in the New Testament: Mere Teaching Model or First Historical Man?* 2nd. ed. Translated by Richard B. Gaffin Jr. Phillipsburg, NJ: P&R, 2012.

Vos, Geerhardus. "The Range of the Logos Title in the Prologue to the Fourth Gospel." In *Redemptive History and Biblical Interpretation: The Shorter Writings of Geerhardus Vos*, edited by Richard B. Gaffin Jr., 59–90. Phillipsburg, NJ: Presbyterian and Reformed, 1980.

Ware, Bruce A., ed. *Perspectives on the Doctrine of God: Four Views.* Nashville, TN: B&H Academic, 2008.

General Index

Scripture Index

The Ultimate Primary
Source Reader for Apologetics

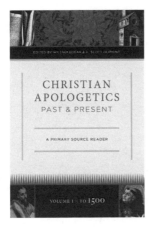

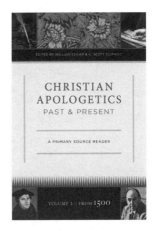

VOLUME 1
To 1500

VOLUME 2
From 1500

With selections from the first century AD to the present day, these two volumes of primary sources include material and explanatory notes from more than 40 renowned apologists such as Justin Martyr, Augustine, Martin Luther, Francis Schaeffer, and William Lane Craig. A valuable resource for all those interested in defending the faith.

"Understanding apologetics as explicating, affirming, and vindicating Christianity in the face of uncertainty and skepticism, Edgar and Oliphint have skillfully selected the best primary sources to introduce us to this ongoing task. Their work fills a gap in scholarly resources and highlights the strength, wisdom, and solidity of the prominent defenders of our faith."

J. I. PACKER
Late Board of Governors' Professor of Theology, Regent College

For more information, visit **crossway.org**.